Sustainable
in Mozambique

Sustainable Development in Mozambique

EDITED BY
BERNARDO FERRAZ & BARRY MUNSLOW

MICOA
in association with

JAMES CURREY
OXFORD

AFRICA WORLD PRESS
TRENTON N.J.

James Currey Ltd
73 Botley Road
Oxford OX2 0BS

Africa World Press
PO Box 1892
Trenton, NJ 08607, USA

British Library Cataloguing in Publication Data
Sustainable development in Mozambique
1. Sustainable development – Mozambique
I. Ferraz, Bernardo II. Munslow, Barry
333.7'09679
ISBN 0–85255–820–1 (James Currey Cloth)
ISBN 0–85255–821–X (James Currey Paper)

Library of Congress Cataloging-in-Publication Data
ISBN 0–86543–748–3 (AWP Cloth)
ISBN 0–86543–749–1 (AWP Paper)

Typeset in 10/10½ pt Bembo
by Saxon Graphics Ltd, Derby
Printed and bound in
the United States of America

Contents

C MECHANISMS

D CASE STUDIES

Preface

This book is the culmination of a long journey. Both editors have been involved in environmental and development issues in Mozambique in different ways over three decades. They began to work together in 1989 and the collaboration has proved an on-going meeting of minds. This current initiative is the most ambitious to date and reflects a long gestation period. Its immediate origins lie in the Rio Earth Summit of 1992 and Agenda 21.

In recognition of the country's proactive engagement in this initiative and efforts to follow it up, a Capacity 21 initiative was launched in Mozambique, the emphasis being on training programmes involving the Council of Ministers, senior national and provincial civil servants and indigenous non-governmental organizations. The best of the written contributions produced were then worked on further to form many of the contributions to the present volume, which also includes chapters by distinguished Mozambican academics who were also involved in the teaching.

Given this pedigree, what we have is a primary research monograph which links together the key issues of the policy agenda into the twenty-first century. These are the actors reflecting on the ideas and the issues. It is a powerful combination. However refined may be the abstracted theoretical and philosophical thoughts of outsiders, this volume combines academic reflections on the problems with the hard edge of credible implementable criteria.

Acknowledgements

Great efforts have been made by many people in the production of this volume. Special thanks go to Mario Souto, the National Director of Environmental Education who gave tireless support throughout. Staff at the Ministry for the Co-ordination of Environment Action were all very helpful in various ways. Marian Hoffmann at the University of Liverpool did a splendid job in producing the manuscript through its many different stages. Many thanks are also due to Frances Christie and Pam Rebelo for undertaking the translations. To these and many other people our thanks our due, needless to say all errors and omissions are our responsibility. The United Nations Development Programme gave generous financial support. Margaret Cornell did invaluable service in the final edit and proof read.

Contributors

Alcinda Abreu has worked extensively in the NGO sector. She was formerly Minister for the Co-ordination of Social Action.

João Alves is head of the investment facilitation division in the Centre for Investment Promotion, based in Maputo. He is an economist by profession.

Gilberto Banze is chief economist in the Ministry of Mineral Resources and Energy.

Issufo Chutumia is a water engineer and head of Mozambique's Southern Water Region.

Luísa Diogo is an economist who is currently the Vice Minister of Planning and Finance.

Bernardo Ferraz was originally trained in physical planning and is the Minister for the Co-ordination of Environmental Action.

Lorna Gujral is a biologist, currently the co-ordinator of the Technical and Scientific Committee of the Research Unit in the Ministry of Health.

Abílio Gune is an agronomist working in the Ministry of Planning and Finance.

Mario Machuale has worked for a number of years on population issues in Mozambique.

Afonso Madope has a veterinary medicine background and is head of the Department of Wildlife in the Ministry of Agriculture and Fisheries.

Isidro Manuel has a doctorate in geology and is Dean of the Science Faculty at Eduardo Mondlane University.

Alexandre Monteiro works in the Ministry of Foreign Affairs and Co-operation.

Oscar Monteiro, a former Minister, is a professor at the Graduate School of Public and Development Management at the University of Witwatersrand in South Africa and also at Eduardo Mondlane University.

Barry Munslow is Professor in the Faculty of Social and Environmental Studies at the University of Liverpool, UK.

Teresa Neto works in the Ministry of Foreign Affairs and Co-operation.

Bie Nio Ong is Professor of Health Services Research at the University of Keele, UK.

António Ribeiro is a forester currently undertaking his doctoral research at the University of Liverpool, UK. He is Director of Forestry Research.

Maria dos Anjos Rosário has qualifications in architecture, physical planning, engineering and civil construction and mining. She has held senior posts in government and in the NGO sector and is currently a special adviser in the Ministry for the Co-ordination of Environmental Action.

Alda Salamão is a lawyer currently working in the Ministry for the Co-ordination of Environmental Action.

Odete Semião is qualified in veterinary medicine and is a technical consultant in the Centre for Investment Promotion.

Eugénio Silva works in the National Directorate of Mines in the Ministry of Mineral Resources and Energy.

João Sitõe is qualified in mechanical and naval engineering. He is assistant director of Marine Affairs in the Ministry of Transport and Communications.

Mário Souto is qualified in education and development and is National Director of Environmental Education in the Ministry for the Co-ordination of Environmental Action.

Sara Taibo is an economist currently working as a technical analyst at the Centre for Investment Promotion.

Atanásio Tivane is the technical supervisor of investments in the Physical Planning Institute.

Rogério Wamusse is a chemist who is currently provincial director in Gaza for the Ministry for the Co-ordination of Environmental Action.

Acronyms

AIM	Mozambique Information Agency
AMDU	Mozambican Association for Urban Development
ARU	Agricultural Restructuring Unit
CASS	Centre for Applied Social Sciences of the University of Zimbabwe
CEF	*Centro de Experimentacção Florestal* [Forestry Research Centre] of the National Directorate of Forestry and Wildlife (DNFFB) located within the Ministry of Agriculture
CIDA	Canadian International Development Agency
CNA	National Environment Commission
DINAGECA	National Directorate for Geography and Maps
DNFFB	*Direcçao Nacional de Florestas e Fauna Bravia* [National Directorate of Forestry and Wildlife] of the Ministry of Agriculture
EIA	Environmental Impact Assessment
EIS	Environmental Impact Study
ESRP	Economic and Social Rehabilitation Programme
EU	European Union
FAO	Food and Agriculture Organization of the United Nations
FDR	Federal Republic of Germany
GNP	Gross National Product
HIPC	Highly Indebted Poor Country
IAC	*Instituto Agrario de Chimoio* [Chimoio Agricultural College], City of Chimoio, Province of Manica, the main forestry training college at diploma level in Mozambique
ICER	Inter-Ministerial Committee for Enterprise Restructuring
ICPD	International Conference on Population and Development
ICRAF	International Centre for Research in Agroforestry
IERO	International Enterprise Restructuring Office
IGEL	Intersectoral Group on Environmental Education
IMF	International Monetary Fund
INIA	*Intituto Nacional de Investigacção Agricola* [National Institute for Agricultural Research], Maputo
INS	National Health Institute
IUCN ROSA	The World Conservation Union, Regional Office for Southern Africa, Harare
Licenciatura	Equivalent to a BSc (Hons) which is generally the first degree at

	UEM after a five-year course and a dissertation submitted and approved by the related Faculty
MICOA	Ministry for the Co-ordination of Environmental Action
NEMP	National Environment Management Programme
NGO	Non-Governmental Organization
NPP	National Population Policy
NRP	National Reconstruction Plan
OECD	Organization for Economic Co-operation and Development
PEC	Privatization Executive Committee
PRA	Participatory Rural Appraisal
PRRA	Participatory Rapid Rural Appraisal
RA	Rapid Appraisal
RWA	Regional Water Authority
SADC	Southern African Development Community
SD	Sustainable Development
SPFFB	*Serviço Provincial de Florestas e Fauna Bravia* [Provincial Service for Forestry and Wildlife] a department of the Provincial Directorate of Agriculture
STD	Sexually Transmitted Diseases
TPIP	Triennial Public Investment Plan
TUER	Technical Unit for Enterprise Restructuring
UEM	*Universidade Eduardo Mondlane* [Eduardo Mondlane University], Maputo
UISS	Health System Research Unit
UK	United Kingdom
UNDP	United Nations Development Programme
UNEP	United Nations Environment Programme
WCED	World Conference on Environment and Development
WWF	Worldwide Fund for Nature

A INTRODUCTION

1 Looking Ahead

BERNARDO FERRAZ
& BARRY MUNSLOW

The modern history of Mozambique has been dominated by destruction rather than by development. Thankfully that is now at an end and the greatest single impediment to building a future of sustainable development has thereby been removed; war has been replaced by peace. The country successfully held its first democratic elections in 1994, which helped consolidate the peace and opened the way for development (Mazula, 1995). They were followed by successive good harvests and a steady growth in the economy. Foreign investors are now showing serious interest in a number of large projects, particularly in the minerals and energy sector but also involving transport and tourism. These all provide optimistic signs for the future in a country where good news has been a rare commodity in the past.

Yet alongside these signs of hope lies a formidable array of constraints. In this volume, we have assembled contributions from a group of Mozambicans who are specialists in a whole variety of areas where progress has to be made if the country is to build a more sustainable future. All of them are experts in their own fields, but in addition they are challenged daily by the problems of developing the country and helping to improve the welfare of the citizens of one of the world's poorest countries. They have all participated actively in the Agenda 21 initiative of the UN Conference on Environment and Development specially designed for Mozambique under the Capacity 21 programme. They include senior civil servants, ministers and leaders of national non-governmental organizations, as well as academics. Each author explores not only the constraints to be overcome, but also the existing opportunities to advance the development process. This book therefore examines not only the critical issues but also how the actors themselves perceive both the challenges that they face and the means to move towards a more sustainable future.

It also aims to provide more than a country case study of efforts to apply the principles of sustainable development in a Southern African context, although it will be useful to all those interested in development processes in the region. It examines broader global issues ranging from debt relief and structural adjustment, democracy and governance, to explaining methodologies such as rapid appraisal and environmental impact assessment and their role in the development process. Hence the intention is to appeal to both the general and the specialist reader.

For a long time now Mozambique's state institutions have often pursued innovative policies, but translating high sounding words into action has proved far more difficult. So much of the state's activity during the long years of war and emergency substituted planning exercises in all their various forms for the actual delivery of development programmes. Emergency operations functioned well enough and all the emphasis on delivery lay in this direction, whilst the task of delivering development remained in the abstract world of planning, strategy and programming.

A volume like this permits an appreciation to be gained of the thinking, and the priorities, of senior professionals in many of the leading development institutions and agencies in the country. The contributions are informative not only in terms of what they say but also in terms of how problem solving is being approached. In the latter case, despite the heavy burden of history and an ingrained element of bureaucratic inertia, efforts are clearly being made to explore new approaches and tackle institutional renewal. Introducing the concepts and principles of sustainable development is leading to a steady re-evaluation of existing ways of perceiving and tackling problems. Whether this new way of thinking will have a significant positive impact on the development process remains to be seen. Inevitably the first decade of the twenty-first century will bring an altogether new wave of insights and development trends. Yet, judging from past experience, many of the best insights gleaned from sustainable development (SD) approaches are likely to be included in the next wave of thinking. They will not therefore go to waste. At the same time, they do not provide a panacea. There is no substitute for creative thinking which is tested and modified in the light of practice, a core value being respect for all who may be affected by new initiatives in the human and the natural world, seeking their support and protecting their interests.

The seemingly all-embracing global adherence to SD in words, it must be said, more often than in deeds, does not disguise the continuing tensions. SD contains a strong economic growth element and at the same time a redistributive element in the form of basic needs provisioning, as well as a concern with conservation of the environment. Managerial and institutional reform is a critical feature. There is an awareness that if we want to keep travelling safely in our planetary vehicle around the solar system, we had better look after spaceship earth in the same way that we look after our own motor car.

The rest of this chapter provides an overview of the contributions to this volume and endeavours to set them in context. The book is divided into three main sections: challenges to sustainable development, mechanisms for its implementation and case studies. A similar approach has been adopted for a 'companion' study looking at South Africa (FitzGerald *et al.*, 1997). Where relevant, the editors have provided a postscript updating the rapidly changing context on the ground in certain key chapters concerning debt, decentralization and the role of the traditional authorities in particular.

Before entering these three arenas, however, Barry Munslow begins by trying to untangle the meaning and significance of sustainable development. He takes the three main texts which have shaped our understanding of SD in the international community and endeavours to extract their central messages. It is the responsibility of each individual country whether or not to apply the core of these messages creatively to the particular sets of national circumstances that exist, and which everywhere will be different. A set of pointers has been distilled, however, that can aid policy-makers and practitioners in their work. Agenda 21 was particularly important in helping to formulate national SD strategies, with its emphasis on cross-sectoral approaches, integrating environment and development in decision-making, participation and partnerships, transparency, setting clear targets and subsuming donor plans into a country-driven process.

A useful starting point is to ask how development organizations can help people to sustain their own livelihoods (Chambers, 1983). Assimilating thinking on sustainable livelihoods is an important beginning. So much points in the direction of prioritizing training, education and general awareness raising. Hence, the message of Munslow's chapter is that sustainable development is essentially about improving the human resource management of the natural resource base. Central to this process is building up institutional and human resource capacity. Existing approaches to policy, programme and project formulation need to be transformed. This requires responding to people's own priorities rather than determining them from the top down, facilitating self-help and working in new partnerships between state institutions and those of civil society.

The relevant stakeholders need to be identified at the appropriate levels, with negotiation and bargaining taking place to maximize the potential usage of a shared natural resource base. Improving the human resource management of the natural resource base means identifying 'win-win' situations, whereby all of the stakeholders stand to gain by co-operating together. Hence it is essential to address the politics of sustainable development.

Challenges

Oscar Monteiro, a principal architect of the country's constitution, contributes the chapter on governance which analyzes the election process, decentralization and the role of civil society. The challenge in relation to the electoral system was how to combine the principles of free and fair elections with a system for integrating the various sectors of society into the management of public affairs in the context of the recently ended civil conflict. Moves towards decentralization, with the introduction of locally elected bodies, provide a key component, which permits groups with a defined regional power base a share in power through formal local government structures.

Monteiro outlines the long struggle to establish democratic structures within the context of an internal armed conflict fuelled from outside the national borders. One important innovation was the hybrid nature of the National Electoral Commission, whose twenty members were appointed by the rival political parties but with a genuinely independent chair person. The electoral process was a mammoth undertaking, involving registering 6 million voters and issuing them with cards carrying both a photograph and their fingerprint. It was successful precisely because the popular will was there to make it succeed and a lot of donor money went into paying for the electoral mechanisms, including extensive civic education programmes. The Presidential elections produced a 53% vote in favour of President Chissano of Frelimo, whilst Renamo's leader won 34%. The parliamentary elections produced 129 seats for Frelimo, 112 for Renamo and 9 for União Democrática. The composition of the votes brought to the fore regional and ethnic considerations, with Frelimo gaining most support in the south and to a lesser extent in the north and Renamo taking the centre of the country. The block party list system inevitably created a weak link between constituents and candidates. The elections were essentially a vital component of the peace process. Whilst the pressures for democratic elections were strongly external as well as internal, interestingly enough no-one now questions the wisdom of adopting multi-party democracy.

Initiatives taken towards greater decentralization have faced no lesser challenges than those towards greater democratization. Constraints include the legacy of colonial centralization, and the lack of competent civil servants, given the exodus of settler monopolized public sector management skills at the time of independence, and an inadequate subsequent strategy of human resource and institutional strengthening in the public service. In the 1990s the central government became increasingly aware of its inability to cope efficiently with local government issues, and its desire to do something about this could mark something of a sea change. The decentralization process began with the 1990 Constitution and has since progressed much further. Recently the government has started intensive retraining courses for district administrators, and there is a positive move towards recognizing the importance of the contribution that the traditional authorities can play. The big initiative, however, is the substantial powers handed to the municipalities, the key challenge being to provide the personnel qualified to implement such a strategy and adequate resources to make it possible.

Under the new municipality law which champions the decentralization initiative, many of the powers with regard to environmental protection, sanitation, land management, public facilities, urbanization, forests and wildlife pass to the municipalities. These are early days, and there is little experience as yet to go on to judge whether the system is operating effectively. What one can say is that these are potentially sweeping changes. Existing human and institutional capacity remains severely restricted and it is by no means guaranteed that the necessary resources will be devolved from the centre to make this bold initiative truly operational. It is clearly important to recognize the potential role of the traditional authorities in improving the management of the natural resource base. In many parts of the country it is the traditional authorities which hold the legitimacy in the eyes of the local community. Building an effective relationship between local government and the traditional authorities therefore takes on considerable importance.

Strengthening local institutional capacity for environmental management holds the key to success. This will require a considerable educational effort in the municipal districts. It will also require a significant reconstruction effort. In 1996, out of 128 districts only 47 had their own offices, 50 had no residence for the administrator, 50 had no means of communication and 3 had no vehicle. The situation is significantly worse at the lower level in the 394 administrative posts, 300 of which had no offices at all, none had any form of communication and nearly all lacked furniture, equipment and supplies. Given that the average-sized district contains 100,000 people and covers an area of 6,000 sq. km., the difficulties are all too easy to appreciate.

Much will depend on the credibility of the new initiative, set in the context of a civil society sceptical of government in the past but slowly growing in awareness of what it has a right to expect. With the churches highlighting declining moral values in public office and in society, the government has set up an institution to investigate corruption. The process of creating elected municipalities with increased powers will remain highly dependent on the Provincial Administrations passing on some of their current powers.

The success of democratization and decentralization in part depends upon a strengthening of civil society; all three initiatives are closely interconnected. Monteiro outlines the various forms of organizations within civil society and the roles they play. A number of challenges have to be confronted in terms of redefining roles and structures of co-operation between the organs of the state and those of civil society. It is still early days and much will depend on the outcome if a renewed development imperative is to be sustained. An important step forward is the government's decision to introduce a new career and salary structure within the civil service from April 1999 onwards, widening wage differentials significantly to improve competition with the private sector in order to attract talented people (AIM, 26 March 1998).

The greatest economic challenge facing the country now that the war is over is the enormous debt burden. Luísa Diogo, Vice-Minister of Planning and Finance, outlines the government's strategy for reducing this burden. Since 1990 the government has tried to cut down on further credits, relying instead on grants. Projects are more strictly monitored to help ensure a better return on investments. Strict adherence to the structural adjustment programmes combined with an intensive effort to negotiate debt relief has produced some positive movement on the side of the creditors. The on-going gap in the balance of payments has been covered by multilateral concessional credit. Essentially the proportion of bilateral debt has diminished and multilateral debt has increased.

The Paris Club of OECD bilateral creditors helped negotiate four debt reschedulings between 1984 and 1993. Since 1989 most OECD creditors have cancelled their external debt. Debt relief negotiations also began with the former Eastern bloc countries. In addition, mechanisms have been put in place to tighten the management of debt. At the end of 1996, further substantial debt relief was negotiated. The stark fact remained, however, that all Mozambique's development efforts, every advance in exports, every saving on expenditure, would come to nothing if the enormous debt burden was not removed (Hanlon, 1996). Finally, in 1998 under the Highly Indebted Poor Country (HIPC) initiative, Mozambique's major debt overhang was agreed to be written off. One of the crucial impediments to sustainable development was significantly removed.

João Alves tackles the critical strategic issue at the heart of the change of direction from a centrally planned to a market economy – privatization. The former nationalization policy was clearly not working and Alves outlines the context in which privatization was put at the centre of the policy agenda. He then examines the record to date. Whilst many privatizations have already occurred, there is no guarantee of the long-term sustainability of many of the privatized enterprises. The process itself has been slow, complicated and bureaucratic. Yet at the end of 1997 the government was able to claim success for the programme, expecting to collect US$23 million from the sale of 13 state owned enterprises in 1997 (AIM, 30 December 1997).

Interim conclusions can be drawn on the basis of the evidence to date. Where foreign companies and capital have been involved, the initiatives have generally progressed reasonably well, as the financial, managerial and technological capacity was available to make them a success. Companies handed over to Mozambicans, on the other hand, (and these are the majority) have generally lacked these necessary inputs. Worryingly, 70% of these have been unable to continue their basic activities. Alves does point to some successes, however, such as the Sabrina clothing factory in Maputo. He makes a series of useful recommendations for improving the privatization process: simplifying and shortening the procedures; setting a realistic selling price to speed up the process; establishing a compensation fund for workers; choosing among bidders only on price and not on subjective criteria; and finally, paying for large companies in cash in order to avoid on-going costs to state revenues.

Odete Semião takes up this theme and examines industrial projects and their role in sustainable development. She charts an increase in direct foreign investment with many attendant benefits through the installation, rehabilitation, expansion and modernization of economic infrastructures and enterprises. Following on from the peace agreement, substantial new investments entered the country, although these mark only a beginning in comparison with what is required. The aim has to be to attract the inward investment whilst at the same time ensuring that it will contribute to the sustainable development of the country and that any potentially serious negative long-term environmental impacts will be minimized. This must involve the treatment of harmful industrial waste and any new projects with a possible negative effect on the environment must undergo an Environmental Impact Assessment. In March 1998 a trade bill was introduced in Parliament to simplify procedures for setting up companies; essentially it involves revoking a 1979 law requiring prior authorization to set up companies (AIM, 18 March 1998). Huge tax breaks were introduced for major investors in such projects as the MOZAL aluminium smelter being built in Boane near Maputo (AIM, 30 March 1998).

Gilberto Banze and Eugénio Silva examine the role of the mining sector, which seems set to grow rapidly in importance, and explore its potential contribution to sustainable development. Both are senior officials in the Ministry of Mines and Energy, and their message is that mining currently offers a significant contribution to economic development throughout the Southern African region. To date, however, it has played a much smaller role in Mozambique, though future prospects look brighter. They identify policy, legislative and institutional fragilities in the system, the main stakeholders involved and the need to bring them together into a constructive dialogue, the extent of current mining activity and a number of promising new developments in the mining sector nationally.

They go on to confront a series of critical issues facing the sector. Unduly bureaucratic obstacles need to be overcome to get all the various components working together to provide the necessary developmental impetus. This is, in fact, a critical area where achieving the right balance in the relationship between the state and civil society is essential. Whilst government regulation can impede economic development, on the one hand, by creating barriers to investors, there is still an obvious need for some state control to avoid the potential environmental, social and economic costs of a totally unregulated scramble to extract the country's mineral riches. Finally, a case study of Manica Province, where many mining endeavours are currently taking place, highlights the importance of minimizing the effects of mining on agriculture, learning from the experience of neighbouring Zimbabwe and ensuring that the polluter-pays principle is put into operation.

Teresa Neto and Alexandre dos Santos Monteiro tackle the problem of how international co-operation can be used to support sustainable development. They see international co-operation as having a very important role to play. Identifying examples of good practice is always a useful starting point, and they pick out the role played by the United Nations Development Programme in Mozambique in this regard and offer it as a case study. Development assistance played a staggeringly large role in the country's economy throughout the extended period of emergency. Hence for some observers the level of aid dependence and the potential for outside manipulation have been of critical concern. Hanlon (1991) has gone so far as to argue that destabilization, the IMF and aid worked together to divide, corrupt and undermine Mozambican society, thus assuming that existing domestically generated shortcomings are exonerated from any responsibility. Whilst admitting the importance of external pressures, it is nevertheless essential to accept that the former domestic policy model was itself profoundly flawed. Of course aid can be a double-edged benefit, with positive and negative potential. But we would argue that aid has often played a highly positive role, not least by engaging in a policy dialogue which helped the country's efforts to avoid past policy pitfalls. It acted as one of the checks and balances within the system.

Neto and Monteiro do not address directly the critique of aid. Rather, they try to show how the best assistance targets the right sectors and programmes to support, in order to reinforce sustainable development, and also engages in meaningful dialogue rather than simply imposing ideas from outside. They identify the critical problems, which stem from the lack of a core ethic of sustainable development on the part of both nationals and the donor community. As a result, policies and strategies of the stakeholders concerned have not been sufficiently clear, coherent and co-ordinated. Debt and poverty add to the burden. A series of recommendations then follow about proactive measures that can be taken.

Alda Salomão explores the vital but complex area of institutional co-ordination and harmonizing formal and customary law in the management of natural resources. She highlights a gap in the government's decentralization policy. Whilst it anticipates the involvement of traditional authorities, there is no clear indication of their specific role or that of traditional law in natural resource management. Unless these are clarified, an essential principle of sustainable development, notably the importance of community participation and tapping the potential of traditional knowledge about environmental management best practices, will not be harnessed successfully to the SD initiative. An editorial update charts the on-going twists and turns of policy and legislation on this issue in relation to the Council of Ministers and the Assembly.

António Ribeiro's chapter takes up this theme and examines the challenges of institutional reorganization in the light of SD principles and approaches, in relation to the Forestry Research Department (CEF). The CEF has a mandate to elaborate policy and appropriate solutions for natural resource management activities as these relate to forestry and wildlife. Once it had embarked on its own agroforestry programmes, the CEF discovered that peasant farmers had already been developing their own techniques in this area. It began learning the lesson that developing more productive systems meant combining the state's initiatives with those of the key members of local communities who were themselves innovators. From an initial focus on industrial forestry alone, the CEF began to reorientate its policy more towards meeting rural people's needs. Hence a strategy was worked out to conduct research with rural communities with the aim of making them the prime beneficiaries, the starting point being to learn about their existing techniques and management strategies in relation to forests and wildlife. The CEF is also working with the private sector which has a dynamic role to play in the country's development; providing technical support here can also provide much needed additional financial resources for the CEF.

Under the former top-down approaches, it was difficult for the state to discover and respond to local realities; local institutions lost the power needed to manage their natural resources and to benefit fully from them. There is a serious lack of communication between local communities and the various tiers of government. A key challenge is to train more professionals in the social and institutional aspects of natural resource management. Ribeiro outlines both the constraints and the opportunities that exist and specifies what will be required in terms of staff development.

Mechanisms

In the opening chapter of the next section of the volume Bernardo Ferraz and Barry Munslow discuss the National Environment Management Programme (NEMP) – a genuinely nationally driven process involving extensive consultation and participation. The process itself was potentially the most valuable feature, as it brought together many different stakeholders and identified crucial individuals capable of making the necessary linkages across the vertical and horizontal dimensions of the environment and development process. Seven key issues are identified in the NEMP document approved by the Council of Ministers. These involve policy, institutional and legal reform first of all. The remaining four areas of critical concern are: environmental education; research, information and documentation; rural coastal problems; and finally the urban environment.

Integrating environmental and development concerns in a practical and beneficial manner to secure a better future requires a clear policy and the correct legislation and institutional structures to carry this through. These had to be the first priorities. Running in parallel is the need to raise awareness of the issues more generally; environmental education is the key, informed by the necessary research and information. The two spatial areas targeted for attention are the coastal strip and the urban areas. It is here that population pressure on the natural resource base is at its most intense.

Ong and Munslow examine the useful mechanism of rapid appraisal. This is a cost-effective participatory methodology used to gain an understanding of the real needs of communities. It enables local people's knowledge and perceptions of their own priority needs to be fed into the development process. Beyond this, however, it can help to mobilize the latent development capacity of individuals and communities. The methodology can be applied to a whole range of problem areas of needs assessment, the emphasis being on a multi-disciplinary and multi-agency approach. The various stages of the rapid assessment process are spelled out and an example provided of how it has been applied in Mozambique.

For a country possessing 2,700 km of coastline, improving coastal zone management will inevitably figure highly on the SD agenda and this is the focus of the study by João Sitoe. He identifies the overall objective as creating the necessary human resource capacity to improve the economic utilization of the coastal zone whilst conserving its biodiversity. A majority of the population live on the coast, the country's principal exports of prawn and cashew are produced there, the new large-scale investments for mining, gas and tourism are located on the littoral and the ports are at the hub of the transit trade for the regional hinterland.

All the potential conflicts and tensions created by competing demands on the natural resource base, exacerbated by excessive population pressures on limited services (health, education and clean water), come together at the coast. Furthermore, there are considerable complexities in securing effective forms of institutional co-ordination either vertically or horizontally, given the diversity of institutions involved and the multiple stakeholders. Hence, juxtaposed with the particularly fragile and vulnerable coastal ecosystems is the challenge of reconciling intensifying economic and social activities with meeting the needs of the dense population concentrations, alongside maintaining the rich biodiversity.

Around 100,000 people are involved in the fisheries sector and fish is a major protein input for the population; yet already there are clear signs of strains being placed on the resource base. Tensions exist between the need to increase exports and to meet domestic needs: this is perceived as tourists using their better equipment to take too many fish, effectively for commercial purposes, against the needs of domestic artisanal fishermen using only the most basic equipment. The major coastal cities deposit untreated sewage which affects the quality of fish for human consumption. Commercial fishing of crustacean resources is the most critical issue; here, it is reaching its limits. Demand for fuelwood and coastal development initiatives destroy mangroves and thereby the nurseries for prawns and fish. With the Mozambique Channel being a major international shipping lane, there is the ever present threat of an oil spill; a number of incidents already serve as a reminder, notably the *Katina P* spill of 1992.

Coastal erosion is proving a problem in specific locations. Most of the coast is of the soft type. There is a particular vulnerability to global warming and possible rises in sea level. Mozambique has been categorized as among the ten countries most at risk. Agriculture, mining, mangrove and soil destruction all contribute to the erosion hazard. There needs to be effective coastal engineering and a conservation management policy. Given the potential magnitude of the problems, there is evidence of some growing awareness that initiatives need to be taken to address a number of these issues. A national coastal zone management policy must be articulated; the necessary mechanisms for improved institutional co-ordination with clearly defined lines of authority need putting in place. Stakeholder participation is a key to success.

Alcinda Abreu examines community welfare issues. She briefly reviews the historical evolution of social services in Mozambique in the present century, identifying the most recent phase, from 1987 onwards, as marking a significant move towards greater decentralization and deinstitutionalization. Both the complexity and the scale of the problems facing the country now require that all potential sources of welfare provision be encouraged, in contrast to the former centralized state form of provisioning.

The Ministry for the Co-ordination of Social Action, working with others, is facilitating a sustainable community development initiative targeted at those groups most in need of support, notably children, women, the elderly, the disabled, displaced people and returned refugees. The aim is to promote welfare by raising living standards and creating opportunities for people to develop their skills. This requires a programme to strengthen capacity for community-based initiatives, and involves training programmes in the strategies and methodologies of sustainable community management. Government and NGO social workers and social activists in the districts will be trained. In every province two or three communities with poor and needy people will be chosen, but they will already possess institutions and organizations around which these initiatives can be based. An additional focus will be the encouragement of inter-sectoral and multi-disciplinary co-ordination. Managing the resource base effectively means finding the appropriate scale for action, and there is a growing consensus that the closer to the grass roots, the more effective the participatory action that can be taken.

One mechanism forming part of an overall SD approach is formulating a national population policy, and this is explored by Fonseca Machaule. Such a policy is relatively new to the country and is still evolving, although the government has agreed publicly with the consensus reached at the International Conference on Population and Development in Cairo in 1994, that population, poverty, development and the environment are closely interrelated and cannot be treated in isolation.

Current levels of basic service provision are unable to cope with an existing population growth ratio of 2.7%, let alone raise the standard of provision so that existing poverty levels are overcome by means of better health care, education, provision of clean water and so on. The key way forward lies primarily with the education of girls and women, which has been shown to have a positive impact on reducing fertility levels. In addition, the government is trying to construct a more integrated population policy with a number of nationwide general programmes, in particular targeting population and development, gender issues, and specific operational programmes focusing on: integrated reproductive, child and adolescent health; education, population, communication and development; and population and the environment.

Rogério Wamusse explores how a capacity for scrutinizing the environment can be built up in Mozambique through the establishment of monitoring and auditing mechanisms. Such measures, if implemented effectively, can save the country huge expenditure on countering the effects of pollution and generalized environmental degradation. Wamusse argues that supervision mechanisms, which exist – if at all – only at the sectoral level, need to be redefined, and he highlights the existing tensions between the current model of centralized sectoral control and the need for more holistic local control.

Mario Souto discusses how to develop the human resource capacity to promote sustainable development. The key impediments identified are the absence of an environmental culture nationally, and the fragility of human resources. Souto identifies four target groups, defined by their functions: policy-makers; technical and advisory people; activists, extension and monitoring workers; and finally producers and communities. Formal education, non-formal training and informal awareness raising can be employed in various ways for all four groups. A programme for building up human resource capacity is required inside the environment ministry to improve its effectiveness as an education and training organization, together with broader initiatives within the government and in civil society.

Abilio Gune delves into ways of establishing sustainability criteria for public investment. These include multiplier effects, ensuring the replacement of the resources used and identifying alternatives to the use of natural resources. He identifies possible criteria including economic, financial, social, technical, institutional, organizational and management, and commercial criteria. He concludes that a consensus is required in the public investment process across all the relevant institutions to design effective methodologies for appraisal and approval. Those involved also need to be trained to effective levels of competence.

Sara Taibo reviews the role of environmental impact assessment (EIA) with a view to including the environmental component in development projects. She defines the various components involved and what they can achieve, and then goes on to review the EIA process in Mozambique, which began in a significant way only in 1994. It begins with an environmental impact study (EIS) for a proposed project. The Ministry for the Co-ordination of Environmental Action (MICOA) lays down the terms of reference for the EIS. The full EIA itself should integrate the relevant sectoral concerns for the management of the natural resource base. A clearly defined legal framework would enormously support such mechanisms. An EIA should add value in a positive way to a development initiative; it should not be seen as yet another bureaucratic obstacle. If EIAs are to become effective instruments, adequate training and streamlined mechanisms need to be devised.

Issufo Chutumia provides a detailed study of the huge challenge of managing water resources in the south of Mozambique. First, there are the difficulties of sharing rivers with upstream neighbours who may take most of the resource or pollute the waters as a conscious or unconscious product of their own development policy. For Mozambique, regional co-operation is essential. Nationally, yet again there is a strong argument for more effective decentralization.

Case studies

Maria Rosario presents an extensive study of participatory development and urban management. She begins by outlining the particular 'ruralized urban' situation prevailing in the country. The war speeded up the flight to the towns and cities, and resettlement back into the rural areas will be hampered by the lack of services and infrastructure.

Most of the urban population live on the verge of absolute poverty. Conditions in the urban areas have declined severely over the past twenty years. Rosario outlines the history of the shortcomings of efforts at urban management, which serves as the backdrop to a case study of a programme of sustainable development in the peri-urban areas of Maputo, initiated by the NGO, the Mozambican Association for Urban Development (AMDU), to promote local initiatives in improving basic services, training and the active involvement of the beneficiaries. Activities include: the self-help construction of social and community facilities; organizing a permanent refuse collection system; rehabilitating roads; tree planting and creating green spaces; organizing income-generating activities; discovering resources and organizing efforts to improve the urban environment; and strengthening local capacity to analyze and manage community problems.

AMDU developed a methodology for monitoring all activities and ensuring that the lessons of experience were built into co-ordinating initiatives. The main components involved were: promoting the complementarity of activities carried out in the various wards by different agencies and institutions; developing the social and community infrastructure required and ensuring its durability; and using local labour and promoting the training and employment of young people and demobilized soldiers.

Over the six years of the programme's life a number of conclusions can be drawn. Participatory development must respect the pace of community life and is likely to be slow. There is a problem of ownership in relation to the infrastructure created. There is an on-going tension between maintaining community facilities and ensuring that they do not become privatized. Maintaining the facilities required a local technical assistance unit to be formed. Finally, the active involvement of the local administration is important.

Lorna Gujral examines the role of rapid appraisal methods as a tool of sustainable development. This methodology provides a functional approach to bottom-up participation which can help managers and policy-makers respond to the needs of local communities as they themselves perceive them. It provides information in an efficient, economical and user-friendly manner. A variety of techniques exist which can be applied in different circumstances and to achieve different ends. Whilst not providing a panacea for all research problems, it does furnish those facing the challenge of sustainable development with a meaningful tool kit.

Gujral provides a concrete study of how this methodology has been applied in a health sector initiative in a suburb of Maputo. The aim was to improve the level of health care for the community by providing the Bagamoyo Health Centre and the city health authorities with information about how the local community perceives its health and sanitation problems. This will help to shape educational campaigns, support the community in understanding and analyzing its own problems, and help guide its search for solutions.

Afonso Madope provides a case study of a recent, and innovative for Mozambique, on-going project of community participation in wildlife management in Tete Province. Inevitably, given the very recent onset of peace, such initiatives are only in the early stages. Whilst there are a number of more long-standing experiences within the southern Africa region, such an initiative is new to Mozambique.

The overall objective is to involve local communities in conservation initiatives by demonstrating that they can market the wildlife resources displayed as the most profitable use of the natural resource base of the area where they live. The rationale for such an initiative is built on the following premises: Mozambique was formerly regarded as a wildlife paradise; the tse tse fly hampers livestock production in two-thirds of the country; both cattle and wildlife were severely reduced by the war; and Mozambique lacks the financial, material and skills resources for accelerated development by other means. The community participation approach builds on the existing human and natural resource base and the lack of viable alternative options, and aims to maximize the potential benefits available locally.

Atanásio Tivane looks at the proposed project to set up a eucalyptus plantation near the southern border with South Africa. The idea was floated primarily for political and military reasons in the late 1980s, and the negative environmental effects were not taken sufficiently into account. Fortunately as a result of pressure, there was a reappraisal and the scheme will not now go ahead in the proposed location. This case study serves to indicate the need for planning processes to take environmental concerns into account if the country is to make the best use of its natural resources.

Isidro Manuel, Dean of the Faculty of Sciences at Eduardo Mondlane University, provides a detailed case study of gold mining exploration in Manica District. Based on original research involving extensive interviews with artisanal miners in the district, a number of important conclusions are drawn. Most gold-diggers are peasants who turn to the arduous and dangerous work of mining out of necessity; for some it is seasonal work only, but for others it is full-time. All the miners maintain their farming base, however, with the full-timers contracting seasonal labour to work on their farm plots. It is not only peasants who work as gold-diggers; there are also teachers, accountants, students, civil servants and demobilized soldiers.

Mining has a considerable negative environmental impact on Manica; it reduces the available agricultural land in prime sites, silts up the rivers, spoils the water quality, and makes significant changes to the natural beauty of the Revue valley. Abandoned wells and trenches of stagnant water are sources of disease and the local fish catch is deteriorating in a number of areas. Peasant farmers appear to be suffering in a variety of ways as a result of both large- and small-scale mining operations. The large-scale operations which have the necessary resources have done virtually nothing to rehabilitate the land. The huge area affected has been transformed from prime to marginal land in terms of agricultural potential.

The important message to emerge from Manuel's study is that proper negotiations are required among the major stakeholders: the local population, the state and the mining interests both large-scale and artisanal. It is particularly important to rehabilitate the degraded land after mining operations cease and to return it to agricultural use, and also to ensure that water quality is restored.

Manuel produces a series of recommendations to ensure that on-going mining activities in the province do not jeopardize other development initiatives or the environment. The mechanisms to facilitate this include: identifying the stakeholders and the key problems to be addressed; bringing all the relevant stakeholders together to discuss the issues and develop a consensus on an action plan; and paying particular attention to helping maximize sustaining livelihoods in ways which are beneficial for people's use of the resource base not only today but also in the future.

Conclusion

The days of grand planning and state orchestrated development are over everywhere in the world. In the 1990s the discussion is about development planning and good governance. Key features include emphasis on: macroeconomic growth but growth that is sustainable; public and private/community partnerships; balancing environmental and development concerns; poverty alleviation; decentralization; participation; gender awareness and equality; improving co-ordination at both vertical and horizontal levels; and last but not least democratization. The move is towards cutting down the scope of government and facilitating the growth of civil society and the private sector.

The gains for government are that it is no longer responsible for doing everything and there is less scope for criticism. The size of the resources at its disposal will depend ultimately on the development of a vibrant, private sector-driven economy, and the tax base this will generate. Aid dependence must be replaced by trade for the country to achieve real economic independence.

Aid dependence represents a serious constraint on developing sustainably. To ensure a successful weaning from such dependence a change is needed in the nature of the aid. Aid provisioning must be linked to the recurrent cost capacity of the government. Local communities also need to be involved in covering recurrent costs. Support for the productive sectors can help stimulate economic development. People are the key to progress, hence human resource development is essential and at every level an effective strategy is required. If aid is to support sustainable development it must be led by nationally driven strategies rather than by aid agency priorities, although there is an important role here for policy dialogue. For this to be effective a greater self-confidence is required in the Mozambican's own capacities and abilities. The new emphasis on partnership means that all the stakeholders need to be identified and involved in order to negotiate 'win-win' situations wherever possible. The current scenario in which around 80% of expenditure goes on administration and 20% on delivery must be reversed. Livelihoods need to be sustained increasingly by production rather than by petty domestic commerce.

References
Chambers, R. (1983) *Rural Development. Putting the Last First*. Longman, Harlow.
FitzGerald, P., McLennan, A. and Munslow, B. (eds) (1997) *Managing Sustainable Development in South Africa*. 2nd edition. Oxford University Press, Cape Town.
Hanlon, J. (1991) *Mozambique: Who Calls the Shots?* James Currey, London.
Hanlon, J. (1996) *Peace without Profit*. James Currey, Oxford.
Mazula, B. (ed) (1995) *Moçambique. Eleições, Democracia e Desenvolvimento*. Inter-Africa Group, Maputo.

2 Sustainable Development: Its Meaning & Significance

BARRY MUNSLOW

Discussion about humanity's natural environment is not a new phenomenon (see, for example, Johnston, 1989). What certainly is new is the urgency and importance of these debates as we move towards the twenty first century. Sustainable development has been viewed differently by the various academic disciplines. Hence, frequently:

- agriculturalists equate it with food self-sufficiency
- environmentalists equate it with proper stewardship of the planet
- for the economist, sustainability is a facet of efficiency
- for the sociologist, sustainability is seen in terms of the preservation of traditional cultural values (see Conway and Barbier, 1990: 9)

The debate about what sustainability means ranges from romantic non-scientific ecological environmentalism to pragmatic environmental management (Johnston, 1989: 5–6). Adams, who has written the most detailed intellectual history of green development, draws a very important conclusion from his study (1990: xiii):

It is no good talking about how the environment is developed, or managed, unless this is seen as a political process ... The 'greenness' of development planning, therefore, is to be found not in its concern with ecology or environment *per se* but in its concern with control, power and self-determination.

This is where the discipline of politics comes in.

The major multilateral agencies all support sustainable development, but their particular expression of it varies. The International Monetary Fund and the Organization for Economic Co-operation and Development (OECD) speak of 'sustainable economic growth'. The World Bank talks of 'sustainable development' and 'equitable development', the European Union of 'sustainable economic and social development', whereas the UNDP promotes 'sustainable human development' (Reid, 1995: xiv).

All national governments have made a commitment to prepare national sustainable development plans and strategies following the 1992 Earth Summit. Most bilateral aid programmes claim to be guided by principles of sustainable development.

The existing development trajectories have brought with them a whole series of problems. How is the improvement of human existence to be judged? This is potentially an area for endless philosophical debate. The first criterion to consider when evaluating any particular pathway is whether it was genuinely successful in bringing about development with rising standards of living. 'Development' and more recently 'human development' are concepts used to denote something broader than simply 'economic growth'. Development encompasses the distribution of the benefits of the growth rather than simply the aggregate rise in Gross Domestic Product.

In many ways adding the word sustainable, and thereby creating the concept of sustainable development, implies refining our ideas still further. Making development sustainable means asking a series of questions about the development process and trying to anticipate, and thereby avoid creating, a whole series of additional problems, which has been our historical experience to date. Rather than ignoring the various tensions which invariably exist within the development process – between short-term and long-term benefits, exploiting or conserving the natural resource base, putting most effort into economic production or social investment – these need to be reconciled. The whole purpose of placing the concept of sustainable development at the centre of development debates going into the twenty-first century, is to try to find ways of turning a myriad of potential conflicts into non-zero sum games. Instead of having one 'winner', say economic growth today, and one loser, the environment, we have a long-term gain in the form of managing the utilization of the natural resource base to ensure development and maintenance of the environment.

In this chapter, we shall take the three most influential texts on sustainable development, and extract the central message each conveys. This is no easy task given the length of some of the texts. The aim is to choose the heart of the message and to demonstrate its applicability.

Prerequisites for sustainable development

For too long there was no meeting of minds between those involved with development and those concerned with the environment. In the late 1980s a major breakthrough took place with the publication of the Brundtland Report (World Commission on Environment and Development, 1987). This brought together a number of important agendas in an innovative and influential way. The development world has its periodic fashions, such as basic needs and rural development in the 1970s. Such fashions never go away entirely but become incorporated in one way or another into the new fashion that supersedes the old one. We use the term fashion not in a pejorative sense – although it is important not to become sucked into flavours of the month – but rather to indicate that in every period certain concerns have dominated the way the world was viewed. The 1980s and early 1990s saw structural adjustment in seemingly unchallengeable hegemony.

The Brundtland Report succeeded in creating a broad consensus around the centrality of sustainable development in development thinking. This enabled it to be embraced by the industrialized and the non-industrialized countries, by the right and the left, by those previously only concerned with the environment and those only concerned with development. The seven central objectives that it outlines for sustainable development bring together a number of different agendas.

The key to its widespread acceptance was firstly that it began with development and the need to revive growth, because existing levels of poverty and degradation were unacceptable. Any attempt to place the environment ahead of development would have guaranteed a rejection by the countries of the South and by economists and influential policy-makers across the globe. Growth is the primary objective therefore. Yet growth alone is not enough. Hence the second objective clearly states the need to change the quality of the growth. This is in recognition of the shortcomings of the past.

The third objective is meeting basic needs, bringing back on to the agenda the social democratic objective of the 1970s, which the first flush of structural adjustment orthodoxy threatened to sweep away in the 1980s. In essence structural adjustment programmes were about reviving growth and this was also the primary objective of *Our Common Future*. Hence its first three objectives are all about development. The next three bring the environment into the equation.

The fourth objective is ensuring a sustainable level of population. This issue has always been a difficult one on which to reach a consensus. Some in the South resent what is seen as the imposition of a Northern agenda of family planning which may often go against existing cultural and religious values. Yet there is no gainsaying the obvious: increasing population growth rates make the process of development in the form of improving people's living standards that much harder. It is a matter of running faster and faster just to avoid slipping backwards in the provision of clean water, health care, education and so on. The demand for basic needs overwhelms the capacity for service provision and children and families suffer the consequences.

The fifth objective goes to the heart of the matter – conserving and enhancing the resource base. Indeed, we shall argue that the essence of implementing sustainable development is improving the human resource management of the natural resource base. All seven Brundtland objectives can be subsumed under this rubric. Human resource management is the key to maximizing utilization of the natural resource base which necessarily includes the human population. Reorienting technology and managing risk, as the sixth objective, is an extension of this concern. Technologies must help anticipate and avoid possible risks.

The seventh and final objective brings together the first and the second sets of concerns when it urges a merging of environment and economics in decision-making. Hence it serves to underline our central argument that improving management is the key within the state and in civil society, for civil servants, entrepreneurs and non-governmental organizations. Managing the existing human and natural resources in ways which minimize potential conflicts and abuse is at the core of improving the quality of development and of the environment.

Interestingly, the second influential document, produced in 1991 by the International Union for the Conservation of Nature, the United Nations Environment Programme and the World Wide Fund for Nature starts the opposite way round. The three multilateral institutions promoting this contribution are very much driven by environmental concerns. This is important and necessary to arrive at an overall balance, because it is all too easy to be driven primarily, and ultimately almost exclusively, by humanity's short-term needs. Their contribution obliges humanity to think not only short-term, which is what it does constantly, but to recognize its current stage of development and the enormous power for good or evil that it has at its fingertips. Such power requires caution and concern to be observed. The best that most of humanity who are privileged to enjoy the recent benefits of longevity and a regular income achieve, is to plan for a pension. Since many can now hope to live beyond the end of their working lives, adequate provision has to be made. But who is looking after the pension provision for the planet? The big operational idea behind the concept of sustainable development is really a strategic management challenge. Who is anticipating the potential pitfalls associated with the business-as-usual scenario dominated by short-term concerns – cash flow and annual profits for the businessmen, the five-year electoral cycle for the politicians? How can these problems, associated with the myopia of the short-term vision, be avoided?

The IUCN/UNEP/WWF document begins with three major environmental concerns, namely: limiting human impact on the biosphere to within carrying capacity; maintaining the stock of biological wealth; and using non-renewable resources at rates which do not exceed the creation of renewable substitutes. Only after the predominantly long-term, environmentally driven agenda has been laid down, does the development-driven agenda come into this document. The fourth point prescribes an equitable distribution of the benefits and costs of resource use and environmental management. Once again we would select this as the essential criterion to reinforce our argument concerning the centrality of improving the management of the natural resource base. The 'equity' within this objective should not be viewed solely within a social democratic, redistributive and poverty alleviation perspective. Equally important is brokering the conflicting interests between sectors, within sectors, between state and civil society, within civil society, between the private sector and NGOs.

The remaining four objectives, in our view, are all sub-sets of this management imperative. They include promoting technologies that increase the benefits from a given stock of resources; utilizing economic policy to maintain natural wealth; adopting an anticipatory, cross-sectoral approach to decision-making (of which more anon); and promoting and supporting cultural values compatible with sustainability.

Strategic directions

This IUCN/UNEP/WWF document is important primarily because it tries to address the question of strategic directions. It identifies three main obstacles to sustainability; lack of ethical commitment; inequitable distribution of power; and separation of environmental conservation and economic development. It then goes on to propose six strategic directions.

(i) **Transforming attitudes and practices.** This is why environmental education has to be the top priority. It should involve responding to people's own priority assessment of their needs, and being able to create forums to discuss these issues in a participatory way. Raising awareness of the issues requires a huge effort in the formal and non-formal education sectors and in the media. Within the structures of the state and in civil society the educational effort has to be transformed into creating new and more effective institutions, structures and practices. Leadership must come from the top to ensure delivery. Transforming attitudes and practices means learning and transmitting the new language of sustainable development, which needs to incorporate all the other current major initiatives of good governance, participation, facilitation and partnerships, in place of the command and control state mentality of the past.

(ii) **Building a global alliance.** This means that international, regional, national, provincial, district and grassroots levels should link up, both horizontally and vertically, with others facing the same challenges. Not all of the challenges can be solved within the framework of the nation state. In the case of Mozambique a number of challenges will require regional and international co-operation. For example, optimizing the use of common river and ocean resources and wildlife management and tourism need to be managed at the southern African regional level; protection against oil spills, the dumping of toxic waste and international crime, in particular drugs and arms, need to be co-ordinated at the international level. Building alliances means identifying the stakeholders who share an interest in the management of the natural resource base and whose interests may at times conflict. Articulating their various constraints and opportunities and creating forums in which these can be negotiated, can give enormous value added to the development process. A further important aspect is shortening the learning curves by encouraging networking and communication at all levels, such that models of good practice are identified and publicized and can thus have the maximum spread effect. Similarly negative experiences can also be shared to avoid further costly mistakes being repeated.

(iii) **Empowering communities.** People must take primary responsibility them-selves for solving their own problems by mobilizing the necessary human and other resources required. In the case of Mozambique, this means going against a long-standing trend of centralized state control, and it is proving a long haul to shift from this mentality. Of course, it is not merely a problem of spreading edu-cation and enlightenment. Self-interest at the level of individuals and institutions operates as an important constraint. When it comes to devolving control over resources, this has proved to be a problem everywhere in Africa, and indeed out-side the continent as well. Yet at the very least, impediments should be removed to allow groups and institutions within civil society to facilitate the management of resources in a more effective manner, including by privatizing former state functions.

(iv) **Integrating environment and development.** This is being encouraged by various means. There are strong advocates for allocating monetary values to envi-ronmental functions (Pearce *et al*, 1989). Others see transforming attitudes and practices as more important. In effect, both will act together. In the North a green consumer consciousness combines with the government's insistence that envi-ronmental costs be covered by companies in their cost accounting. Integrating environment and development has not been a habit in the past, with the negative results now there for all to see. If development goes ahead with utter disregard for the environment, time and again a heavy price has to be paid.

(v) **Stabilizing resource demand and population.** This implies a change in lifestyles and family planning. The need to limit population growth within the constraints of current resource availability, given present levels of social organi-zation and technology, makes good sense if people are to enjoy a reasonable qual-ity of life.

(vi) **Conserving the variety of life.** Conserving the variety of life is both a moral virtue in itself and a hedging bet for humanity's current and future benefit. There is a powerful utilitarian logic in not destroying anything which may eventually benefit humankind through medical or technological discovery from the treasure chest of biodiversity. On the other hand, and reinforcing this, is the ethical prob-lem of who are we, mere humankind, to play God over all other life forms? Respect for nature was part of the ethos of pre-colonial societies; however, colonization did much to undermine this. Now is the time to reassert pre-colo-nial societies' own environmental ethical code, as part of re-evaluating Africa's roots and rooting development more firmly in each country's social and cultural base.

Sustainable development involves a process that will secure adequate levels of con-sumption of basic needs and the income to obtain them for our generation and for our children, both today and also in the future. Security and adequacy imply the need for environmental sustainability. If we take care of nature, then nature will take care of us. If we do not, then we are simply storing up problems for ourselves when the crops, livestock and fish catch diminish. Beyond basic needs, sustainable develop-ment also implies increased leisure, an evolving cultural identity and an expanding range of choice. Only food independence can release human beings to realize their full potential. An empty belly drives out other ambitions.

Sustainable development, then, is concerned with meeting people's basic needs for food, clothing, shelter, work, health care and education as minimum requirements. This can best be achieved by using natural resources wisely. Knowledge of the local environment is absolutely essential for this. Traditional knowledge of the environment exists amongst farming communities and is a rich treasure house providing a foundation stone on which to build (Richards, 1985).

Sustainable development is all about people learning how to improve their lives. Hence people need to be well informed so that they can do things themselves rather than waiting for the government or aid agencies to do them for them. Tapping the traditional knowledge base is the place to begin for peasant farming communities. Building upon it to improve and maximize the benefits of natural resource usage is the challenge.

Start with food and the farmers

Food self-sufficiency is a good starting point. This means encouraging rural development efforts, locally led by the farmers, which are sustainable and spreadable. Agriculture cannot be run by outside experts from abroad or even from the capital city or provincial headquarters. It has to be run by the farmers themselves, with their own organizations articulating their needs. The job of government extension services and aid agencies is to support and facilitate the efforts of rural farmers. The nature of extension needs to be both dramatically expanded and transformed. For too long the task in Africa has been seen as taking solutions to the peasants. This has to be reversed. Peasant farmers' problems have to be taken to, and assumed by, the researchers. The extension service must become the agent of the farmers rather than of the government. Farming systems research represents one such initiative. In Zimbabwe the extension motto is: 'Build on what farmers have and use what they know'. This is not simply a populist policy deemed appropriate only for developing countries. This approach is the one that dynamically transformed agriculture in the United States in the early part of the twentieth century.

Lloyd Timberlake (1988) examined the reasons for past failures in agricultural policies in the late 1980s. A decade later it is salutary to ask what has changed? The following five reasons he deemed to apply in general in Africa:

(i) **Neglect of agriculture.** In the period 1978–82, nine out of ten African governments studied by the FAO spent less than 15% of their annual budget on agriculture, whilst agriculture accounted for an average 40% of their GDP. The general belief of governments was that economic development meant urbanization and industrialization.

What will be the comparable figures twenty years on from this for the period 1998–2002? In the 1990s the structural adjustment agenda moved from encouraging the state to spend more on agriculture, to the state withdrawing in the main from the agricultural sector. The question remains, who will fill the gap?

Falloux and Talbot, senior environment advisers in the World Bank, reconsider (1993, Chap. 18) the role of rural development in what they term the era of the environment. Rural development had its heyday in the 1970s and early 1980s. It then sank from view as the fashion changed. Critics argued that these integrated approaches were too complex, and the idea of the multi-functional development agent was abandoned in favour of sectoral initiatives. Yet at the beginning of the 1990s a major World Bank review of the rural development experience concluded that a very reasonable 60–70% of these projects actually achieved their economic objective, and as Falloux and Talbot go on to say:

To these economic results, measured directly by the increase in agricultural production and revenues, must be added the benefits derived from the improvement in living conditions from better physical and social infrastructure. (1993: 244)

The two authors draw four important lessons from the rural development experience for the environmental era. Complexity is inescapable. A multi-sectoral approach and eliminating poverty remain essential. They reaffirm the importance of participation. Finally they underline the need to link information and action.

(ii) **Urban bias** The balance of political power and influence lies with the urban areas, hence government policies were oriented towards urban interests and spending went on towns and industries.

The state bureaucracy was frequently parasitic and industry inefficient. The only genuinely productive sector was agriculture. Exchange rates were overvalued to the benefit of urban consumers, and the peasants suffered through cheap food imports plus food aid generated by the North's need to dump food surpluses.

Prices to farmers were kept low to provide cheap food for the cities. Low peasant incomes cannot provide a market for manufactured goods. Low set prices are a disincentive to market through official channels. There was neglect of rural roads and infrastructure.

A generation later there is little evidence that the urban bias has been significantly reduced, at least in the mentality of the political and civil service elite who tend to view rural problems with detachment as they themselves live in an urban milieu. Of course the heavily subsidized state industries are dissolving under the pressure of structural adjustment. An administered price regime for peasant products is being replaced by free market bargaining. But it seems to be a long and tortuous uphill struggle.

(iii) **Northern biases.** Northern technologies and approaches were overvalued and African ones devalued, i.e. encouraging monocropping rather than intercropping, whereas the latter is generally better suited to Africa's environment. Traditional farming knowledge was ignored.

This assessment by Timberlake was part of a populist backlash in the late 1980s against the modernization orthodoxy. It raises profound questions for the twenty-first century and the era of globalization. To what extent does it make sense to create an 'either/or' situation between commercial farming methods and building on traditional farming knowledge? Both can have a role to play, the only important test is effectiveness. It is certainly the case that far more can be made of building on the best practices of traditional farming methods. Yet as population pressures and land scarcity grow these are not always the most appropriate solutions.

(iv) **Top-down approaches.** The top-down approaches legitimized Northern agricultural biases. In Mozambique, Angola and elsewhere, given the Cold War alliances of the time, this led to the expensive disaster of state agriculture. State ownership of natural forests, rangelands and wildlife reduced community control. Policies were framed without consulting the people and therefore did not command enthusiastic support.

President Nyerere said in 1979

> The best intentioned governments – my own included – too readily moved from a conviction of the need for rural development into acting as if the people had no ideas of their own. This is quite wrong ... people do know what their basic needs are ... if they have sufficient freedom they can be relied upon to determine their own priorities of development. (Timberlake, 1988:)

Greater efforts are being made today to avoid excessive top-down approaches. The difficulty is in finding the right balances to strike. It remains to be seen whether innovative schemes such as community wildlife management initiatives, say, will develop a proven track record of success.

(v) **Aid often mis-directed.** Projects are often highly import-dependent. Aid donors are reluctant to cover local costs. When aid dries up, projects inevitably collapse.

Aid can indeed strengthen centralization, sustain unpopular governments and inflate bureaucracies. Generally there has been insufficient emphasis on capacity building in terms of both human resources development and institutional strengthening.

The WCED Report (1987) looked at the challenge of food security and recommended:

- turning the terms of trade in favour of the farmers through better pricing policies for food;
- investing in the agricultural sector by providing farm support services (credit and extension) and better market infrastructures;
- making better use of the resource base through land reform, expanding the technological base (especially through renewable energy inputs) and implementing integrated development schemes. If this is not achieved, the poor have no alternative but to over-use the resource base;
- governments introducing a three-fold classification of land:
  i) 'enhancement areas' capable of sustaining intensive cropping and higher population and consumption;
  ii) 'prevention areas' not to be developed for intensive agriculture or, where this already occurs, converting to other uses;
  iii) 'restoration areas', once productive land now in need of restoration;
- better water management;
- developing alternatives to chemical fertilizers and pesticides, including organic plant nutrients;
- instituting more and better agroforestry schemes;
- introducing fish farming to compensate for over-fishing.

Initiatives have been taken to put some of these ideas into practice, but much work remains to be done.

Sustainable livelihood thinking

This is proposed by Robert Chambers (1988). The starting point is human survival but the focus is much broader than food security alone. Poor people want command over their assets and income. To diminish population growth and the flight to urban centres, the living conditions of the rural poor must be improved. The poor must be transformed from being the problem to being the solution. Traditional knowledge resources need to be tapped. Chambers puts forward the following agenda:

i) to secure sustainable livelihoods sources of income need to be diversified;
ii) ensuring sustainable livelihoods means respecting traditional practices, valuing them and building upon them;
iii) sustainable livelihood policies require:
   - land redistribution and greater resource equity
   - granting some form of tenure
   - preserving access to common resources and ensuring greater equity of returns
   - supporting diversification
   - ensuring good prices

- extending all support facilities
- encouraging small-scale irrigation to provide all-year employment plus increased intensification
- decentralising power in a meaningful way;

iv) supporting professionals who encourage this view;
v) research and development undertaken by rural people themselves. There is much to be gained from sharing the traditional knowledge base and the successes that occur.

Given the huge disruptions to the social fabric caused by wars, as in Angola and Mozambique, with communities torn apart and massive population dislocations, rediscovering the traditional knowledge base is a first priority. Where are the individuals who possess this knowledge? They have to be located and their knowledge recorded and shared as a community-based educational effort. The situation may be such that the knowledge base is lost altogether. For instance, massive social change engineered for more than a century in South Africa effectively destroyed most of the peasantry. Separate development and later apartheid wrenched the black population from their land and from a farming livelihood.

How can the potential be tapped? First of all, Africa has an incredible diversity of farming systems. These have to be carefully studied prior to making interventions. We can find many of the ingredients for success amongst existing farming systems. These involve four main methods of intensifying production to produce higher yields by means of: i) irrigation; ii) agroforestry; iii) organic recycling; and iv) soil conservation (Harrison, 1987). The Chagga on Mt Kilimanjaro in Tanzania developed very sophisticated systems incorporating all four.

The successful intensified agricultural systems exist in pockets. If these could be generalized, this would go a long way towards tackling the problem of sustainable development. One reason why they are localized is that farming systems are complex ways of managing crops and soils, and have to be taught. The challenge is to generalize the traditional knowledge of these systems.

Over time, as population densities increase, intensification of production will occur, according to the Boserup (1965) thesis. But the clock is ticking away and unless the process can be accelerated people will suffer and the land may become irreparably eroded. The only way out is for Africa's farmers to intensify before population density compels them to do so. To achieve this requires:

i) incentives
- improved incomes
- inputs available to exchange for crops marketed
- devices to improve efficiency.
ii) A more rapid diffusion of intensive and soil-conserving techniques via extension efforts which build upon pockets of existing farmers' knowledge combined with improved methods that build on what is there, in an incremental manner that does not require the peasant farmer to engage in excessive risk.

What about a green revolution in Africa? With the exception of hybrid maize in South Africa, Kenya and Zimbabwe, the green revolution has been slow to affect much of Africa. The evidence suggests that with the spread of HYVs (high yielding varieties) rural economic differentiation has increased and that access to capital inputs has been biased in favour of richer farmers.

The major barriers to innovation are: i) labour constraints; ii) poor supplies of associated inputs; and iii) market uncertainties. Where these barriers have been removed innovations have spread rapidly, but only where they are appropriate to farmers' needs, and where research, extension and other back-up services are in place. The removal of these barriers has been a reflection of greater integration into the market economy at the local, national and international levels. Opening up to the global market appears to make overcoming these barriers easier. In practice it is likely that modern high technology farming will go ahead, especially in the private sector. Yet for the vast majority of small farmers this will not be a viable option. The answer for these people is to build on indigenous farming methods.

There have been success stories. What is the nature of Zimbabwe's agricultural success story of the early 1980s? On the eve of independence peasant farmers produced 7% of marketed grain; by 1985 it was 50% (1.78 million tonnes). Since independence services previously exclusive to settlers have been extended to peasant farmers:

- maize collection depots were moved from railheads to be closer to the farmers and there have been lower transport costs
- high yielding seeds and fertilizer packages have been distributed
- there is improved access to credit for small farmers
- working together through farmer groups has been encouraged
- high maize prices have been instituted to provide incentives
- fertilizer prices have been kept down
- there is good infrastructure especially roads and rail, and
- good back-up services and structures (extension and research, also working farmers are used in extension) (Harrison, 1987: 87–97)

Zimbabwe has advantages – some good land on the high and mid-veldt. Maize is both a cash and a food crop. The Master Farmers have their own organizations and are a vocal pressure group through the National Farmers' Associations. Robert Bates (1981) has argued that African countries which have done well agriculturally are those where farmers are a potent political force. Farmers need organizations to speak to governments on their behalf.

Policy and institutional challenges: formulating a national strategy

The 1992 Earth Summit significantly helped to move forward the impetus to develop national strategies. A huge level of written output ensued and what follows once again draws out the essentials (see Grubb *et al*, 1993 for a summary). This is the third influential text on sustainable development that we shall consider.

There are three systems basic to any process of development: the biological or ecological resource system, the economic system, and the social system. Human society applies a set of goals to each system; for example, in the ecological system to protect biodiversity, in the economic system to increase production of goods and services, and in the social system to ensure broad public participation in decision-making.

The objective of sustainable development is to maximize the achievement of goals across the three systems at one and the same time through an adaptive process of trade-offs. The process is adaptive because individual preferences, social norms, ecological conditions, and the state of development change over time. Agenda 21 of the 1992 World Conference on Environment and Development repeatedly emphasized these three systems and the need to apply an integrated approach to them.

Chapter 8 of Agenda 21 outlines the key objectives in helping to formulate a national strategy for sustainable development. These objectives include:

- the integration of environment and development at all levels in decision-making;

- a long-term coherent and cross-sectoral approach;
- systematic and on-going review, monitoring and evaluation of the development process and the environment;
- participatory development and social partnership;
- greater accountability, transparency in decision-making and access to information;
- setting clear, achievable, costed and time-bound targets, goals and objectives;
- defining ecological and other constraints on human and economic activity;
- rationalizing and integrating existing national planning exercises, and where relevant subsuming donor action plans into a country-driven process;
- creating a framework for implementing Agenda 21;
- creating a framework for accountability and transparency on environmental and development issues;
- examining the interface between national development and environmental and international factors.

To achieve these objectives it is essential that coherent and long-term training programmes for sustainable development be initiated. These must incorporate decision-makers at the national, provincial, district and grassroots levels.

There is growing world-wide recognition of the vitally important role to be played by environmental education in understanding, preventing and solving environmental problems. We now know that the key to solving these problems lies not in technological fixes alone but primarily in changing the values, attitudes and behaviour of individuals and groups in respect of the environment. Environmental education should simultaneously transmit information, create awareness, develop knowledge and skills, promote values and habits and provide standards and guidelines to facilitate sustainable development decision-making and problem solving.

In response to these challenges, a national strategy for environmental education and training should seek to achieve the following:

i) the implementation of effective models of environmental education, training and information gathering and dissemination;
ii) general awareness of the causes and effects of environmental problems;
iii) general acceptance of the need for an integrated approach to solving these problems;
iv) training of the personnel needed at various levels for the national management of the environment, with a view to achieving sustainable development at community, regional and national levels.

Capacity must be built up for integrating environmental concerns with development initiatives across all sectors. Knowledge must be improved about the environment and development problems of the country. SD solutions must be devised with an emphasis on intersectoral approaches. People need to learn basic environmental, natural resource and sustainable development concepts to facilitate free exchange of ideas and the formation of interest groups in the democratic process.

The hardest challenges to making development sustainable confront those countries which are poor in an absolute sense – with an extremely low per capita GDP. Not only are the people the poorest of the poor; beyond this, some countries have experienced long and bitter internal wars which have destroyed countless human lives both physically and psychologically, tearing apart the social fabric of society. One of the ironies of the situation is that, whilst war is the ultimate anti-development force, it may also act in some measure as a conservation factor for the environment by limiting for the time being the extent of the economic utilization of the natural resource base.

An additional burden upon these poorest of the poor countries is that their very poverty and marginalization within the global, market-based economic system contributed to the radical socialist development option some have taken in the past. Mozambique stands alongside Angola, Ethiopia, Vietnam, Cambodia and Laos and others in this respect. This trajectory, for a wide variety of reasons, proved to be a developmental *cul-de-sac*, foundering on the harsh realities of the fundamental economic and political weaknesses of the existing Marxist-Leninist model. The sustainable development challenge that these countries collectively face is highly complex. Their economies are shattered; they represent what is portrayed in the media as the ultimate 'basket-cases' of the international system. At the same time, their previous experience had highly positive dimensions in terms of preventative health care, mass education and in some degree – albeit short-lived – the widespread use of political participation as an empowering developmental force. These are important dimensions of the current sustainable development agenda, and their positive legacy should not be lost. A subsequent ossification of these initially promising traits under the democratic centralist system heralded the final demise of the Marxist project. Subsequently, there has been a massive swing in the opposite direction into a free market free-for-all. The ruling parties both in Angola and in Mozambique succeeded in maintaining their hold on government because the principal opposition parties in the democratic elections had significantly less moral authority, associated as they were with allying themselves with the South African apartheid government and condemned by the electorate for the brutality they exercised against the civilian population.

Changing our approaches for policy, programme and project formulation

It is essential to move beyond narrow sectoral planning. If this does not happen, each sector's plans and activities will never be able to succeed properly because of the potentially adverse effects of a lack of co-ordination. These can take many forms: the necessary land, labour, capital, water, tourists or investors may not be available as required because of competing demands from other sectors or there may be negative environmental effects resulting from a failure to co-ordinate with other sectors and among the state, the private sector, NGOs and citizens in general.

The WCED Report, *Our Common Future* (1987), gave some clear directions about how to change existing approaches. These provide a workable set of guidelines that can be used on a day-to-day basis. They are as follows:

i)   improving intersectoral co-ordination for better management of the human and the natural resource base;
ii) responding to people's own priorities of their needs;
iii) helping groups to articulate their needs and to engage in dialogue over the constraints and opportunities;
iv) paying special attention to the most disadvantaged whose voice is weakest: women, the unemployed, the elderly, the poorest;
v)   prioritizing meeting people's basic needs: shelter, water, food, health, education;
vi) ensuring sustainability.

Improving intersectoral co-ordination is essential. The government, the economy and education are all divided up into sectors and disciplines which are tightly compartmentalized. Real life is never divided up so neatly. The peasant farmer operates his/her farm on the basis of integrated land use. Land is used for habitation, crop production, livestock grazing, hunting and gathering, and trees and shrubs – known collectively as woody biomass – providing fuelwood, timber for house construction, tool-making and fencing, medicinal ingredients, and a habitat for the spiritual and ecological world of the peasant farmer. Local farmers manage their *machambas* (farms) as integrated units. Advisers from outside make a specialism out of a discrete part of their integrated universe. All the external advice comes in as though this segment was the only thing that mattered and that this was the ultimate priority. But this can never be determined from the outside. The only place to start has to be people's own priority needs, which they will, of course, adapt somewhat, according to the potential package which appears to be on offer from outside.

Problems arise because what happens in one sector can negatively affect others. Hence it is essential to obtain the broader vision, which allows the key actors to recognize and identify where the potential conflicts lie in the common use of the natural and the human resource base. It does not take a genius to recognize what has to be done once this central problem is identified. In sum, there has to be better management of the human and the natural resources base to overcome potential conflicts.

Solutions can be found once the reality of existing conflicts is recognized by the parties involved. The nature of the conflicting interests has to be identified in order to provide an agenda for negotiation and resolution. It is possible to alert sectoral groups to the negative effects upon themselves of poor management practices within and between sectors. Thereby, political and economic pressure may be brought to bear to obtain an amelioration of such activities within or between sectors. The array of mechanisms available to achieve this is important to survey. These can include tax incentives, a proactive investment code and polluter pays principles. Yet there are serious impediments to political decision-makers' taking the right options.

Politicians with their short-term electoral horizons are little concerned with the interests of generations yet unborn. Only a sufficient concern amongst an electorate for their children's well-being and their own total quality of life, rather than a narrow income and tax calculation, can help resolve this. UNCED took place in the midst of a severe world recession. 'The standard of living of the American people is not up for negotiation' is President Bush's famous quote concerning UNCED. Businesses are likely to be concerned with short-term profit maximization. What conditions can be created to help businesses think and act for the long term?

Building for improved intersectoral co-ordination for policy and planning requires a number of steps to be taken. Key professionals in the civil service, NGOs and businesses as well as politicians have to be convinced of the value of such an approach. A hard analysis is required of each of the sectors and where the potential intersectoral conflict in the management of the human and the natural resource base might lie. Explorations of the interface can identify options for improved synergies from better integrated efforts. Beyond this, the negative effects of existing practices can be scrutinized to discover if better options exist, to minimize pollution, say. The aim is to try to find win-win situations, or, at a minimum, to identify least bad options. These can then offer some guidance as to meeting the first principle of the WCED report.

The other five guidelines listed can be tackled in significant measure by pursuing an active process of decentralization and of supporting a strengthening of civil society. An all-powerful central government with weak national-level interest group articulation is unlikely to be able to respond effectively to people's own priorities of their needs and to prioritize meeting basic needs, with special attention paid to the most disadvantaged. Ensuring sustainability has to begin at the local level, anything else is unviable. At the national level, a legislative framework can be put in place and training programmes initiated. What follows is some guidelines for helping ensure project success and sustainability at the local level.

Secrets of project success
i)   Beware the large-scale projects: big dams, factories or irrigation schemes.
     Sometimes they are unavoidable but look for the low cost alternatives.
ii) Wide reach is necessary to escape the pilot project or show-case village.
iii) Local initiatives are important as they guarantee participation, but they need support.
iv) Dynamizers are needed to give good leadership at all levels.
v)   Flexibility is needed, and a practical approach of trial and error.
vi) Respect for the people and their knowledge and ideas is essential.
vii) There must be meaningful participation through all stages, especially in the
     execution of projects and the commitment of people's own time and resources.
     People must feel they have both invested in the project directly themselves and
     obtained the rewards. Project management is also important. The World Bank
     believes that project beneficiaries should gradually assume increasing responsi-
     bilities for project activities during implementation and particularly following
     completion.
viii) Self-reliance is essential.
ix) There should be low risk, re: labour time, land use, and costs. Spreading the mes-
     sage is important (Harrison, 1987).

A checklist for project sustainability
   Asking the right questions of projects is vital.
i)   Does it meet people's needs?
ii)   Is there a definable target group?
iii) Is there local control?
iv)   Does it use local human resources?
v)   Does it use local material resources?
vi)   Is it sustainable?
vii) Is there limited external aid?
viii) Is there a shift of power to the disadvantaged?
ix)   Is there adequate regional co-ordination? (adapted from Ben Wisner, quoted in
      Timberlake, 1988)

The basic principle is to encourage human activity which works with nature rather
than against it. Human settlement, mining and cultivation should be discouraged on
steep slopes, river banks, coastal dunes, around lakes and where damage can be
inflicted on water catchment sources. Protecting environmentally sensitive areas is an
important concern.

Conclusion: facing the challenges

Sustainable development is an attempt to reconcile environmental conservation with
development, and this will remain a problem into the foreseeable future. Human
greed and self-interest make it unlikely that the better sentiments of humanity – a
concern for the poor, future generations and other species – will prevail, unless an
improved widespread education effort is undertaken combined with serious government intervention to modify the rules of the free market game.

   Politics has to be at the very heart of creating sustainable development policies.
This means leaving the realm of the ideal to enter the world of material interests. Self-
interest is always elevated to high principle in public debates over development issues.
Creating the conditions for sustainable development means identifying the key elements or stakeholders that need to be included in the policy dialogue and locating an
organizational form of interest articulation with which to discuss the main issues and
engage the major players. This process, of course, creates enormous disparities in

terms of both the organized articulation and relative power of the various potential interest groups.

Once interest groups are identified, the process of negotiation can begin. Here, the South African case is particularly rich and insightful (see FitzGerald *et al.*, 1997). The limitations of relying upon a benign, single party political system are now very apparent. In essence the interests are not adequately articulated or synthesized; the compromises are not made to ensure that all of the identified key groupings feel that they have a positive stake in the system.

Unless the *politics* of sustainable development is addressed it will be extremely difficult to introduce economic solutions such as those advocated by Pearce *et al.* (1989). The reason is quite simple: no legislation will be introduced unless it is acceptable to the interests of the key power brokers. In other words, the broader political framework will determine whether the space exists for economic initiatives for 'costing the Earth'. Here we enter another domain of problems. So many developing countries are undergoing structural adjustment programmes, whilst most of the remainder lie under the shadow of a similar fate, unless the prescribed remedial measures are taken. In the eyes of the critics, duplicity lies at the heart of some of the multilateral donor agencies, in that they proclaim the importance of taking the environment into consideration in development initiatives, yet the bottom line remains the same: export more—which usually means mining the natural resource base – to improve the external balance of payments situation; and spend less internally to balance government deficits – which invariably implies cuts in health, education and more general human resource development expenditure. To its credit, the World Bank is on an appreciable learning curve, and within the organization there is now an on-going debate to redress former imbalances. Yet these unresolved tensions are likely to continue for some time to come.

References

Adams, W.M. (1990) *Green Development, Environment and Sustainability in the Third World*. Routledge, London.

Bates, R. (1981) *Markets and States in Tropical Africa: the Political Basis of Agricultural Policies*. University of California Press, Berkeley, CA.

Boserup, E. (1965) *The Conditions of Agricultural Growth: The Economics of Agrarian Changes under Popular Pressures*. Allen and Unwin, London.

Chambers, R. (1988) 'Sustainable rural livelihoods: a key strategy for people, environment and development', in C. Conroy and M. Litvinoff (eds), *The Greening of Aid: Sustainable Livelihoods in Practice*. Earthscan, London.

Conway, G.R. and Barbier, E.B. (1990) *After the Green Revolution: Sustainable Agriculture for Development*. Earthscan, London.

Falloux, F. and Talbot, L.M. (1993) *Crisis and Opportunity: Environment and Development in Africa*. Earthscan, London.

FitzGerald, P., McLennan, A. and Munslow, B. (eds) (1997) *Managing Sustainable Development in South Africa*, second edition, Oxford University Press, Cape Town.

Grubb, M *et al.* (1993) *The Earth Summit Agreement*. Earthscan, London.

Hanlon, J. (1991) *Mozambique. Who Calls the Shots?* James Currey, London.

Harrison, P. (1987) *The Greening of Africa*. Paladin, London.

IUCN, UNEP, WWF (1991) *Caring for the Earth: A Strategy for Sustainable Living*, IUCN, Gland, Switzerland.

Jacobs, M. (1991) *The Green Economy: Environment, Sustainable Development and the Politics of the Future*. Pluto Press, London.

Johnston, R.W. (1989) *Environmental Problems: Nature, Economy and State*. Belhaven Press, London.

Madeley, J. (1991) *When Aid Is No Help: How Projects Fail and How They Could Succeed*. Intermediate Technology Publications, London.

Pearce, D., Markandya, A. and Barbier, E.B. (1989) *Blueprint for a Green Economy*. Earthscan, London.

Reid, D. (1995) *Sustainable Development: An Introductory Guide*, Earthscan, London.

Richards, P. (1985) *Indigenous Agricultural Revolution*. Hutchinson, London.

Timberlake, L. (1988) *Africa in Crisis*. Earthscan, London.

World Commission on Environment and Development (1987) *Our Common Future*. Oxford University Press, Oxford.

B CHALLENGES

3 Governance & Decentralization

OSCAR MONTEIRO

Introduction

Mozambique is emerging from a long period of conflict with millions displaced and the economy ravaged. Elections for the Head of State and a multi-party National Assembly took place in November 1994. Peace has been restored and new institutions are functioning without encumbrance. At the same time the economic situation remains precarious and the debt burden heavy. The country remains extremely poor despite its undeniable potential. The challenge for Mozambicans is to build a sustainable system of governance in these conditions. In this chapter we deal with three of the components of governance: the election process, the process of decentralization and the role of civil society.

Good governance implies an electoral system that is not only free and fair but which should also aim at integrating the various sectors of society into the management of public affairs. In other words, it needs to be inclusive. As this always proves difficult to achieve even in highly homogeneous and integrated societies, various avenues need to be found for political integration. One option is participation in locally elected bodies. Minority groups and in particular regional interest groups can obtain their share of power in formal structures through decentralization, if such a process is conducted with a view to providing real opportunities and effective power sharing. Formal powers enshrined in the law must be underpinned by actual capacity, both in terms of qualified manpower and financial resources or the legal means to procure them, specifically powers of taxation.

More and more, formal institutions have to rely on the co-operation of both organized and non-organized sectors of civil society. Democratization and decentralization are not proving to be the panacea for the chronic ills of maladministration and lack of commitment on the part of civil servants or elected MPs or councillors, whilst an atmosphere of crisis and distrust continues. Despite the fact that the main actors tend sometimes to see themselves as the standard bearers for democratization, the strength of the democratic process rests ultimately on the combined efforts of all, which inevitably implies a certain degree of conflict and the capacity to manage it. Openness and tolerance are essential for success.

We shall try to identify in the Mozambican experience the various features of the processes, showing that through a sometimes slow build-up, the difficulties and the contradictions may themselves contribute to the emergence of democracy in society.

Election process

From one-party to multi-party democracy

Recognition of pluralism did not come easily within the existing Mozambican political landscape. The successful outcome of the national liberation process with the proclamation of independence in 1975 led to an attempt to incorporate into the new political dispensation and the management of public affairs the values that had been the source of success in the previous phase, the liberation struggle. This incorporated a fair measure of participation, particularly in the first years of independence, but it always remained extremely centralized. So there was the co-existence of a heavily top-down approach, culminating in the adoption of the one-party system, combined with participation expressed through a plethora of meetings and structures operating at every level from neighbourhoods to government departments. This period left indelible marks on the pattern of Mozambican political culture and continues to permeate present political life.

Inconsistencies, or perhaps incompatibilities, between participation and top-down approaches, although not immediately perceived, were at the basis of the eventual crisis of the system. This led to a period when a political vacuum existed in which the one-party system was no longer seen as providing a solution, whilst fear of the unknown created a conservative reaction to change.

One of the stronger arguments for one-party states in Africa lay in the concern that opposition parties would be a front for regional interests leading to secession. The Biafra syndrome influenced the thinking of the first generation of nationalists, only to be replaced by an awareness that excessive centralization and the lack of space for any expression of differences of opinion were in turn undermining national unity. Finally, the fact that Mozambique was facing a war waged with support from external forces (former Portuguese settlers allied with Rhodesian and South African military and political powers) also contributed to the maintenance of the *status quo*.

The challenges facing the democratic process in Mozambique are how to combine pluralism, understood as being the acceptance and recognition of diversity with the formation of political parties, with the search for solutions, namely the definition of public policies, and with the space to be granted to regional and in some cases ethnically based interests; and finally, how to deal with all of them in a positive way, while allaying fears of national disintegration.

The principle of multi-party elections was enshrined in the Constitution approved in 1990. The original draft proposal submitted to the public did not take a position on the issue. The eventual decision was finally taken only after an extensive national debate that lasted for six months. This initiative was a result of the evolution of political thinking within the ruling party itself that the prevailing system was running out of options. In addition, new social classes had emerged within the Party demanding economic liberalization to pursue their interests. Despite its name, the Frelimo party was in reality a continuation of the liberation front. In fact, economic liberalization had begun in practice in a limited way from 1980 onwards.

The international context marked by the failure of the Eastern European Marxist-Leninist socialist political system also had a bearing on the model of development and organization, combined with Western influence which became stronger, in particular insofar as it was linked to the negotiations for debt relief. Changes were also taking place in the political systems of many African countries, including neighbouring countries such as Zambia. The one-party state model was being challenged as never before.

Most of the opinions expressed in the national debate on the Constitution coming from the rural areas were in favour of maintaining the *status quo*. The most vocal sectors in the urban areas were in favour of multi-party democracy. While this was probably a minority view at the time, it was decided that the existence of such political sentiment should be accommodated and the multi-party system was adopted. It is interesting to note that since the elections, while criticism of the existing political forces and personalities remains rife, and is in some cases exaggerated, no one now questions the idea of a multi-party system. Sectors of civil society take the existing shortcomings of the system as a challenge to discover various forms of democratic renewal.

The formal approval of the Constitution was followed by the passing of a number of implementing laws that gave it substance and made it meaningful: the law on the freedom to constitute political parties, (Law 7/91, 23 January 1991); the law on associations; the law on freedom of political demonstrations (Law 9/91, 18 July 1991); the law on freedom of the press (Law 18/91, 10 August, 1991); the law on free trade unionism (Law 23/91, 31 December 1991); and the law on the right to strike (Law 6/91, January 1991). These were all passed in the course of 1991 and allowed the development of multi-party life and stimulated the growth of civil society movements.

From war to peace

In the meantime negotiations had started in Rome with a view to putting an end to the war. From the official point of view, there was at first no connection between the two processes, internal democratization being seen by the government as part of an internal process of political evolution unrelated to the war. At that point in time, the government did not portray Renamo as a legitimate political force but rather as an agent for destabilization. On the other hand, the government was confronted with the difficulty of implementing the democratization programme in a situation of war. Renamo, essentially a military movement, in the meantime issued its own political manifesto, calling for multi-party elections. This created a potential common ground that ultimately provided a basis for both parties to end the war: let the people decide.

But issues such as the fate of the contending armies and the arrangements to be made for the demobilized soldiers delayed the signature of the peace agreement and therefore had a bearing on the pace of the democratization process. There is in fact an in-built danger in the procedure followed, namely, to end a war through elections. Whilst a post-war situation requires a peaceful environment that does not interfere with the demobilization of soldiers and a toning down of conflicts, an electoral campaign tends to raise tensions and tempers. The holding of elections immediately after the end of the war courted these risks. The fact that elections were postponed for a year to allow total demobilization to take place, in order to avoid a repetition of the Angolan scenario, in the end contributed positively to the electoral process.

It was feared that the military as a group would be a serious obstacle to peace. They represented a significant constituency on both sides and their role in society had grown enormously as a result of the war. Would they resent the end of the conflict and thereby of the special status they enjoyed? Could they draw support from other sectors of society? What could be done to avoid a resurgence of acts of banditry that would jeopardize the democratic and development processes?

The alternatives considered were either keeping a large number of men in the army or demobilizing many soldiers with a programme for their reintegration into the productive sphere. The number of soldiers from both sides who volunteered for the new army proved to be considerably below expectations. Most of the former military went to their regions of origin, with 18-month severance pay but without any real prospects of economic reintegration, given the protracted economic crisis facing the country. This factor, together with the fact that the technical training provided failed to reach the majority of the soldiers, constitutes probably the single most important on-going threat to the democratic process and stability in the country.

Definition of the electoral system

The definition of the electoral system and the adoption of the electoral law went through a number of phases:

i)   The Constitution adopted by the one-party Assembly incorporated the basic principles of free and fair elections, the freedom to vote, and the role of political parties. It laid down the conditions for the election of the President of the Republic and the members of a one-chamber Parliament and adopted the majority voting system.

ii) During the negotiations in Rome some guiding principles were agreed. The following were the most important:
*   simultaneous elections for the President and the Assembly;
*   elections should take place within a year after the signature of the peace agreement, although allowance was made for the possibility of postponements;
*   there should be a voters' roll;
*   there should be a National Electoral Commission composed of personalities guaranteeing 'balance, objectivity and independence', one-third of them to be designated by Renamo;
*   constituencies would be drawn on the basis of the existing Provinces;
*   a proportional voting system would be adopted, which entailed a major change in the Constitution;
*   the threshold for representation in Parliament would be established in the Electoral Law within the limits of 5% and 20%;
*   international observers would be invited.

iii) A Consultative Conference of all parties, including Renamo, was convened by the government to draft the Electoral Law, according to one of the agreements reached in Rome. The Conference lasted for months without reaching consensus on all issues. Nevertheless it served the purpose of allowing new political parties to air their views on electoral issues.

iv) Parliament adopted the electoral law (Law 4/93, 28 December 1993), taking into account the peace agreements and the positions expressed at the multi-party conference.

v)   A crucial decision concerning the immigrant vote on which no consensus had been found, was left to the National Electoral Commission. Opposition from Renamo meant that the Commission was unable to reach a consensus, and the significant Mozambican community in neighbouring countries (and elsewhere) were deprived of their voting rights.

Organization and supervision

Organization of the electoral process was entrusted to a National Electoral Commission. It would also decide on complaints.

In Rome it was established that Renamo would appoint one-third of the members. During the multi-party conference the composition of the Commission led to protracted discussions. The government argued that it should have a sizeable representation, and in the end the Commission was composed of 10 representatives from the government, and 10 from the opposition parties, 7 of them from Renamo. In spite of what was stated in the Peace Agreements, some members appointed by the political parties were political leaders, particularly in the case of Renamo. An Electoral Court was created to adjudicate any complaints arising from decisions of the National Electoral Commission, comprising two judges from the Supreme Court and three international judges appointed by the United Nations, who were to choose the President of the Court. A judge from the Mozambican Supreme Court was elected. The Court was not challenged.

Whilst arguably an independent National Electoral Commission could have been seen as advisable, the weakness of civil society, on the one hand, and the fact that these first elections were highly charged politically led to the creation of a hybrid system. Twenty members were appointed by the parties but they had to agree on an independent Chairman. The choice of Barzao Mazula, a former Education official and academic with no known party connections, was successful as an acceptable moderator, able to steer a course through the atmosphere of mistrust and achieve the remarkable result of having most decisions adopted by consensus. Plaudits must also be given to members of the Commission who took very seriously their task of being members of an independent body. Yet the rule of consensus that was to guide the proceedings of the Commission remains problematic in a situation where quick decisions are required. Whether in the future electoral commissions are made up of representatives of political parties or independent personalities, the weight of independent bodies such as the judiciary and public opinion will remain important in any context of strong disagreements.

Complexity of the system

The whole exercise started in an atmosphere of extreme distrust. This implied the use of a very complex and expensive system. The existing administrative structures were not used as the organizational basis for the elections, because they were seen as being linked to the ruling party. Instead, a cumbersome and expensive machine reproducing the national set-up at both provincial and district levels was created, composed of provincial and district commissions and an independent Technical Secretariat for Electoral Administration that had to be created from scratch. For the same reasons, lessons were not drawn from previous one-party elections. This was an expensive exercise in terms of both human and financial resources and will be difficult to replicate in the future.

Most of the members of these institutions received a subsidy for their work, including the delegates of parties who attended the polling stations. The idea was created that all work involved in elections would be remunerated, contrary to what had happened in previous one-party elections, and this raises an important challenge for future elections. A revival of the ethos of voluntary work and civic responsibility is called for, which will only be possible when the present phase of economic hardship is overcome. The present model may not be financially sustainable.

Over 6 million voters were registered and issued with water-proof voters cards which carried a picture and fingerprint, an extraordinary feat, taking into account the poor state of the roads and the dispersion of the population over a large territorial area. It can be interpreted as an expression of the will for peace on the part of the organizers and the population. There were 2,600 polling stations, 52,000 members of the respective boards and 35,000 listed delegates.

The government made a US$5.4 million contribution to the exercise and the international community contributed US$59.1 million. To these costs must be added other expenses involving the lists of delegates, the initial costs incurred by the government including the multi-party conference and civic education carried out by NGOs and religious organizations amounting to US$7.7 million, making a total of $72.2 million. Most of the activities were undertaken by national citizens with some external technical support (17 advisers and specialists and 43 UN Volunteers) (UNDP, 1995). Elections for the Head of the State and for the Assembly were held simultaneously and this did not prove to be particularly difficult.

Civic education
Three aspects have to be considered: first, the exercise of the right to free speech and the role of civic education in promoting the idea that no undesirable consequences would result for any individual speaker; secondly, preparing both winners and losers to accept results that might not respond to their expectations; and thirdly an explanation of the different registration and voting mechanisms. In Mozambique the process involved explaining that everyone was entitled to her/his own opinion even within the family, and that not even a sorcerer, to use one of the examples, would be able to unveil the secrecy of the vote. Use was made of appropriate social communications mechanisms geared to an illiterate public, such as theatre, short films, comic strips and rallies. In some areas the parties were very effective in enrolling and educating their members to vote. Special workshops were held for journalists to encourage fair and accurate reporting of the electoral process.

Apart from the ruling party (and even here there were difficulties), none of the candidates or parties was prepared to sustain the financial implications of an electoral campaign. Three alternative financing options were available: through voluntary or private funding; through the State budget; or through the international community. The first stood little chance of success, given the seriousness of the country's economic crisis. The second – subsidies from the State budget – was already enshrined in the Law of the Political Parties, but only for parties represented in Parliament. The Electoral Law broadened it to include candidates. A precedent for the third option was opened up when, simultaneously with the signature of the Peace Agreements, the international community, and in particular Italy, accepted the responsibility of funding the transformation of Renamo from a military force into a political party. A Trust Fund was created, administered by the UN Special Representative together with the donor community. Once officially registered, all candidates and parties were entitled to the same subsidy. This was an attempt to level the playing field. It seems that there was no alternative. The fact that conditions for admission to the race were relatively easy to accomplish – 10,000 signatures for a presidential candidate and 2,000 members for the creation of a political party – gave rise to a certain opportunism, which in the end was regarded as a relatively minor price to pay.

Results
12.6% of registered voters did not take part in the election and a significant 6% to 8.5%, depending on which election, voted blank, which can be explained by lack of voter education. Around 150,000 votes, 2.76%, were invalid (*Mapo Oficial,* 1994), 50% of them simultaneous votes for both main presidential candidates. Brazao Mazula (1995) drew the conclusion that these simultaneous votes represented mainly a 'cry for peace' – we vote for both of you for the sake of ending the war.

The results of the elections for the President of the Republic were as expected in the polls, with the incumbent President gaining 53.30% of the vote against 33.73% for the next candidate and a sprinkling of 10 other candidates with 0.49% to 2.87% of the vote. Overall, the ruling Frelimo Party had an overall majority of 44.3% against 37.78% for Renamo and 5.15% for Uniao Democrática. The Parliament is composed of 250 MPs, 129 Frelimo, 112 Renamo and 9 Uniao Democrática. Frelimo won 3 seats more than the majority of 126. Changes to the Constitution require a two-thirds majority, hence consensus and negotiation will be necessary.

This leaves 12.74% of the voters without parliamentary representation. Although a proportional representation system has the theoretical advantage of allowing for the emergence of new political forces, the voting threshold of 5% for parliamentary representation – demanded in Rome by Renamo, who feared that the small parties were a creation of Frelimo to manipulate voters dissatisfied with the government – contributed to this effect. Small parties were unable to mount an effective challenge to this rule, neither were they able to build a coalition that would allow for their representation.

Elections and regionalism
Elections are essentially about democracy and pluralism. Usually multi-party democracy is about political pluralism. The Mozambican case only partly reflects the expression of political pluralism. While the ethnic factor does not seem to be excessively dominant, one cannot dismiss the possible significance of a regional vote that surprised the political establishment. The vote was overwhelmingly in favour of Frelimo in the southern provinces of the country and moderately so in the most northern provinces, while Renamo had the majority in the centre of the country, with strong support along the Beira Corridor and a more balanced although clear edge in the centre-north. Frelimo gained 59% of the urban vote against 29% for Renamo (Brito, 1995).

Thus the 1994 elections brought to the fore important factors in the political equation, namely, regional and ethnic components that had previously been denied or ignored. Despite the fact that most parties did not appeal to ethnic or religious considerations, or claimed afterwards their right to speak for one sector of the population, the strong bias in favour of Frelimo in the south and of Renamo in the centre can be said to be linked to the origin of their respective leaderships and the historical conflicts between the two regions, whilst the regional factor seems to have played a role in the centre-north because of a widespread perception that the south was accorded a larger share of power, privilege and access to education. Voting in the most northern provinces can be linked to an historical factor – the fact that the liberation struggle by Frelimo started in these two provinces. Nevertheless, this did not mean that for the time being politics had become completely dominated by ethnic or regional considerations; at least when they became manifest these factors tended to cut across party barriers. While in major issues party discipline prevails, interest groups composed of MPs from all parties are emerging with a view to promoting the defence of regional interests. Fears of a crystallization of regional conflicts through the parties have not materialized so far.

Candidates, parties and voters
Votes were for political parties in party block lists. Candidates were in some cases chosen by party caucuses, but the introduction of changes by party bureaucracies to accommodate different interests surprised voters at the last minute. José Norberto Carrilho, Vice President of the Supreme Court and a constitutional expert, argues that a combination of a national block list and regional constituencies with multiple choice candidates would ensure better representation (Carrilho, 1995). The main point is that in the present system the linkage between the electorate and the MPs has become somewhat tenuous.

Others from opposition parties not represented in Parliament, disadvantaged by modern electoral systems which require a strong party machine and finance, recall the positive side of previous elections in which candidates had to stand in front of the electorate and present their biography and their proposals.

The future evolution of the political scene is difficult to predict. On the one hand, differences in Parliament do not express themselves very strongly in terms of political philosophy, hence the Programme of Government for the legislature was approved by a unanimous vote. On the other hand, the two main parties are strongly rooted in their own history and constitute political families or brotherhoods. Some renovation is taking place from within, more pronounced at a parliamentary level in the case of Renamo which had to recruit new members to serve as MPs. A significant factor could be the evolution of the smaller parties that are struggling to survive. The fact that small parties are not represented in Parliament deprives them of financial support from the state, which is allocated on the basis of the respective numbers of seats. In one way this clears the ground of unrepresentative groups, but it may also hinder the renovation of the political landscape. The question remains of whether or not an electoral system should encourage the emergence of new political forces necessary for a full pluralistic political life, overcoming the present polarization. While bearing in mind the risk of political fragmentation and ungovernability, there is reason to rethink the present threshold of 5%. On the other hand, the high costs incurred in the current electoral process could be financially unsustainable; hence a simpler and less expensive system may be required as the level of external support does not seem likely to be sustained in future elections. Also financing of candidates and parties according to the existing very loose rules, while explicable by the concern not to exclude anyone, led to a proliferation of candidates that potentially jeopardized the seriousness of political life.

Conclusions
Elections remain linked in the collective memory to the end of the war. This is in one sense positive, but in another way it does not help to gauge the extent to which the new democratic political philosophy is embedded in political life, from political parties to civil society. In a way, the fact that war had drained the country of all resources, leaving everyone mentally exhausted, influenced participants. The message from the population was unmistakably clear. It is the one case where destruction finally played a positive role in winning what initially seemed the difficult challenge of putting an end to war through elections. The discussion on whether the democratic changes were brought about by indigenous change or international pressure will rage for a long time. In a sense no one is immune to pressures – and these existed, even when applied gently as suggestions. No clear divide is possible between what you have to do under pressure and what you genuinely feel has to be done.

The importance of the discussion lies in the fact that it is the strength of the internal elements that determines the sustainability of the new model, taking into account the dynamics of the process. The transition from a one-party system to a multi-party democracy started as an interaction between government and society, and for some time the leadership of the process remained essentially in the hands of the government. The introduction of multi-party democracy was achieved by the adoption of a new Constitution by the existing National Assembly and not as a result of national conferences as in Benin's model,[1] nor can it be said that it resulted directly from the peace agreements or the war situation.

On the other hand, it is also true that once the dynamics of multi-party democracy came into force, the ruling party could not lead the process alone and felt the need to incorporate other forces. This was done through multi-party conferences and later through Parliament where the opposition started to play a more significant role. Civil society made only timid forays into the process, such as through the personality of the

---

[1]Faced with a crisis of the system in Benin, a conference of all political forces was convened chaired by an archbishop. It drafted the new Constitution and adopted a multi-party system of government.

Chairman of the National Electoral Commission, through COMPOL, a supervisory body created *ad hoc* to supervise the impartiality of the Police during the transitional period and composed of civilian personalities, through the role of the Churches in appealing for tolerance as well as by NGOs in civic education, but such forms of participation were not organically sustained. Regional changes, particularly in South Africa, created a favourable environment, as the new authorities are committed to a peaceful evolution in the sub-region.

No one any longer questions the wisdom of adopting multi-party democracy. Criticism can sometimes be heard of the real representativeness, and concerns are expressed about the commitment of elected or non-elected office bearers. The challenges to the democratization process come from different sources: the economic hardships suffered by the population and the fact that immediate improvements resulting from the end of the war are not materializing, and the fact that economic decline has not been reversed, unemployment has been on the increase and the social divides are greater with no proper and efficient mechanisms of social protection for the poor.

There is no immediate answer to these questions in the political field. New institutions created after the elections will not be accepted *per se* but only insofar as they measure up to people's expectations and become institutionalized in social life. This will require sound decision-making, a recognized concern for the problems of the common man and certainly a fair amount of education by example. The role of the political establishment is to prevent demoralization and cynicism amongst the citizens. Civic education, on the other hand, means upgrading the degree of popular understanding of the difficult problems and sometimes impossible choices of political life; this will lead to more enlightened contributions from the citizens. Civic education which has been associated with the electoral process has to become wider and to encompass political education for the political democratic process to become sustainable and less prone to failure. Political stability is not an end in itself, it must result in more investment, more efficiency and improved economic conditions. The road ahead is still a long one.

Decentralization

Inherited centralization

Mozambique inherited at independence a centralized structure of government, with a higher degree of dependence upon the metropolitan centre than was usual in other colonies. The process of granting autonomy under pressure from the independence movement was late to start and was then mainly concerned with the settler sector of society. Limited autonomy was granted to the areas occupied by settlers, cities and towns with an appointed mayor and elected councillors. Urban institutions dealt mainly with traditional urban issues like refuse collection, road maintenance, and urban planning and collected their main resources from the sale of land. Important public services like the railways, a mainstay of the economy, made a significant contribution to urban resources, over US$500,000 a year in the city of Maputo and about $150,000 in Nacala, the equivalent of all the salaries of the education and health sectors in that city. The municipal area was limited to the European areas with a modicum of service provision for the adjacent African township.

Independence brought an ever greater demand for service provision, in terms of both numbers and the area served. Moreover, in response to the growing demand for existing services that accompanied independence, the scope of service provision was enlarged to include health and education, amongst others.

The administration in the rural areas was totally centralized with Provincial

Governors and *Administradores* (Commissioners) at the level of the district and below (*posto administrativo*), all appointed by the central government in Portugal. These *Administradores* were trained in a central school for all colonies based in Lisbon.

A difficult transition

At independence, all Provincial Governors were replaced for political reasons by political appointees, most often former regional Frelimo commanders, who had the qualities of leadership and legitimacy considered important at the time but who lacked a formal professional background and who received no specialized training at all. Most Portuguese *Administradores* left. Their replacement occurred in two phases: in the first phase Mozambicans belonging to the secretarial services were promoted; later they were largely replaced by a new brand of political appointees, who had undergone rapid training at a Public Administration School set up in 1977.

In 1978 a new law was enacted the main features of which were:

- similar types of institutions in the whole country in both urban and rural areas;
- local assemblies at every level;
- insertion of all structures within the same hierarchical administration;
- creation of hybrid bodies with district and city administrators appointed centrally, assisted by an executive council chosen by the National Assembly.

Human resources and training

All civil servants remained appointed centrally. *De facto* exceptions referred to support personnel for the cities, which remained in the hands of the city administrations. Attempts in 1980 to decentralize this function to Provincial Administrations without preparing local conditions resulted in a breakdown in the system, with uncontrolled appointments. The strategy then adopted was to centralize, restructure, train managers in human resources and begin a transfer of powers to the provincial level.

To date, the academic level of administrators is fairly low but has been compensated for by their experience and empirical knowledge of the district reality. The disparities in living conditions between the capital and the provinces is such that most university or technical institute graduates tend to stay in the cities. The most notable exception was in the health services where in the first years of independence all districts had a trained general practitioner.

Mozambique had 105,000 civil servants in the mid-1990s, 73% of whom worked in services related to health and education; 17% of the personnel worked in central government institutions in the capital, while 83% worked at the Provincial and District level. In 1991, on average, 67.7% of District Administrators had six years of formal schooling, while 21% had nine years and 11% a lower level. These data have improved subsequently but not significantly from the point of view of officers in the Ministry in charge of Local Administration (Cuereneia and Guambe, 1993).

Training was mostly in the form of executive courses lasting from a few weeks to three months. Simultaneously a medium-level technical course of three years, after nine years of formal education, was instituted. In recent years a retraining programme for all district administrators has begun. The government is preparing to face the challenge of decentralization by upgrading the level of training: new curricula have been drafted and two new medium-level training centres in the centre and the north are in train. The problem remains that the new office bearers will be elected and it is not clear how many of the trainees will remain in similar positions.

Innovation

City councils have played an important role in promoting urban agriculture in the periphery of the cities, in an attempt to provide an answer to some of the problems stemming from rapid urban growth without concomitant job creation in industry or services, the rising costs of transport and the breakdown of a supply system previously in the hands of the Portuguese. In a certain way it also responded to the peculiar nature of African cities, where there is no clear distinction between the urban/industrial and tertiary sectors and rural/agriculture, but rather a continuum exists. A department for urban agriculture was created in the municipalities. In Maputo, its role has been instrumental in upgrading production in the wide Maputo Green Zone, improving the livelihood of 70,000 producers (family, co-operative, private) and increasing productivity from under 1 to 6–7 tons per ha., with a tax yield of about US$60,000.

Obstacles to implementation

Three main obstacles prevented full implementation of the model: one was the decision to centralize the budget administration. This was made for two main reasons: to overcome the loss in financial management capacity after the departure of the Portuguese municipal officers; and to prioritize a centralized resource allocation system. All municipal resources were channelled to a central budget and reallocated to the cities as subsidies. This did not encourage the cities to look for their own revenues and the collection of fees started to fall into disuse.

The second obstacle of a political nature was the change in one democratic feature of the proposed political system: members of the Executive Council who were supposed to be elected by the local assembly and who make up the Executive Council together with its appointed executive head, were replaced by the heads of city or district Departments, all appointed centrally. The bureaucracy effectively took over the role of elected officials. This reflected a certain lack of enthusiasm about entrusting ordinary citizens (albeit elected) with the management of public affairs. Thus, assemblies at district and city level were not allowed to play the limited democratizing role they had been assigned.

The third factor was lack of follow-up: the government tended to envisage reform as the approval of laws and the setting up of new structures, then moving on immediately to new or more pressing matters. Strategies for training, monitoring the functioning of new institutions, redesign or even pilot experiences were techniques unfamiliar to the new leadership.

Criticism of the model

In the course of time, the new model came under a series of criticisms. The all-encompassing functions defined for the cities were considered too ambitious for existing capacities, and it was felt that city and town administration should resort to what concerned urban life more immediately. The fact that the area of the city was no longer restricted to the previous white modern area and now incorporated poor areas which contributed little to city resources through the tax base represented a further strain on scarce resources. Criticism in the urban areas mainly concerned the poor quality of urban services, although their quality could have been considered fair by normal African standards.

The new model created a duplicate structure of command, both central and local, as area Directors were appointed and subordinated both to their respective Provincial Directorates and to the local Administrator.

There was a lack of financial resources resulting from the loss of traditional urban revenue in the form of land sales. Of the new resources – rents from nationalized buildings, for instance – only 15% was transferred back to the cities. Larger transfers were made in favour of education, health and national defence at the cost of the maintenance of costly urban infrastructures. The lack of own powers to levy taxes prevented the cities from responding in a timely way to new demands. Officials' lack of democratic representativeness was seen as the reason for their lacklustre performance and the demand for more local representation. In fact, because of the different levels of development in the country, most *administradores* tend to come from the southern region. Finally, there was a total reliance on central subsidies.

An objective assessment of what the cities and districts achieved should, of course, be balanced by taking into account the on-going confrontation, first with Rhodesia and then with South Africa, with the Renamo insurgency. The degree of economic hardship can be gauged by the fact that GDP fell by one-third from 1982 to 1986.

The need for change

After 1988, a move developed away from excessive power concentrated in central bodies. The challenges facing the central government and its manifest inability to cope efficiently with local issues led to an awareness that more power should be handed down to the lower levels. At first the pressure came from Provincial Administrations who, although appointed by the central government, were acting more and more as representatives expressing regional grievances.

The first move took the form of deconcentration: more powers were granted to Provincial Administrations in terms of both human resource management and revenue collection, as well as in the issuing of permits for economic activity. At the same time a new thinking developed concerning the lower tiers: the cities, towns and districts. The process of decentralization was enshrined in the 1990 Constitution, albeit with a certain degree of ambiguity reflecting the absence of a consensual and coherent view of the matter. Only with the signature of the Peace Agreements were conditions created to proceed further with the design of a new model for local government. In the meantime some provisional measures were adopted, such as the gradual appointment of locally born Provincial and District administrators.

A major challenge was the integration of regions under the control of Renamo into one unified administration. It was agreed in Rome that all officers would be appointed by the central government, but appointments for the areas previously under Renamo control would fall to people residing in these areas. The Ministry of State Administration undertook the training of local leaders and integrated them into the administration, although in some areas challenges to the central government are still taking place.

Political change and the new philosophy

With the widespread political change and a greater demand for democratization, on the eve of the elections the government introduced at the one-party National Assembly a bill proposing radical qualitative changes in local administration. In its initial formulation former cities and rural districts were all to become municipalities with an elected Municipal Assembly and a directly elected Mayor.

Decentralization is envisaged as a gradual process. The original bill was the subject of prolonged debate and transformation, involving an amendment to the constitution and nine separate laws being passed. Parliament decided in the constitutional amendment that, in the first instance, only the urban areas would have elected local government. Whilst the towns and cities are governed by municipalities, the district administrators retain control of the rural areas. The basic argument for limiting elected government to the urban areas is the lack of capacity, infrastructure, logistics and means to ensure effective participatory rural local government for some time to come.

The 1998 municipal elections involved 33 towns and cities, with almost 1.5 million potential voters. Initially, the government proposed elections only in the 23 cities but later amended this to include one town in each province. Designated areas of expansion for future elections involve the remaining 106 towns and 394 administrative posts. Hence initial elections in 33 locations should eventually be expanded to 533 elected councils. As envisaged at present, future elections in the rural areas will initially involve only the headquarters of administrative posts, designated as *povoações*. The rest of the rural areas will remain under the control of the district administrators.

Voters will elect a Mayor as the president of the Municipal Council and representatives to the Municipal Assembly. The Mayor will be assisted by a Municipal Council appointed by him. Its members are known as *vereadors* and half of them must be chosen from within the ranks of the Municipal Assembly.[2] The *vereadors* are full- or part-time officials who receive a salary. The Municipal Assembly is the elected representative legislative body, whereas the Municipal Council is the administrative or executive branch.

Under the constitutional amendment the municipalities are given responsibility for encouraging local development. They develop the plans and organize the budgets. Their responsibilities involve the following functions, many of which are simply inherited from the previous executive councils: electricity distribution, water, sewerage and rubbish disposal, public transport, pre-school education and primary schools, roads, parks, cemeteries, markets, street traders, shop licences, the local police and fire services, street lighting, libraries and museums, sports facilities, ground-level health facilities, and low-cost housing. The challenges are formidable to ensure implementation of the decentralization initiative in a sustainable manner. Interestingly, the power of the central government to intervene is restricted to instances of the local councils breaching existing laws. The municipalities are allowed to create their own companies operating along commercial lines. They are also allowed to receive outside aid.

Inevitably a variety of problems remains to be resolved, not least because massive urban growth has made a nonsense of the former territorial boundaries upon which local elections are based. In the ten towns included in the first wave of elections in 1998 elected mayors and appointed district administrators will have to negotiate shared terrains of responsibility.

Challenges at management level

a. **Human resources management.** The new law had adopted an 'autonomous' approach to the question of the management of human resources. Many still argue that autonomy in terms of deciding on the recruitment of human resources will benefit the developed regions and further contribute to the weakening of the less developed regions. This is, for instance, the rationale behind the creation of the Unified Local Government Service in Botswana (Ministry of Local Government and Lands, Botswana, 1990).

The system prevailing in Mozambique had fallen prey to privileging civil servants originating from the areas of the country where training facilities both academic and specialized existed. In order to correct this imbalance regional training schools are being revitalized and upgraded. But even within the more developed regions of the country inequalities exist. How to attract qualified personnel to the least developed areas? Most probably, the central government will have to be prepared to second qualified personnel to the least endowed municipalities – at their

---

[2] The *vereadors* perform the role of 'ministers' in local government.

request – combining this policy with adequate incentives. This will mean defining a policy of recruitment, training and secondment which is currently lacking.
b. **Financial.** Studies undertaken in the course of the preparation of the law on local finance have suggested the transfer of certain taxes as well as some automatic transfers. The objective is to grant municipalities a larger share of the revenue generated in their respective areas, to improve tax collection and to develop a sense of the costs and mechanisms of financing activities other than through grants and subsidies that have been completely lost.

The executive councils which preceded the municipalities raised on average half of their budgets locally. The municipalities will rely on a poll tax on everyone aged between 18 and 60 with the exception of housewives, female peasants, students and the sick and infirm. The level of taxation is determined by the municipality but cannot exceed 20% of the minimum monthly wage. In order to encourage local revenue raising, the national subsidy to municipalities will be undertaken by means of a compensation fund in direct proportion to the poll tax collection rate. The compensation fund will be between 1.5% and 3% of government receipts. Transfers to local governments will be based on a formula determined by area, population, and level of development as well as collection rates of the local tax. In addition, a number of national taxes will be shared with local councils, including a section of income tax for people working locally, three-quarters of the vehicle tax and 30% of the tourism tax collected locally. A property tax will be levied but only on permanent buildings. Exemptions here include a 15-year grace period for those either building or buying their own property. Undoubtedly guaranteeing the financial resources to ensure the sustainability of the local government initiative is one of the biggest challenges.

The challenge of decentralization
Decentralization is such a complex process that it took a long time to be enshrined in law and implementation was very slow thereafter. Decentralization requires a combination of solid political will, legislative mechanisms, financial evaluation and expertise, management capacity and favourable reception by the community. Training at all levels is absolutely vital to its success.

No sudden change will occur by the mere fact that elected bodies have taken control. Both national and international experience show that capacity and motivation are crucial factors for both officials and politicians. Local bodies must be representative and democratic but must also be able to attract qualified members such as local professionals, entrepreneurs and charismatic and imaginative leaders capable of motivating people and producing results with limited means. Expectations that the constitutional change will bring results of itself court serious disillusion. Motivation is only possible if citizens trust public officials. That is where the values of openness, fairness and transparency take on a concrete meaning.

Efforts have been made under the new legislation to limit opportunities for nepotism and corruption. Any issue which involves their family members (broadly defined) excludes the participation in discussions of Council presidents, *vereadors* and local assembly representatives. These local government representatives and officials are also forbidden from being active in private companies having dealings with the state and local government. In addition, paid local government officials are not allowed to take other paid employment, nor are they permitted to exercise any decision-making power over local government by virtue of their position in higher tiers of government.

Civil society

Three predominant social forms of organization can be identified within civil society: traditional forms of authority, based on heredity; natural or otherwise informally legitimized and accepted forms of leadership; and new or modern forms of organization.

At present, voices are raised concerning the compatibility between tradition and change in relation to the traditional authorities. José Luis Cabaço, a sociologist, points to potential conflicts between societies where traditionalism prevails and modern interest groups such as trade unions and churches which express a will for change in society (Cabaço, 1995). Most probably there will be a situation of flux within communities in a differentiated way according to the regional and local contexts before a stable policy can be devised.

The second grouping, natural-informal forms of social organization and leadership, has a long tradition in Mozambique and is probably the most solid form of social organization, incorporating traditional, sometimes spiritual, legitimacy and procedures, blended with modern perceptions. It reflects in a way the society itself, because no man is fully traditional or modern. In Mozambique, where the process of cultural exchange and change has always been very dynamic, the grouping stretches from self-help organizations dealing with support for the bereaved, to house building, crop collection and cultural groups which are very much alive everywhere.

Both hereditary leaders and less formal natural leaders are an integral part of civil society. They are the depositories of the social values that hold society together. The crisis of values in modern society is counterbalanced by the survival or revival of these values at the neighbourhood or community level. These institutions do not wait for a law to operate, and their legitimacy rests within society. The challenge for the formal state is to know how to recognize and support their role without subordinating or emasculating them. Fora with these organizations are starting to take place, where the formal leaders listen rather than issuing directives as was the previous practice.

The modern NGO sector has a tradition in urban areas stretching back to the colonial period, but it has gained considerable momentum in recent years. After independence mass organizations were created under the aegis of the ruling party for women, youth, trade unions, teachers and journalists. With the new political dispensation, most of these organizations were liberated from party oversight. Some of them, such as the trade unions, split and gave rise to independent trade unions. The new brand of organizations includes regional associations, professional, economic, media, cultural, regional development, gender and environmental interest groups.

Many regional associations have been formed, grouping people originating from a certain area. The proffered objective is to promote the interests of the region of origin, although the dividing line between them and a regional political association is sometimes thin. The oldest of these is the *Associaçao dos Amigos de Ilha de Moçambique* started in 1982 and relatively alone in the field. Its concern was the preservation of the island's historical heritage, a point of exchange of African, Arab, Asian and European cultures with impressive physical features and buildings, which was proclaimed by UNESCO in 1991 as a historical heritage of mankind. In a highly innovative approach for Mozambique, heritage was not assimilated to the mere rehabilitation of buildings but sought to comprehend the economic and social context that would contribute to the modern revival of the island. Its activities are concerned with mobilization of support for the rehabilitation of basic infrastructures (water supply, telecommunications, electricity) and improving means of livelihood for the inhabitants (e.g. fishing equipment), training (of local artisans in traditional techniques) and improving basic services (education and health).[3]

Other groups deal with the promotion of rural development in the most disadvantaged areas of the country. *Associaçao Progresso*, for instance, runs programmes in education and health aimed mainly at rehabilitating the infrastructure. It works closely with the local populations rather than importing qualified external manpower and makes use of local techniques (schools are rehabilitated with local materials and upgraded with a final layer of cement). It does not create its own schools or community schools; rather it tries to build on what already exists and to boost existing capacity within public services or community organizations already in place.[4]

Social organizations are playing an increasing role in the management of public affairs. Carlos Cardoso considers that this is due to the failure of the state to address many relevant issues; hence economic organizations such as the Association of Private Entrepreneurs will play an increasing role in public life and in the definition of economic policies.[5]

Among the organizations created during the period of the liberation war, one of the most dynamic is the women's organization. Women are also particularly active in the co-operative agricultural movement and the Secretary General of the *Uniao Geral das Cooperativas* is a dynamic woman, Celina Cossa. A group of women lawyers promoted an association, Women, Law and Development, that fights for recognition of equal rights in terms of both legislation and legal education and equality in the courts. Women are one of the most vibrant forces within civil society, yet their potential is still hampered by tradition, lack of formal education and outright discrimination.

Up to 1991, all the media were the property of the state. These included two daily newspapers, three weekly publications including a sports one, one national radio station transmitting in Portuguese and national languages, one TV station and one news agency. Since the introduction of the law on freedom of the press in 1991, two new weekly newspapers have been published on a regular basis, and one private TV broadcaster has emerged as well as various radio stations. The first initiative for the creation of non-official media was the work of co-operatives of professional journalists. For the time being most of these initiatives are based in Maputo. Religious broadcasts, notably from a Brazilian church, have a radio station and also buy most of the prime time of the private TV station.

A highly successful venture was the launch of a bulletin distributed by fax (*Mediafax*) which is well informed and has become very influential (it can be found on the desks of officials, bankers and businessmen). It is sent by fax in an A4 format and can be easily photocopied. Its example was emulated by another group, which tends to be highly critical of the government.

Religious organizations represent the most structured form of non-governmental organization and have networks of lay people working in different fields, providing social, health and education services. A Catholic University has also been set up.

Relations with the state
Both foreign and national NGOs operating with external funding have resources far superior to those of the district authorities where they operate. This can be explained by the difficult financial situation of the official administration; in some districts and towns the budget merely allows for recurrent expenditure without any provision for equipment or investment. Relations between the project of the NGO, even a national one, and the local authority therefore have to be carefully balanced. A solution found in recent years is to draft integrated regional plans that include support for both com-

---

[3]Interview with Louis Filipe Pereira, Vice-President and founding member of the Associaçao dos Amigos de Ilha de Mozambique.
[4]Interview with Elisabeth Sequeira, Executive Director of Progresso.
[5]Interview with Carlos Cardosa, editor of *Mediafax*.

munities and official institutions. In some cases this has been achieved by the twin-ning of cities and towns with other cities abroad. Apart from these minor problems, relations have been free from tensions, as the work of these NGOs is generally seen as making an important contribution.

NGOs were initially foreign-based and a considerable number of them operated in Mozambique, especially in emergency relief. Their *modus operandi* was similar to that of official aid, with consultants, projects and the chronic problem of unsustainability once the external funding dried up. The development of national NGOs started from the perception that civil society was, first and foremost, citizens taking upon them-selves their own responsibilities.

A law on freedom of association was adopted in 1991, and recognized associations were formed with a minimum of ten members and subject only to registration with the Ministry of Justice. Associations can also benefit from a privileged fiscal position if their social goals are acknowledged by the state. A law on philanthropy was adopted to encourage donations but it has not been very effective, given the lack of experience and the financial difficulties of potential donors.

It is accepted that, while the internal activities of associations can be supported through voluntary work, most substantive activities require external funds. In Mozambique there was no notable charity tradition and in the present situation few enterprises can afford to give subsidies. Hence civil society relies heavily on resources from foreign donors. This is the dominant trend currently and it runs the danger of dependence on the political perceptions of donor countries.

Some feel that an effective civil society requires a certain degree of autonomy. The most significant attempt to create a sustainable basis for NGO activity was under-taken by the Association for Community Development chaired by Graça Machel. It is in fact a foundation in being and its aim is to encourage and finance civil society organizations working for the promotion of socially disadvantaged communities. In 1992 the Association promoted the first regional meeting of NGOs from Southern Africa to help develop awareness of the importance and possible role of civil society organizations, and this gave a boost to their development. Together with the Christian Council of Churches it promoted in 1993 a workshop on National Reconciliation, and continues to be very active.

References

Brito, L. (1995) 'O comportamento eleitoral nas primeiras eleicões multipartidàrias em Mocambique' in Mazula.

Cabaco, L. (1995) 'Concertacao social e governacao', Maputo (mimeo).

Carrilho, N. (1995) 'A legislacao eleitoral em Mocambique e a realizacao política' in Mazula.

Cuereneia, A. and Guambe, J. (1993) 'O processo de decentralização em Mocambique e o seu enquadra-mento no actual sistema de Administracção Publica', Maputo (mimeo).

Mapo Oficial do Resultado dos Eleições (1994) Commisao Nacional dos Eleições, *Boletim da República,* Série I, No. 47, 23 November.

Mazula, B. (ed.) (1995) *Mocambique. Eleicoes, Democracia e Desenvolvimento,* Maputo.

Ministry of Local Government and Lands (1990) *Personnel Handbook for Local Authorities.* Department of Unified Local Government Service, Gaborone, Botswana.

UNDP (1995) *Apoio ao Processo Eleitoral em Mocambique. Relatório Final.* UNDP. Maputo, March.

4

A Strategy for
Reducing the External Debt

LUÍSA DIOGO

Since 1987 Mozambique has been implementing a structural adjustment programme, with the help of the international community and the Bretton Woods institutions, with a view to revitalizing the economy. During this eleven-year period a successful transformation has been achieved from a centrally planned to a market-based economy. The major causes of macroeconomic disequilibrium have been corrected and at the same time the role of the state in the economy has been reduced thereby encouraging greater private sector investment.

This process has been implemented in spite of formidable difficulties inherent in the war situation which lasted until 1992 and which was accompanied by various natural disasters. Notwithstanding these constraints, the restructuring of the economy was undertaken, with rates of growth attaining an annual average of 9% in the period 1993–5. Yet these rates of growth were insufficient to outweigh the extent of the destruction caused by the war, including the massive population movements, with the return of around one and a half million refugees. The country's GDP per capita is thus one of the lowest in the world, equivalent to only about US$80.

During the structural adjustment process, external donations and credits have constituted the most important financial support facilitating the liberalization of the economy and laying the foundation for development. Since 1990 in particular, the government has pursued a steadfast policy of limiting new borrowing, endeavouring wherever possible to use donations rather than credits, even though these loans are offered on concessional terms. Accompanying this strategy there have been initiatives to improve investment efficiency, through a better selection of projects and tighter control over their execution.

Following a dozen years of successive rescheduling, the external debt relief conditions obtained, although concessional from the viewpoint of the creditors, have continued to have a negative effect on the government budget and the balance of payments, thus perpetuating Mozambique's dependence on external resources. Parallel with the rescheduling initiatives, debt reduction activities include debt buyback, debt cancellation and debt conversion into the capital of Mozambican enterprises or the purchase of enterprises within the national privatization programme. At the same time, non-concessional loans have been severely restricted and the relevant portfolio is currently being revised. Reflecting this strategy, the balance of payments gap has been covered by resorting to multilateral concessional credit.

This chapter reviews recent developments and government initiatives in the management of the external debt and outlines the strategy for establishing the necessary conditions for the country's effective economic development in the future.

Impact of the external debt

Nature of the external debt

On 31 December 1995 the stock of external debt totalled about US$5.3 billion, US$1.1 bn of which was overdue, including interest mainly resulting from the lack of rescheduling. Of the overdue debt, 4% was owed to Paris Club creditors and the remaining 96% to other official creditors. The evolution of the debt stock is shown in Table 4.1.

Table 4.1   *Evolution of the stock of foreign debt: 1985–95 (US$m.)*

1985	1987	1989	1991	1993	1995
2794.3	3898.2	4391.4	4994.8	5011.2	5331

Note: These figures do not include military debt to the former Soviet Union nor private debt, in the main involving the Cahora Bassa hydroelectric dam.
Source Ministry of Finance 1996

The debt stock grew substantially from 1985 to 1990, at an average rate of 12.4% per year. From then on, the pace slowed to 2.4% per year, except for 1993 when it fell by -1% over the previous year.

Multilateral debt. The debt stock with multilateral institutions grew considerably over the decade to 1995, rising from 4% of the total in 1985 to 30% in 1995. This growth was dictated by the financing requirements of the Economic and Social Rehabilitation Programme and by the fact that the country's indebtedness allowed it to resort only to credits from these institutions, since they are more concessional than commercial loans. Table 4.2 presents the multilateral debt by creditors.

Table 4.2   *Multilateral creditors*

Institution	% of multilateral debt	% of overall debt
World Bank/IDA	55.0	16.6
ADF	14.3	4.3
IMF	12,5	3.8
African Development Bank	4.6	1.4
Other[a]	13.6	4.0
Total	100	30.1

[a]Includes Nigeria Trust Fund and ADF, AEADB, the European Investment Bank, OPEC and Kuwait.
Source Ministry of Finance 1996

The World Bank/IDA, the ADF and the IMF are the largest creditors, with one quarter of the overall debt. Although these are concessional credits, without rescheduling the debt service with these institutions will continue to grow into the new millennium.

Table 4.3 examines the expected evolution of multilateral debt service without the debt forgiveness envisaged in the Highly Indebted Poor Country initiative. This scenario reflects the debt service to be paid during the period 1997–2015. Multilateral debt payments are likely to rise by 61% between 1997 and 2002, from US$ 58.6 million to US$ 94.4m. Over the period 2002–10 the debt service is likely to fall, but from 2010 onwards it will grow substantially. World Bank, IMF and ADB debt will contribute to the rise over the 1997–2002 period. World Bank debt will increase from US$11.8m. to $27.4 m., while that with the IMF will rise from $13 m. to $18.1 m.

Table 4.3 *Expected evolution of multilateral debt service (US$m.)*

	1997	1999	2001	2003	2005	2015
Total	58.6	87.9	90.6	81.6	68.1	92.1
ADH Group	19.6	20.3	19.1	17.1	14.0	19.4
IMF	13.0	33.1	29.5	6.6	–	–
World Bank	11.8	18.0	24.3	32.6	42.4	70.4
Others	14.2	16.5	17.7	25.3	11.7	2.3

Source Bank of Mozambique and Ministry of Planning and Finance (January 1996)

Bilateral Debt The stock of bilateral debt grew annually by 11% on average over the period 1985–91 (see Table 4.1). Since 1991 the growth has mainly been the result of outstanding debt-service payments being included in the agreed subsequent rescheduling.

Over the same period debt buy-back operations, debt cancellation and the more favourable rescheduling terms from the Paris Club detailed below, have had a positive effect on the stock of bilateral debt. The contracting of new loans has been gradually reduced and there have been none with the OECD group since 1994. No loans have been contracted with other official creditors since 1990 (see Table 4.4).

Table 4.4 *Bilateral loans contracted, 1986–95 (US$m.)*

	1986	1989	1990	1991	1992	1993	1994	1995
OECD	135.3	75.1	49.2	24.7	3.4	5.1	0.0	0.0
Other Official Creditors	50.3	41.8	0.6	0.0	0.0	0.0	0.0	0.0
Total	185.6	116.9	49.8	24.7	34	5.1	0.0	0.0

Source Ministry of Finance 1996

OECD countries which subsequently cancelled part of the debt arising from their loans include France, Italy and the Federal Republic of Germany (FRG), which cancelled all loans except those from the former GDR. In the other official creditor group, loans up to 1990 were provided essentially by the former USSR.

Mozambique's most important bilateral creditors are Russia, France, Italy, Brazil, Portugal, Germany and Algeria (see Table 4.5). These countries account for about 60% of the overall external debt. Of these countries, France, Italy, Portugal and Germany are members of the Paris Club.

Table 4.5 *Main bilateral creditors*

Countries	% of bilateral debt	% of overall debt
Ex-USSR	21.0	14.7
France	14.0	9.8
Italy	12.1	8.5
Brazil	10.4	7.3
Portugal	9.2	6.4
Germany	7.4	5.2
Other	25.7	18.0
Total	100	69.9

Source Ministry of Finance 1996

Relationship between external debt and other macroeconomic variables
Since 1993 the stock of foreign debt has represented about four times GDP. In 1985 it was only 84% of GDP, but it deteriorated from that year onwards.

Over the 1990–95 period, payment of interest on debt averaged about 13% of current expenditure. In 1994 this percentage fell after the fourth rescheduling signed with the Paris Club in March 1993, covering the period from January 1993 to December 1994. Under this rescheduling, Mozambique started paying about 12.1 million contos in 1994 instead of 15.5 million contos in 1993.

External debt service (capital and interest) during the period in question averaged 16% of total expenditure. This involves current expenditure plus the local component of investment expenditure. In 1995, debt service was aggravated by the payment of retroactive interest on the fourth rescheduling, for which the bilateral agreements were only signed that year.

Measures taken to maximize external debt relief

Between 1984 and 1993, four external debt rescheduling agreements were signed with the Paris Club. The amounts and terms agreed at the multilateral meetings are summarized in Tables 4.6 and 4.7. The Toronto conditions put in place in 1990 were as follows:

Option A: cancellation of one-third of the consolidated debt and rescheduling of the remaining two-thirds in 12 semestral payments with a grace period of 10 years. This option was taken by France and Sweden.

Table 4.6 *Amounts and terms agreed with the Paris Club, 1984–93 (US$m.)*

				Payment conditions	
Date of Agreement	Consolidation period (months)	% of debt consolidated	Amount consolidated (million)	Amortization (years/months)	Grace period (years/months)
25.10.84	12	95	312	10.6	5.0
16.06.87	19	100	506	19.3	9.9
14.06.90	30	100	844	Toronto	Toronto
23.03.93	12	100	497	London	London

Source Ministry of Finance 1996

Table 4.7 *Cancellation of external debt by 1996 (US$m.)*

Country	Amount
Belgium	0.2
Denmark	11.8
USA	52.9
Finland	3.0
France	382.8
Italy	191.8
Netherlands	20.5
Germany	152.2
Sweden	2.0
Total	817.2

Source Ministry of Finance 1996

Option B: rescheduling over 11 years, with a grace period of 16 years at the market interest rate. This option was taken by Belgium, Finland, Spain and United States.

Option C: rescheduling over 6 years with a grace period of 10 years at the market interest rate less 3.5%. This option was taken by Australia, Germany, Italy, Japan, Portugal and the UK.

The London conditions put in place in 1993 consisted of the following:

Option A: cancellation of 50% of the consolidated amount and rescheduling of the remaining 50% over 23 years of amortization, including a 6-year period of deferment with interest paid at market rates. This option was agreed by Austria, Belgium, Spain, Italy, Japan, Portugal and the UK.

Option B: rescheduling of 100% of the consolidated amount over 30 years of amortization, including a grace period of 12 years, with concessional interest rate payments. This option was for all of the official development assistance loans eligible for rescheduling.

Option C: rescheduling of 100% of the consolidated amount over 25 years of amortization, including a grace period of 16 years with concessional interest rate payments. This option was agreed by the US.

Option D: rescheduling of 100% of the consolidated amount over 10 years with a 5 year grace period and a market rate of interest.

Since 1989 most OECD creditors have cancelled the external debt. The total amount cancelled over this period is about US$817m.

Debt cancelled up to 1996 essentially involved loans granted on highly concessional terms. The result of the cancellation only affected the debt stock, since the loans had low interest rates and long maturity periods, often more than 20 years. US$11.8m., in nominal terms, of Paris Club debt with Portugal and the UK was converted into investment projects and the acquisition of shares in Mozambican companies. In each case the debts were insured by COSEC and the Export Credits Guarantee Department (see Table 4.8). In the case of Portugal, a tranche of US$17m., equivalent to 25% of the amount eligible for the second rescheduling, was allocated for debt conversion into shareholdings. In the case of the ECGD, the possibility of conversion was agreed and was noted in the fourth bilateral rescheduling agreement signed with the UK.

The conversion of about US$10m. of the debt with Portugal has still to be effected. Debt conversion into investment has involved only small amounts, given the need to respect the constraints of monetary and fiscal policy under the structural adjustment programmes.

Table 4.8 *Paris Club debt conversion into investment or the acquisition of shares in Mozambican companies*

Creditors	Amount of debt (nominal) (US$m.)	No. of projects	Sectors
Portugal	6.8	6	Agriculture, Construction Ind., Food Ind.
UK	5.0	1	Construction
Total	11.8	7	

Source Ministry of Finance 1996

Agreements on terms comparable to those of the first rescheduling with the Paris Club were agreed with the former USSR, Bulgaria, Romania, Hungary, Czechoslovakia, Cuba, Algeria, South Africa and the former GDR, on terms comparable to the second rescheduling with the former USSR, Cuba and South Africa, and on terms comparable to the third rescheduling with Brazil and South Africa. Agreements on paying the debt through exports on more favourable commercial terms than other markets were made with Hungary and Cuba. There have been various negotiations with Russia on alternatives for liquidating the Mozambican debt. In the October 1995 negotiations, Russia expressed its willingness to consider a debt buy-back operation at a substantial discount.

In December 1991 the Bank of Mozambique concluded a debt buy-back operation involving 24 banks and international institutions, most of which were located in France and the UK. This eliminated US$124m. of capital and cancelled $118.9m. in interest, and was totally financed by external grants provided by the World Bank and four donor countries, namely, France, Sweden, the Netherlands and Switzerland. The operation eliminated a substantial part, about 64%, of the commercial debt. The remainder, mostly debt with Brazil, was subsequently rescheduled together with the official debt, on terms comparable to those of the Paris Club.

Management of the external debt

Following the introduction of the economic rehabilitation programme, the foreign debt had to be subject to greater control in order to provide the necessary input for other macroeconomic targets such as those concerning the budget and the balance of payments. The Ministry of Planning and Finance (MPF), through its Public Debt Department, and the Bank of Mozambique, through its Exchange Control and External Debt Department, have shared responsibility for monitoring and controlling the external debt. Up to 1988 this was done by the Bank of Mozambique. With its DAMS (Debt Analysis Management Systems) computer software, it systematically gathered data on the external loans contracted. Since 1988, multilateral loans have been monitored and controlled by the MPF.

These two institutions have received technical assistance from the Commonwealth Secretariat, which has provided CS-DRMS software. This has helped to improve the data base and thus facilitate both reconciliation with creditors and improved debt management at various levels of decision-making. In addition, regular information flows have been established in order to ensure regular monitoring and supervision of debt service. Simultaneously, debt management at the macroeconomic level is monitored by the various co-ordination groups working in this field.

From the early 1990s onwards the contracting of new loans has been strictly curtailed. During this period, whenever possible the government has substituted credits by grants to meet its import needs. The government has been contracting loans which are concessional in terms of either interest rates or maturity periods. Since January 1996 they have had a degree of concessionality equal to or greater than 35%. With the re-establishment of peace, government loans have been slowly replaced by private ones, thus reducing government responsibility for debt service in the future. The loan portfolio is being revised in order to assess its priority in the context of the government's programme and the performance of the projects concerned. The aim is to reduce credits and increase grants, to allocate amounts to other priority projects and even to cancel loans.

Since 1984, measures have been taken to liberalize and consolidate the foreign exchange market. At the moment the exchange rate is determined by the free play of demand and supply, with Central Bank intervention limited to regulating and establishing norms for the market. Various policy measures have been taken to stimulate the confidence of economic agents in the exchange market and make the supply of foreign exchange more fluid. These include, in particular, retaining 65% of export revenues in foreign currency accounts in the national banking system. In 1996, the foreign exchange interbank market involving commercial banks began operations. This market was later extended to other operators, such as exchange houses.

One of the central objectives of the Economic and Social Rehabilitation Programme is the stabilization of domestic prices. Fiscal policies have therefore been restrictive, at the same time reflecting the government's reduced intervention in the production system. Consequently, measures have been taken which include the following:

- Reduction and control of the budget deficit. In 1996 the budget deficit before grants as a percentage of GDP was scheduled to fall from 20.3% to 16.5%.
- More rigorous management of public funds, ensuring transparency in their allocation and use.
- Greater control over public expenditure.
- Establishment of a hierarchy of public expenditure priorities, including payment of debt service.
- Greater efficiency in launching and collecting taxes through the expansion of the tax base.
- Contracting private companies for pre-shipment inspection and the management of customs.

Other measures were also put in train, such as the reformulation of the customs tables, in order to ensure protection for national industry in a context of liberalized foreign trade practices.

Alternatives for external debt relief

After years of successive rescheduling of the official debt on terms comparable with those of the Paris Club, Mozambique's debt was still unsustainable at the beginning of 1998. The characteristics of the Mozambican economy, and in particular the effects of the war, were not taken into consideration in the terms negotiated during previous reschedulings. The government has continually informed the international community that the viability of the country's external debt demands a reduction of the debt stock.

Bilateral debt
Based on World Bank and IMF initiatives, the following scenario was prepared by the government in 1995–6 based on the stated assumptions. This demonstrates why a more radical debt write-off was required.

For some Paris Club creditors the Naples terms would be applied, for flows with the following options:

Option A: France, Germany and Sweden. This option comprises the cancellation of 67% of debt service and the rescheduling of the remaining 33% over 23 years, with a 6-year grace period at market interest rates.

Option B: Austria, Italy, Spain, Portugal and the UK. This option comprises the reduction of the debt service to a level equivalent to the debt reduction in Option A. The remainder would be rescheduled over 33 years without any grace period.

Option C: The US. Consideration of a rescheduling over 40 years with a grace period of 20 years.

The debt service resulting from the London terms (fourth rescheduling) is not covered by the Naples terms. For the creditors which are not members of the Paris Club, rescheduling on terms comparable to the Paris Club, Option A, have been assumed.

Based on the above assumptions, the resulting debt service is presented in Table 4.9.

Table 4.9 *Projected bilateral debt service (US$m.)*

	1997	1998	1999	2000	2001	2002	2003	2004	2005
Total	85.5	61.0	73.3	86.8	94.1	102.4	110.4	110.7	111.1
Capital	3.4	3.8	11.6	20.3	21.1	23.5	26.2	21.6	17.6
Interest	82.1	57.2	61.7	66.5	73.0	78.9	84.2	89.1	93.5
Paris Club	48.5	38.2	48.8	61.3	62.0	73.3	78.9	76.6	74.7
Other Creditors	37.0	22.7	24.4	25.5	32.0	29.1	31.4	34.0	36.4

Source Ministry of Finance 1996

Total debt service over the period 1997–2005 is presented in Table 4.10.

Table 4.10 *Projected global debt service, 1997–2005 (US$m.)*

	1997	1999	2001	2003	2005
Bilateral	103.6	90.5	115.0	126.8	123.5
Paris Club					
Pre-Cut-off	48.5	48.8	62.0	78.9	74.7
Post-Cut-off	18.1	17.3	21.0	16.5	12.8
Other	37.0	24.4	32.0	31.4	36.0
Multilateral	58.6	87.9	90.7	81.6	68.1
Total	162.2	178.4	205.7	208.4	191.6

Source Ministry of Finance 1996

From 1997 until 2003, average annual debt-service payments will be US$190.6m., compared with an average $57m. over the 1990–95 period. This represents a rise of 234% in average payments. Over the period 1997–2005, average debt-service payments will be $115.8m. Under this scenario, average debt service would be 3.3 times higher than during the 1990–95 period.

The impact of debt service on the macroeconomic figures is presented in Table 4.11. The following conclusions can be drawn:

Table 4.11 *Impact of debt service 1997–2005 (%)*

	1997	1998	1999	2000	2001	2002	2003	2004	2005
Debt service/exports goods and services[a]	31	29	29	29	27	26	23	19	18
Debt service/total expenditure	33	33	35	39	44	44	40	35	34
Debt service/fiscal revenue	37	33	31	33	32	32	29	24	23

[a]Excludes debt service on new loans and private debt.
Source Ministry of Finance 1996

Debt service/exports: According to recent analyses of sustainability, a ratio between 15% and 20% is considered sustainable. As Table 4.11 illustrates, in Mozambique the ratio is always above these parameters (excluding new loans). In addition, fluctuations in export prices and other risk factors must also be taken into account.

Debt service/total expenditure and debt service/fiscal revenue: These ratios show the impact of debt service on the budget. The debt service/total expenditure ratio shows that, throughout the period in question, the budget will have to allocate roughly double the current amounts for debt payments. This will be extremely prejudicial to the government's objectives and priorities, in particular with regard to poverty reduction. The need to channel resources to debt payments will have a negative effect on the allocation of resources to the social sectors and on the growth of investment. In addition, the need to generate the amount of revenue able to support debt service, could oblige the government to increase current tax levels, which would have a negative effect on attracting private investment and on growth and consequently on employment levels.

Multilateral debt initiatives
The government has been asking multilateral creditors to provide debt relief, given the heavy burden (see Table 4.3) this represents for the budget and the balance of payments. It has also appealed to donors to provide funds for the payment of debt service or for debt buy-back operations, so as to enable it to reallocate its budget lines towards such priority sectors as education, health and the judiciary. Denmark recently made available about US$28m. to pay part of the multilateral debt service. The Netherlands has also shown interest in buying part of the IMF debt.

New opportunities arose with a report of the Director General of the International Monetary Fund and the President of the World Bank, in April 1996. The main issues are set out below:

i)   In October 1995, the Development Committee and the Interim Committee instructed the World Bank and the IMF respectively to carry out studies analyzing the debt problems of highly indebted countries.
ii) In cases where current mechanisms are inadequate for putting the country in a sustainable debt situation, the Bank and the Fund should present new proposals for action.
iii) Following analyses by staff of the two institutions, it was concluded that a reasonable number of highly indebted poor countries faced a debt situation which, irrespective of their development efforts, was unsustainable in the medium term with the current relief mechanisms.
iv) A precondition was that the debtor country should (a) have adhered to a structural adjustment and stabilization programme; (b) have explored all possibilities at the bilateral level; (c) be currently contracting debt only on concessional terms.
v)   Three groups were thus established:
     ● those which could return to a sustainable situation;
     ● those which would only return to a sustainable situation within 5 to 10 years (5 countries);
     ● those which would not be sustainable even in 10 years (4 countries).
     Mozambique was included in the third group.
     Pre-requisites include the following:
     ● the need to work case by case on the basis of the total debt;
     ● the debtor country should have a good track record in the adjustment process and have made good use of foreign aid;
     ● the new effort should be based on current mechanisms;

- the additional effort should be a joint one with creditors with equitable participation;
- the character and nature of multilateral creditors should be protected, ensuring the possibility of their continuing to finance other members;
- there should be guarantees on the concessionality of new credits.

In the case of Mozambique, the decision as to which phase it is in – point of entry (phase 1) or point of decision (phase 2) – is very important. It is widely accepted that the country is one of the poorest and most indebted in the world and the wrong decision could aggravate the debt situation even further. In addition, the fact that Mozambique has had an uninterrupted IMF programme for well over 10 years is a recognition of the pre-requisites regarding growth and a good track record. The results for the on-going programme are encouraging, despite the constraints that the country is facing.

In Mozambique, efforts have been made to improve the debt management policy on contracting new debt, reviewing loans linked to projects and strengthening the structures linked to the management of the external debt and reserves. In this context, donor assistance was requested for the following:

i)   Obtaining maximum relief from creditors, through debt cancellation where possible, debt buy-back and other operations which achieve the same results;
ii) Channelling of donor resources to facilitate debt buy-back operations with Paris Club members, given the heavy weight of this debt in the overall debt structure;
iii) establishing a debt fund, where donors can channel their resources for debt payments or buy-back operations.

The debt fund will have two distinct parts: Fund A for debt-service payments; and Fund B for buy-back operations. The purpose of both funds is to help increase social expenditure, which would rise by an amount corresponding to that received in Fund A and, as regards Fund B, would comply with the fiscal and monetary programming parameters. The resources of both funds would be operated through a special account managed by the Bank of Mozambique, in the name of the Ministry of Planning and Finance.

Donors will receive quarterly reports containing the following information: donor contributions to each fund; the list of projects and disbursements made; payments made to creditors; and the available balance and forecasts on payments and expenditure in the following quarter. The report will be discussed with all donors each quarter in the Budget Group. Donor contributions are essential to the improvement and sustainability of the debt situation and consequently for improving the revenue and export indicators.

Table 4.12 *Impact of debt service taking into account phase 1 – point of entry (%)*

	1997	1998	1999	2000	2001	2002	2003	2004	2005
Debt service/export goods and services	31	29	29	29	27	26	23	19	17
Debt service/total expenditure	35	34	37	41	45	45	42	36	35
Debt service/fiscal revenues	39	35	33	34	33	33	30	25	24

Source Ministry or Finance 1996

Table 4.13 *Impact of debt service taking into account phase 2 – point of decision (%)*

	1997	1998	1999	2000	2001	2002	2003	2004	2005
Debt service/export goods and services	28	27	27	28	26	24	21	17	16
Debt service/ total expenditure	32	32	35	39	43	43	39	33	31
Debt service/ fiscal revenues	35	33	31	32	31	31	28	23	22

Source Ministry or Finance 1996

Postscript and update (by the editors)

The government has convinced the World Bank and the IMF of its sincerity of intent through its adherence to the tough structural adjustment programmes implemented in the face of serious criticisms, both at home and abroad, of the social costs associated with these measures. After a considerable period of hardship, positive results have begun to show through. In 1997 the economy grew by 6.6%, exceeding the 5% growth target set. A similarly impressive set of figures were recorded in relation to inflation, where a target figure of 10% was well beaten by an actual performance figure half this. More astonishing still, there was only a 1% devaluation of the national currency, the metical (AIM, 12 January 1998).

Adherence to the programme combined with active negotiation resulted in significant steps forward being taken. Multilateral concessional credit has been forthcoming to cover on-going balance of payments deficits. The proportion of bilateral debt has been reduced with the aid of the Paris Club. Most creditors in the club have cancelled the external debt. In September 1997, the boards of the IMF and the World Bank agreed in principle to make Mozambique eligible for the important new Highly Indebted Poor Countries (HIPC) debt relief initiative. Given that servicing the debt alone accounts for 30% of annual export earnings and that debt repayments consume a third of the government's revenue, in the words of Finance Minister Tomas Salomão, 'All our efforts will be useless, really useless, if the debt problem is not solved' (AIM, 8 September 1997).

Following this agreement in principle, it took longer than expected to reach final agreement with all of the creditors on the debt figures, in particular with Russia.

In January 1998 the Paris Club announced that it had agreed to write off 80% of Mozambique's debt to the members of the Club. Whilst this was obviously a most welcome step in the right direction, critics were arguing that it would still be inadequate to ensure future sustainability. The Bretton Woods institutions define sustainability as a debt-service ratio of 20–25%. According to their figures, Mozambique's debt service ratio between 1996 and 2005 would average 30%. The debt stock to export ratio for sustainability would be in the range of 200–250%, whilst the most optimistic estimate for Mozambique's ratio would be over 400% (AIM, 26 January 1998).

The important breakthrough came in early April 1998. The World Bank and the IMF along with other creditors announced an agreement providing 'exceptional support', amounting to nearly US$3 billion in nominal terms in debt-service relief for Mozambique. The actual figures agreed were $1.442 bn of debt cancelled under HIPC calculations as the Net Present Value (NPV) at the completion point of the agreement. Under the HIPC rules there is a 'decision point', which was Tuesday 7 April 1998, and a 'completion point', in June 1999 when the debt relief is actually implemented. The NPV is significantly magnified when calculated in nominal terms, as this includes the interest that would have been paid on the debt stock which has been cancelled. This raises the total debt relief to US$2.9 bn.

The NPV debt relief figure represents over 70% of the country's GDP, which in 1997 was just under $2 bn. Of course, the agreement requires the continued implementation of the reform agenda and was made subject to confirmation by all Mozambique's other creditors. In effect, the combination of this latest initiative with the on-going traditional debt relief mechanisms reduces the country's external debt from $5.6 bn in NPV terms towards the end of 1996, to $1.1 bn at the completion point in June 1999. The debt stock will have been reduced to 200% of exports, compared with 466% in NPV terms without the initiative. These figures are based on the past three years of goods and services exports. The debt-service ratio then drops to around 20%, and, according to the World Bank, may optimistically drop to under 10% by 2002. This remains to be seen. Undeniably this marked a hugely significant milestone along the path to a more sustainable development future for the country.

Announcing the initiative, the World Bank stressed that Mozambique's case was special, and required an exceptional effort beyond what was originally envisaged by the HIPC initiative. Earlier debt relief initiatives had not covered both debt stock and the interest owed, combined with a joint effort on the part of both multilateral and bilateral creditors. The multilateral creditors have granted $526m. and the bilateral creditors $916m. Mozambique's Finance Minister stated that, although the country would have liked to receive total debt forgiveness, this move was indeed a positive step forward.

References
All the statistical material was supplied by the ministries cited.

5 Privatizing the State Enterprise Sector

JOÃO GODINHO ALVES

Foreign investment, whether in the commercial, industrial or agricultural fields, and whether individually or in co-operation with local partners, is seen as the most secure and lasting way to ensure and consolidate production for the domestic and foreign market. On the whole, between 1976 and 1989 the state enterprise sector in Mozambique functioned badly and was unsustainable both economically and socially. Agro-industrial plants lacked equipment and the companies were decapitalized. They operated well below their installed capacity owing to a shortage of raw materials and spare parts, a lack of technicians, the constant breakdown of equipment which was never replaced, assembly lines which did not function coherently, and frequent power cuts. Weak domestic demand and the impossibility of competing with the quality and price of foreign products also hampered the development of the state-run agro-industrial sector at that time. These problems were linked to and compounded by the following factors: supply difficulties stemming from a shortage of funds; inadequate financial autonomy; and the state companies' heavy indebtedness to the banks and the Treasury.

Following a reappraisal of the country's post-independence economic performance, in 1983 the government approved an Action Programme for the three years 1984–6. Under this programme, a series of measures were taken to deal with the country's economic and financial imbalances. However, given the magnitude of the internal and external imbalances, more extensive policy measures had to be introduced to stimulate the recovery of production and the gradual realignment of the internal and external accounts. This initiative resulted in the government adopting the Economic Rehabilitation Programme (ERP), which began in 1987 and has subsequently been complemented by other measures of a social nature, resulting in the later introduction of an Economic and Social Rehabilitation Programme with the Portuguese acronym of PRES.

The new Constitution, adopted in November 1990, established a market economy based on giving due value to labour, market forces and the initiatives of economic agents. This context included the approval of an important legislative package regulating the restructuring of the state enterprise sector, and in particular the commercial privatization and transfer of companies, establishments, installations and shareholdings owned by the state.[1] The privatization of the state sector in Mozambique remains an on-going process.

The privatization process

This section will examine the privatization process and analyze whether it has been successful and, given the overall macroeconomic policies, if it is on a path which will really guarantee sustainable development. Without going into too much detail, it will also examine and analyze in general terms how the process has operated.

Broadly speaking, the privatization process in Mozambique has involved two sectors: small and medium-sized companies which, under the Mozambican classification, employ between 50 and 200 workers; and large companies, which normally employ more than 200 workers. The privatization of small and medium-sized companies, which are selected by the various line Ministries, is co-ordinated by National Evaluation and Alienation Committees (NEACs) and is authorized by the Provincial Governor and the Minister of Planning and Finance together with the respective line Minister and the Prime Minister. There is also the Industrial Enterprise Restructuring Office (IERO), which assists the NEAC responsible for restructuring companies in the industrial sector, and the Agricultural Restructuring Unit (ARU).

The restructuring of large companies identified by a decree of the Council of Ministers is co-ordinated by the Technical Unit for Enterprise Restructuring (TUER). In addition to this responsibility, the Unit ensures that the Ministry of Planning and Finance participates in the Technical Council of the Inter-Ministerial Committee for Enterprise Restructuring (ICER) and in the Committee secretariat, and finally in taking decisions on the companies to be alienated.

The Prime Minster decides on the alienation of these companies, establishments and shareholdings owned by the state. In the case of alienation, this is done by public tender. The Prime Minister appoints a Privatization Executive Committee (PEC) comprising representatives of the line Ministry, the Ministry of Planning and Finance, the Bank of Mozambique and the Investment Promotion Centre. For each of the large companies to be privatized it has the following functions: the pre-selection of candidates; the evaluation of bids; and negotiations with the candidates selected.

Under current legislation, the restructuring and privatization of state assets can take the following forms, either individually or in combination:

- alienation by public tender;
- public offer and sale of shares;
- negotiation or restricted tender preceded by pre-selection;
- private investments in state companies;
- alienation or sale of state shareholdings to managers, technicians and workers;
- exploration and management contracts.

Between 1989, when the legislation on enterprise restructuring was published, and September 1995, the government had restructured about 502 small and medium-sized companies through the NEACs. Of these, 53% were companies in the industrial, commercial and tourism sectors and 21% were in fisheries and agriculture. The alienated companies comprised 423 units, and over 90% were sold to Mozambican entrepreneurs. There were also 54 exploration-management contracts. By September 1995 the TUER had handled the restructuring of 59 large state companies. Between 1992 and 1995 a total of 45 new companies were established as the result of privatization.

The net revenue earned from privatization had reached about US$65 million by September 1995, with guaranteed investments at that time of almost $120m. over the following ten years for rehabilitation and new equipment. The privatizations since 1992 have included most of the economy's productive sectors, involving cement production, building materials, metallurgy, plastics, soap and oils, fisheries, beer factories, clothing, cashew processing and the retail trade. Although more than 90% of the companies privatized have been acquired by Mozambican companies or citizens, approximately 60% of the funds from the sales have come from abroad, from:

Portugal, South Africa, the UK, the Netherlands, Denmark, Zimbabwe, Swaziland and Mauritius.

Whilst privatization has certainly moved ahead in terms of the number of privatized entities, there is no guarantee as yet of the longer-term sustainability of these enterprises. A summary analysis is presented below of the essential sustainability issues within the privatized companies.

Constraints
Analyses by the World Bank indicate that the privatization of the so-called large companies in Mozambique has been very slow. As a result, on the one hand, the restructuring of the country's entire industrial plant has been delayed, and on the other hand, there have been negative repercussions for macroeconomic stability in general, especially since privatization has been declared to be the only way of reorienting the state enterprise sector.

The slowness of the privatization process can be linked to various factors. A World Bank report, of 22 August 1995, by the Macroeconomic, Industrial and Financial Division of the Southern Africa Department, which makes an exhaustive analysis of the enterprise sector in Mozambique, identified the following difficulties:

- slow preparatory processes;
- labour-related problems;
- the transparency of the process (tenders and other sale modalities);
- time-consuming administrative procedures in banks and at the customs;
- weak financial capacity on the part of the people and companies involved in the process and inexperience in handling such a complex situation;
- a fragile and virtually non-existent national capital market;
- absence of inter-institutional co-ordination;
- lack of financial, administrative and productive capacity on the part of the new agents involved in the process (adjudicators);
- imperfections and imprecision in current macroeconomic policies;
- incompatibility between credit periods (for working capital) and the production cycle;
- unfavourable interest rates for credit;
- few fiscal incentives;
- the unfavourable nature of the new exchange management policy;
- and the concentration of industries in towns.

In this chapter we focus on why the process has been so slow. This is directly related to the fact that the government announces in advance the companies which are to be privatized, which makes it difficult for them to carry on business as usual. Henceforth, credit is limited and their clients are usually reluctant to enter into commercial contracts. During this phase, companies targeted for privatization normally suffer losses, their access to bank finance declines and they are unable to meet their current expenditures and salary bills. This period of uncertainty can last for three years or more, as in the case of Navique, a maritime navigation and coastal transport company.

Procedures for the privatization of companies in Mozambique are both slow and complicated. The diagnosis of restructuring potential requires far too much information, and too long a time is taken to consider this and reach a decision. Indeed, the 1995 World Bank report states explicitly that the diagnosis has gathered much more information than is required, and that the evaluation methods for determining the reference price of the company being put up for privatization have been both subjective and excessively complicated. The normal method now used for determining the reference value involves calculating the current net value of the company's projected cash flow, assuming a certain amount invested. The World Bank considers that the determination of a company's reference value should be based on its market value, that is, its real price. Hence the determination of the reference price using a subjective model usually leads to under- or over-valuation of the company. This situation has meant that, following the publication of the respective sales memoranda, the privatization process is delayed, thus discouraging potential purchases.

There is also the labour issue, which has two components, the first related to the payment of salaries and the second to the existence or not of a strong trade union movement in these companies. Given the scarcity of funds, various state companies have been unable to pay their workers' salaries. Consequently, many companies ask their workers to stay at home until the situation returns to normal. This has not been the most appropriate solution, however, since the company is accumulating further debts for its salary bill, thus increasing its fixed cost component.

The existence of surplus labour, the accumulation of salary debts and the consequent paralyzation of companies through strikes created numerous problems for the privatization process. Current policies and practices surrounding the sale of state companies effectively transfer these problems from the government to the private sector. For example, the NEAC has made the maintenance of the same workforce a condition for bidders for small and medium-sized companies. According to the NEAC, the maintenance of the labour force after adjudication is mandatory. Indeed, any bid which offers a good purchase price but intends to reduce the labour force is immediately rejected.

In the case of large companies with many workers, when privatization is handled by the TUER there are compensation mechanisms. The company which takes over all the workers receives a discount on the adjudicated price and any workers fired receive compensation. The purchaser must give priority to paying compensation calculated from the date the company was paralyzed. The World Bank considered that the Labour Law in Mozambique was out of date and not in keeping with a period of transformation towards market policies.

The macroeconomic impact of privatization

In the field of macroeconomic performance, budget policy has been positively affected by privatization. Up to September 1995, the most important developments in budget policy can be seen in Table 5.1.

Table 5.1 *Impact of privatization on the budget 1995 (in meticais)*

Reduction in finance	million contos
Revenue	–235
Collection of countervalues	–381
Foreign investment finance	–320
Privatization revenue	+56
Total	–880
Reduction in expenditure	
Current expenditure	-287
Investment expenditure	–405
Total	–692

Source: Government of Mozambique 1996

Table 5.1 shows that from January to September 1995, for a financing deficit of 880 million contos, the negative adjustment on the expenditure side was 692 million contos. The difference between these amounts, about 188 million contos, represents the saving in the state bank deficit, a significant and positive contribution of privatization.

The evolution of output up to September 1995, arising from the contribution of privatized state companies and the resulting revenue, shows an overall rise of 2.5%, almost one percentage point less than planned. Although this outcome was relatively low, the economic sectors, excluding services, experienced a highly satisfactory growth rate of 8% up to September 1995. The main reason for the slow overall growth is the expected decline in the production of government services.

Companies whose privatization involved foreign entities and capital have had no difficulty in implementing their projects, since they have financial and technological capacity and know-how. Companies which have been handed over to nationals have faced problems related to insufficient capital and the use of outdated technology, management and know-how. Although most privatized companies have been adjudicated to nationals, 70% of them have not been able subsequently to continue their basic activities.

What usually happens is that a company is bought in order to resell the plant installation or to turn the buildings into warehouses, places of worship or of entertainment, among other functions, to the detriment of the workers and the economy in general. Another problem faced by national economic agents is that of technology. The technologies adopted to revitalize paralyzed companies have not always been the most appropriate. They are often outdated and produce goods without any competitive edge in the market. For example, a group of Mozambican entrepreneurs bought an industrial unit for producing and bottling beer, with a turnover of about US$1m. As it was necessary to raise capital to invest in new machinery, the group was obliged to contact a foreign company specializing in beer production. However, since the factory's technology was considered out of date, the foreign company turned down the offer of shares in the company.

The Sabrina clothing factory in Maputo provides a more positive example. Privatized under law 15/91 as one of the sub-units of Soveste, which has mixed capital, it has been performing well, in both the quality and quantity of its output. The quality of the Sabrina product has been compared to that of Malaysia. In terms of output quantity, the company has managed to achieve a return to 1973 levels of production.

Recommendations

The following recommendations are intended to help make the privatization process in Mozambique more effective and help establish the foundations for sustainable development.

i)   The requirements of the Diagnosis of Restructuring Potential should be redefined and considerably simplified. Consultants hired to prepare the diagnosis should be instructed to complete the work in two months.

ii) The World Bank recommends that during the privatization process the assumed sale price should be as reasonable as possible. It should be evident that the main objective of privatization is to restructure Mozambican companies on a basis of sustainable development, by transferring assets to more productive hands. It must be borne in mind that the longer privatization takes, the more money the companies concerned will drain from the government budget and the economy in general.

iii) A compensation fund for surplus workers should be established as an emergency measure to ensure sustainable living conditions for workers.

iv) Successful bidders should be chosen exclusively on the basis of price and not according to subjective criteria, such as, for example, proposals on the company's future development. The bidder's technical capacity should be evaluated during the tendering pre-selection stage.

v) Large companies should be paid for in cash so that the state no longer has any connection with the future of the company.

Endnote 1

- Decree 21/89 of 23 May, *Government Gazette* 1st Series No. 20 permitting the sale of state assets by public tender and establishing the procedural and administrative mechanisms for such a transfer (alienation).
- Law 13/91 of 3 August, *Government Gazette* 1st Series No. 31, Supplement, establishing that companies where the state had taken over could either be privatized or closed down, thus revoking Law 18/77, of 28 April.
- Law 15/91 of 3 August, *Government Gazette* 1st Series No. 31, 2nd Supplement, establishing norms for the restructuring and rescaling of the state enterprise sector, including mechanisms for such transfers.
- Decree 28/91, of 21 November, establishing the Inter-ministerial Committee for Enterprise Restructuring (ICER).
- Decree 28/91, of 21 November, regulating Law 15/91, defining in detail the juridical-administrative framework for the restructuring process for state companies.
- Law 17/91, of 14 October, *Government Gazette* 1st Series, No. 42, 2nd Supplement, clarifying doubts as to the interpretation of Article 1 of Law 15/91.
- Law 20/92, of 5 August, *Government Gazette* 1st Series, No. 32, Supplement, creating the *Economic Rehabilitation Support Fund*, establishing that part of the net profit from privatization which should be used to support small and medium size national entrepreneurs.
- Ministerial Diploma No. 87/92, of 24 June, *Government Gazette* 1st Series, No. 2, assigning to the Technical Unit for Enterprise Restructuring (TUER) the function of co-ordinating the privatization of large companies.
- Decree 20/93, of 14 September, *Government Gazette* 1st Series, 3rd Supplement, establishing the procedures to be followed for managers, technicians and workers to receive shares.

References

Government of Mozambique (1996) *Plano Economico e Social a Politica Orçamental para 1996*. Maputo.

World Bank (1995) *Impediments to Industrial Sector Recovery in Mozambique*. Report No 13752-MOZ. Macroeconomic, Industry and Finance Division, Southern Africa Department, World Bank, Washington, DC.

6 Industrial Projects for Sustainable Development

ODETE SEMIÃO

Introduction

The growing internationalization of the world economy is one of the most striking phenomena of our age. It means that economic agents must find new, dynamic ways of responding to market behaviour and to political conditions, which ensure more security and incentives for investors. In this context, direct foreign investment (DFI) is an important instrument for promoting growth in developing countries, and helping to overcome the various limitations of government, entrepreneurs and investors in these countries. A strong government commitment to development can transmit a message of confidence and, if followed up with practical measures, can provide an attractive package for foreign investors. Welcoming and encouraging the development of private business can also inspire greater political stability.

The procedures for national and foreign investment in Mozambique are governed by Law 4/84 of 18 August and 5/87 of 19 January (for investment projects authorized between 1985 and July 1993) and by Law 3/93 of 24 June for projects authorized from August 1993 onwards. Following the government measures of 8 August 1995, which simplified the procedures for presenting and approving such proposals, capital investment in ventures in Mozambique has grown substantially.

The general evolution of DFI in Mozambique over the 1985–95 period has been one of positive growth, despite declines in 1987, 1991, 1993 and 1995, and this growth is expected to continue at an even faster pace in the future. One important aspect of the clearly positive situation of DFI is its effect on the country's economic development through the installation, rehabilitation, expansion and modernization of economic infrastructures, and the creation of new companies producing goods and services, 70% of which have national partners. The introduction of new technologies and improved entrepreneurial productivity and efficiency, the diversification and stimulation of exports, the creation of jobs for Mozambican citizens, import reduction and substitution and the consequent positive effects on the balance of payments, and the fight against tax evasion on the borders, are just some of the ways in which DFI contributes to the Mozambican economy. This whole dynamic involves important beneficial synergies for more accelerated economic and social development.

The influx of DFI, in turn, promotes and favours the internationalization of the Mozambican economy. This process has been advancing, albeit gradually. Exports have been reactivated and a growing number of national products and services are being placed in overseas markets, both regional and international.

The conclusion of the General Peace Agreement and the greatly improved prospects for stability and democratic development in Mozambique have had a very positive effect on the inflow of foreign capital. This is evident from the number of investments authorized between 1993 and 1995: more than 320 projects, totalling US$600 million, compared with 116 projects totalling $334m. approved in the 1985–92 period. Whereas the 24 investment projects approved in 1992 were worth $188m., the 124 projects authorized in 1994, the year the first multi-party elections were held successfully, reached $412m. The number of approved projects continued to grow in 1995, reaching 174 projects worth about $280m. This trend continued throughout the second half of the decade.

Once the right conditions have been created, Mozambique has strong economic development potential and the capacity to achieve growth levels which will enable the country to free itself from its extreme dependence on external aid if the existing heavy burden of unpayable debt is removed. Some mega-industrial projects are now starting to appear, such as the proposed Beira and Maputo Aluminium Project. The Prime Minister actually laid the foundation stone of the aluminium foundry in July 1998 (AIM, 20 July 1998). It represents a US$1.3 billion investment. Given its size and potential impact, appropriate environmental norms need to be taken into account.

The industrial sector has so far attracted the largest volume of foreign investment, thus making it possible to accelerate the country's development. Since production levels in this sector have fallen considerably in earlier years, industry has received special attention from the government. It has faced a variety of problems, from a shortage of raw materials to the small size of the domestic market and to its inability to compete with imported products. However, the privatization programme and assistance to new small and medium-sized industries could facilitate industrial recovery in the medium term. By 1998 the privatization programme was virtually completed.

Constraints

The growing industrialization of the SADC member states combined with the political changes in South Africa (the most industrialized country in the region) will intensify the impact of industry on the region's environment. Donor agencies, international creditors and the Ministry for the Co-ordination of Environmental Action (MICOA) now require development projects, including manufacturing industries, to take environmental concerns into account. Consumers in industrialized countries can boycott the products of companies which fail to do so.

Industrialization is an essential indicator of economic growth in developing countries, and all countries need economic growth. Although the growth resulting from industrialization can have positive effects on human health, it can also create adverse conditions which may directly affect workers and the population in general, or affect them indirectly through a deterioration of the environment.

As is the case currently with economic analysis and engineering viability studies, a preliminary Environmental Impact Assessment should form part of the toolkit for managers who have to take decisions on development projects or new investments. Over the past decade many industrial development projects have faced serious problems because they did not pay sufficient attention to their relationship with the environment. Following this experience, it is clearly very risky to finance or approve any development project without first considering its environmental implications and without designing the project in such a way as to minimize any adverse impact.

For example, before implementing any project the following questions need to be asked:

- Can it operate safely, without serious risk of dangerous accidents or long-term effects on the health of the population? One example here is the Retreading Tyres Project, which is operating in a garage below an apartment block on Karl Marx Avenue in Maputo. In addition to its waste products, the chemicals used in the production process can be a serious health risk to the people living there.
- Might the project's proposed location conflict with land use in surrounding areas, or prevent the development of the surrounding areas at a later date? For example, the location of the Maputo cement factory did not take into account the expansion of the city's residential areas. When it was built the disposal of waste from the production process had no negative effects because no one was living near the factory at that time. But these problems are arising now because of the city's expansion.
- Can the local environment absorb the effluent and additional pollution to be produced by the project? Here we have the concrete case of the União de Curtumes de Moçambique (UNICUM) project. Given the nature of the project, it has to be located near rivers. But it is also recognized that before the effluent is discharged into the rivers it needs to be treated, since the preparation of skins involves chemical substances such as chrome acid, amongst others. Failure to treat the effluent could pollute the river and affect natural habitats.
- How do waste products affect fishing reserves, agricultural land and other industries?
- Can the existing local infrastructures (roads, railways, sewers, etc) support the project?
- What human resources will be required by the project and what social effects might it have on the community?
- How much energy, water and other resources will be consumed by the project and will there be enough of these resources?
- What accidental damage could the project cause to national wealth such as beaches and tourist areas, or areas of historic and cultural interest?

These are just some of the aspects which, depending on its type and size, need to be considered when establishing an industrial initiative intended to ensure sustainable economic development.

Another aspect to be considered in the development of the industrial sector is the elimination of industrial waste. MICOA usually recommends investors to establish mechanisms which minimize all harmful environmental effects of such waste, by ensuring the availability of an appropriate disposal system. But companies are often not prepared to comply in full with these demands, nor is the Ministry always able to inspect the projects to check whether or not investors are complying.

Industrial waste has become an increasingly undesirable feature of our daily lives, and will undoubtedly continue as such in the future, given the seemingly unrestrained increase in the consumption of industrial goods. For example, the SOSUN (Coca Cola) project has had a number of positive impacts, including reducing imports, providing employment, and to some extent, reducing the disposal of soft drink cans on beaches and in towns. Since Coca Cola is the cheapest soft drink, most people drink it and the bottle is recycled and reused, thus diminishing litter.

Colgate Palmolive is another project which to some extent helps reduce imports of toothpaste and soap, but it does not have the production capacity to supply the whole domestic market.

The production of waste which is subsequently dumped in the surrounding area can cause serious environmental problems affecting the cycle of living organisms, fostering the incorporation of contaminating agents into the biological chain and involving their subsequent spread and the further aggravation of the problem. In addition, the growing generation of waste products implies a parallel consumption of raw materials, most of which exist only in limited quantities in nature, to the detriment of their use for other productive purposes.

In order to try and resolve the problem, the Use of Waste project was approved. Its aim is to collect, process and transform waste and rubbish in order to obtain benefits from the resulting metal substances and glass, and from the energy and organic fertilizers retrieved from the respective selection and decomposition of inorganic and organic rubbish. The project has a positive social impact in that it should help resolve the problem of filth in the towns. However, in an ealier version of the project, the investors planned to import rubbish for subsequent treatment, which could cause severe ecological damage. Also, if there is inadequate control and inspection capacity there is the risk of toxic or contaminated waste being imported, since Mozambican businessmen have no environmental culture and only consider the profit component.

Conclusions and recommendations

The industrial recovery and development strategy must deal with the overall challenges facing the Mozambican economy as a whole, namely, resolving the main macroeconomic problems of economic growth and development. Sectoral agreements between business associations and the environmental management companies should be drawn up and implemented so that the application of the law does not prejudice economic activity, and the objective of reducing industrial waste is pursued.

MICOA, in collaboration with the Industrial Association, must find an interim solution for the problem of industrial waste, until an integrated system for recycling it can be set up. Methods for treating industrial waste should be introduced such as, for example, secure land-fills for special waste with similar characteristics to domestic rubbish; incineration; injection of waste into deep wells (land fills); and physical-chemical treatment, among others. An environmentally aware industry needs to be created in order to ensure the future growth of the industrial sector in the SADC region, since the consumer will prefer goods which take into account the environmental factor.

All industrial projects with any negative effects on the environment (no matter how small) should be subject to an Environmental Impact Assessment (EIA) before being implemented, in order to ensure an environmentally sustainable production system and that any potential environmental problems are anticipated and dealt with in the initial phase of project planning and conception. All the relevant people or groups should be involved – for example, those who will manage or undertake the EIA, those with the authority to permit, control or alter the project, and those who can contribute to the study in one way or another with facts, ideas and their concerns, including scientists, environmentalists, political economists, community representatives, in sum, all of the stakeholders and relevant experts. The EIA should be conceived in such a way as to present clear options for project planning and implementation and should present clearly the probable results of each option for reducing the impact and for effective management of the environment.

Industrial policy should aim to promote small and medium-sized projects which have minimum negative effects. Appropriate strategies should be developed for planning and controlling industrial activities with the aim of minimizing health and environmental problems and hence maximizing the benefits of industrialization. A project inspection committee should therefore be established without delay, since it is widely recognized that, given the fragility of the country's economy, MICOA's policy is not to reject projects but to recommend measures which might minimize their negative environmental effects. There is thus a need to monitor whether these measures are being implemented or not.

The development of Industrial Tax Free Zones would be of considerable assistance for economic development, since at least 80% of the goods produced under this system would be for export and this would make an important contribution to the state budget.

7 The Mining Sector's Contribution to Sustainable Development

GILBERTO BANZE
& EUGÉNIO SILVA

Introduction

Throughout history, the improved use of mineral and energy resources has marked the most decisive transformations in human development – from the Stone Age through to the Industrial Revolution and on to the current rapid industrialization of many developing countries. The *per capita* consumption of mineral products or oil is a clear indicator of the level of a country's development (Franciso, 1995).

The mineral resources sector is a cornerstone of the economies of Southern Africa and the one which often makes the largest individual contribution to both Gross National Product and exports. Mining activity has its own unique characteristics, some of the reasons being:

- it is an activity which extracts non-renewable resources;
- its development requires large financial resources and a long time-frame for preparation and for a return on investments;
- it is a high-risk activity;
- it frequently results in comparatively high rates of return on investments;
- it is an important and essential basis for socio-economic development in general and industrial development in particular; and
- it interacts with the environment in a particularly intensive way.

This chapter begins by providing a brief description of mining activity in Mozambique to indicate the most striking features of this sector of the economy. It then goes on to formulate some suggestions as to how to minimize its negative aspects in the economic, social and environmental fields. The chapter then discusses the case of mining in Manica Province.

Mining in Mozambique

The region's tradition of mineral exploitation dates back to 96–212 AD when gold, silver and copper were extracted and processed by the Ziwa peoples and later by the Shona. The colonial period was characterized by deliberately weak progress in the geological-mining sector compared with that in neighbouring countries. The Department of Geological Services was created only in 1928. Until then, the limited basic geological work was undertaken by the Royal Companies, in particular the Mozambique Company.

The advent of the armed liberation struggle forced the colonial administration to undertake some geological mapping and mineral inventories in the Zambezi valley, in Manica, Tete and the Alto Ligonha region as part of the Mining Development Plans. These were intended to develop mineral resources only to the extent required for the expansion and consolidation of the colonial presence and to contain the spread of the armed struggle. At independence the country inherited a weak mining industry in which the only major undertaking was coal mining. The other operations were only small and medium-scale and lacked consistent geological data, clear technological orientation and adequate resources. The sector's participation in the economy has always been marginal.

Following independence what was by then the Directorate of Geology and Mines was reorganized and specific programmes were launched in order to:

- increase geological research and mineral inventories;
- undertake basic geological cartography through regional aero-geophysical, geological and geo-chemical surveys;
- establish the hydrocarbons sector and begin geological research in this field: and
- evaluate the reserves of known mineral occurrences.

These activities culminated in the creation of the Ministry of Mineral Resources in 1983 and the revision of legislation relating to the sector.

However, the war interrupted many of the on-going initiatives and projects and many mining units were completely destroyed. Throughout this period about 1,000 basic, middle-level and graduate technicians were trained for the civil service (excluding businesses) (Francisco, 1995).

During the 1976–84 period alone, more geological work was undertaken than during the whole colonial period, as shown in Table 7.1.

Table 7.1 *A comparison of geological mapping before and after 1975*

	Activity	Before 1975	1975–94	Total	% of country
Geological cartography	1/120,000	476 420	478 590[a]	747 504	93.51
	1/100,000	123 540	349 000	472 540	59.11
	1/50,000		173 200	173 200	21.67
	1/250,000	511 360		511 360	63.97
Aerogeophysical surveys	1/100,000		476 650	476 650	59.63
	1/50,000		12 675	12 675	1.59
	1/250,000	134 700	238 300	373 000	46.66
Geochemical surveys	1/100,000		66 000	66 000	8.26
	1/50,000	6 630	7 075	13 705	1.71

[a]Includes 198,506 km^2 mapped for the second time
Total area of the country – 799,388 km^2
Source Ministry of Mineral Resources 1995

The legal framework for mining

The Mines Law provides for the issue of the following mining titles: Prospecting and Investigation Licences; Mining Concessions; Quarry Permits; Mining Certificates; and Minerals and Precious Metals Trading Licences.

The Prospecting and Investigation Licence gives the holder the right to undertake geological reconnaissance and research on specific minerals in a clearly defined area where he does not have exclusive rights and where there can be other users or occupants of the same piece of land. A Mining Concession gives the holder exclusive rights to develop, extract, process and trade specific minerals in a clearly defined area.

It does not substitute for a Land Use and Benefit Title but rather enables the holder to obtain one. By law he may negotiate with eventual users or occupants of the same piece of land and also has priority in relation to other forms of use and benefit from the land. The Quarry Permit authorizes the exploitation of mineral resources destined for building materials. The Mining Certificate is specifically for small-scale geological mining activity and is issued in areas designated by the state. The Minerals and Precious Metals Trading Licence authorizes the holder to transact business in gems and precious metals which do not result from exploitation under a mining title, in a defined area.

The mining licensing process essentially involves the submission of a request giving the precise identity of the petitioner, specification of the intended object(s), location and minerals, a presentation of technical capacity (a satisfactory work programme for mineral development) and proof of financial capacity to cover the basic budget for the work proposed. After the request has been examined by the appropriate sectors, announcements are published in the largest circulation daily newspaper, followed by a period for any objections to be presented. If there are none, then the requested title can be issued.

The fragility of the systems

The system for checking the availability of a given area is undertaken manually, and is slow and subject to imprecision. The announcements receive insufficient publicity (which is only as extensive and efficient as the distribution of the newspaper in question). The indication of the geographical co-ordinates in the announcements is not sufficiently illuminating, but other methods, such as publication of the accompanying topographical outline, are rather complicated and expensive.

The administrative system for mining mapping should be computerized so as to ensure speed and precision, as well as providing a basis for efficient communication between institutions. Conflicts of interest inevitably arise, given the multiple forms of occupation and use of the land and the resources it contains. Delays and imperfections in the licensing system only serve to aggravate such conflicts. A variety of different, not necessarily compatible, interests surround the development of mineral resources:

- On the one hand, there is the state, which is struggling to promote investment and the subsequent development of mineral resources in harmony with environmental protection and the rational use of mineral deposits.
- On the other hand, there is the local business sector, which is, of course, motivated by profit and seeks to position itself in the sector, but which usually does not have the necessary material resources or experience in this field.
- There are also the potential foreign investors (small, medium and large), whose involvement is essential if mineral resources are to be developed, since this usually requires heavy investments. This group usually seeks incentives and satisfactory guarantees before investing.
- The population in the areas subject to geological-mining activity are another group with specific interests in the sector's activity. It involves their vital space and operations can either threaten their presence in these areas and the quality of the environment or they can become a development centre and employment opportunity.
- Small-scale operators, commonly known as panners, who do not always have formal authorization, are yet another group interested in taking advantage of mineral resources. This group usually comprises local people or those from not far away who are attracted by the discovery of accessible deposits and undertake

mining to complement or substitute for their agricultural work. They do not gain much profit and merely hand over their products to middlemen, or traders, for low prices or much sought after goods. They usually mine voraciously, sometimes devastating valuable deposits and rendering them worthless through disorganized excavation and the uneven extraction of only the richest parts.

● Illegal traders in mineral products, normally or solely gems and precious metals, play a significant role in the sector and have distinctive interests and forms of behaviour. They can be nationals or foreigners and operate close to mining areas. They are usually intermediaries in the illegal export of the illicitly traded products, exploiting the immediate shortages of the panners and the weak or non-existent commercial network in such areas.

The current situation

The Ministry of Mineral Resources and Energy has issued more than 400 titles, more than 80% of which are Prospecting and Investigation Licences for gems in the provinces of Zambezia, Nampula and Cabo Delgado. In numerical terms, these are followed by Prospecting and Investigation Licences for gold in the provinces of Manica, Niassa and Tete. Few Mining Concessions have been issued, due in part to the substantial technical and financial requirements which petitioners must satisfy in order to obtain them.

Industrial mining activity is limited to a very small number of operations, namely:

● mining and processing of bentonite in Boane, Maputo;
● mining and processing of graphite in Ancuabe, Cabo Delgado;
● extraction of marble on Montepuez, and subsequent cutting and polishing in Pemba, Cabo Delgado;
● mining of gold in Manica (two operations, two companies); and
● some quarries, claypits and sandpits mainly in Maputo province.

A number of geological research, viability study and rehabilitation projects, differing in scale, pace and nature, are being conducted in the country. The following are the most important:

● a research project on heavy minerals in the coastal sands of Congolone, Nampula;
● a research project on heavy minerals in the coastal sands of Moebase-Mecalonga, Zambezia;
● a research project on heavy minerals in the coastal sands of Xai-Xai-Chongoene, Gaza;
● the Moatize Coal Basin development project;
● research and rehabilitation projects for the tantalite and niobium mines of Morrua, Muiane and Marropino in Zambezia;
● a research project for gold in the Braganua/Chifumbazi mines;
● a research project for gold in Cazula.

There are considerably brighter prospects for mining activity in the future.

Given the relative impotence of state institutions intended to regulate the industry and sometimes even of the holders of mining rights themselves, illegal activity by panners predominates in the gem and alluvial gold fields. Gems and gold of enormous value are being illegally siphoned off abroad without any benefit to the panners, other national operators or the state.

Critical issues

Mozambicans holding mining rights face severe technical and material constraints in developing mineral resources. Even for small-scale operations this activity involves much larger investments and risks than in other industrial fields. Consequently, many title holders give up without having had the chance of implementing even a part of their proposed work programme, or they lose their rights for not carrying out the obligations laid down in the title.

Many people without the necessary technical and financial capacity acquire mining titles so as to legitimize their trading in minerals and precious metals, or seek finance for the investments, usually in association with foreign enterprises.

The performance of operators is hampered by the substantial bureaucratic hurdles they encounter, from the initial licensing process to the industrial production phase. Rights established by law are not observed where they apply or there are excessive delays in granting them. The obstacles are due in part to the following:

- various people and institutions are unaware of the importance of the mining sector, as the country has no mining tradition;
- lack of co-ordination between institutions;
- inadequate human resources, in number and quality, in the sectors responsible for support and control;
- other problems common to the civil service in general.

There is a significant problem of illegal mining and trade, for a number of reasons:

- the absence of control mechanisms (material and human resources in particular);
- the situation created by the war which ended only recently;
- the impossibility of agricultural production in many areas (because of war and drought);
- strong inducements by foreign agents, many of whom are in the country illegally;
- the inflexibility of the sector's legal framework; and
- the very nature of the minerals concerned (low weight and volume and high commercial value) have encouraged the illegal production and trade in gems and gold.

Technical safety and environmental protection form another problem area. There is a lack of adequate means and technical knowledge to ensure that both of these concerns are properly addressed. The situation is worsened by the pressure of extreme poverty and the insecurity of 'exploration rights'. All of the above factors have contributed to the disorganized assault on deposits, resulting in voracious mining, which renders rich deposits worthless, the destruction of rare and valuable gems, constant exposure to death, and enormous unmarked, abandoned craters and extensive denuded areas, among other damage.

The beginning of any large-scale operation, as in the case of heavy sands projects on the coastal dunes for example, will radically alter Mozambique's economic prospects, giving the mining sector a prominent position in the economy and bringing employment and development to the areas in question.

Recommendations
The development of mineral resources requires the creation of institutions, the provision of continuous and appropriate training for the sector's cadres and the material resources for each institution to be able to do its job properly. One could cite as an example the establishment of a computerized data base for the administration of the mining register and for recording mineral occurrences and deposits, among others. This data base would be complemented by the Geographical Information System (GIS), with as much georeference material as possible.

A strong inspection body with appropriate means of transport would help to minimize economic and environmental crimes. The creation of a technical assistance body and the implementation of pilot projects where there is a proper balance between commercial and learning aspects would complete the efforts aimed at the sustainable development of mineral resources.

In the future, mineral taxes should include a clear and unequivocal percentage for geological mapping work and mineral inventories, a task which is the exclusive responsibility of the state. Without this the promotion and development of mineral resources will rest on shaky foundations.

In addition to merely paying compensation and/or resettling people elsewhere, large and medium-sized operations must give priority to involving local people and the eventual occupants and/or users of the land. Whenever possible, marginal parts (in size or content) of large deposits, which would otherwise not be used rationally, should be handed over to small operators from among the local population so that they can be developed with a minimum of technical guidance and the benefits can be shared.

Comprehension of the nature of the mineral resources sector by all those directly and indirectly involved and affected by it is crucial for a positive synergy to occur between mining and other economic activities. It is therefore important to publicize its potential and discuss the risks of this activity with all sectors of society and all institutions, making use of all available instruments.

There is a need to establish and/or strengthen co-ordination among all the institutions directly or indirectly involved in promoting, licensing and controlling mining activity. This is undoubtedly one of the key aspects for achieving a rational equilibrium among the economic, ecological and social vectors of geological-mining operations.

In addition, there is a particular need for articulation between different levels within the same institution, starting with the conception of sectoral policies and continuing through the detail of implementation. Horizontal co-ordination is also required to ensure harmonization of the roles of different institutions and fluid communication between them. These will all help to provide the conditions necessary for the sustainable development of mineral resources. Civil society must always be not simply informed but also consulted on all matters of vital interest and importance.

Some legal mechanisms, intentions and decisions take far too long to implement because of bureaucracy or inadequate material and human resources. Streamlining the issuing of Mining Certificates would resolve some of the difficulties in integrating small operators, and the prevalence of illegal mining. Similarly with the Trading Licence, this would help to minimize the problem of illegal traffic in precious metals and minerals, as well as the inopportune granting of Prospecting and Investigation Licences and Mining Concessions to agents without the necessary commercial experience and capacity.

Environmental impact of mining activities

In recent times, the environment has emerged as a major area of concern worldwide. Pollution is perceived as a serious threat in the industrialized countries, where the quality of life had previously been measured mainly in terms of growth in material output. Meanwhile, natural resource degradation is becoming a serious impediment to economic development and the alleviation of poverty in the developing world. In the final part of this chapter we shall focus on the environmental aspects of mining activities in Manica Province.

Mining activity has gone on in Manica for centuries, since the time of the Monomutapa Empire. The Manica region is rich in gold and its associated minerals such as silver, bronze, copper, bauxite, fluorite, etc. Mining activities since independence have been undertaken by MAGMA, a parastatal mining enterprise, on a medium scale for gold, copper and fluorite. In 1990, a private company started to produce bauxite, with an average production of 8,000 tonnes per year. In Manica there is also small-scale mining, mainly concentrated on gold, involving hundreds of miners called 'garimpeiros' (see Chapter 25).

The aim of this case study is to review how mining activities affect the environment and the use of natural resources (both mineral and biological) as well as man-made capital and human resources, and the extent to which activities are actually jeopardizing the environment, creating a potential constraint for long-term sustainable development. Special attention is paid to soil and water management and conservation. Proposals are made to help overcome some of the problems identified.

It is important to place the specific problems facing Manica Province within a broader global and historical context. Mohan Munasinghe of the World Bank has usefully provided the following overview:

Mankind's relationship with the environment has gone through several stages, starting with primitive times in which human beings lived in a state of symbiosis with nature, followed by a period of increasing mastery over nature up to the industrial age, culminating in the rapid material-intensive growth pattern of the twentieth century which resulted in many adverse impacts on natural resources. The initial reaction to such environmental damage was a reactive approach characterised by increased clean-up activities. In recent decades, mankind's attitude towards the environment has evolved to encompass the more proactive design of projects and policies that help anticipate and avoid environmental degradation. The world is currently exploring the concept of sustainable development – an approach that will continue improvements in the present quality of life with a lower intensity of resource use, thereby leaving behind for future generations an undiminished or even enhanced stock of natural resources and other assets. (Munasinghe: nd)

There is an important interaction between the need for economic development and the need for environmental conservation and management, mainly in relation to the use of the natural resource base. Governments of different countries have been facing the dilemma of which comes first or what is more important. Many have undertaken appropriate measures to mitigate the worst effects on the environment resulting from human activity.

Economic policies, both macroeconomic and sectoral, play a significant role in determining the rate of depletion of natural resources and the level of environmental degradation. Fiscal and monetary policies, structural adjustment programmes and stabilization measures all have an effect on the natural resource base. In developing countries the interactions between the economy and the environment are complex; however, some governments have set up policies for environmental management and have traced the most important impacts of environmental problems, at least in a qualitative way and wherever possible, quantitatively as well.

In Mozambique, environmental policies have been drawn up; however, their effective implementation requires greater social awareness throughout all sectors of the economy and improved institutional co-ordination between different sectors. These are the biggest challenges currently facing the country in this area.

In general there are three types of industrial pollution problems affecting developing countries, including Mozambique. Principal air pollutants include sulphur dioxide, carbon monoxide, nitrogen dioxide, ozone and toxic pollutants such as benzene, vinyl chloride, hydrogen sulphide and other toxic gases.

In gold and bauxite mining activities in Manica, there are no major problems of pollution in relation to these common air pollutants. The main pollutants in Manica are dusts resulting from earth movements for the treatment of alluvial gold and pollution related to the use of diesel and fuel oil in the equipment for producing and processing the ore, because all operations occur in open-cast mines. Water pollution is one of the most serious negative environmental impacts of mining in Manica. Manica Province is well endowed with rivers, so the discharge of industrial effluents, for example heavy metals, some organic and inorganic chemicals, fuel oil, suspended solids and nutrients into water bodies without treatment and/or pre-treatment pollutes the water and is a major cause of concern. Pollution in the rivers often leads to changes in their courses, mainly as a result of the activities of the small-scale miners who work in a disorganized manner and without following mining rules. In this case, fines should be applied for those who discharge waste into the rivers without prior treatment. The problem in the case of small-scale miners is the fact that they are not officially registered and consequently do not hold a mining licence.

Classically, there is a range of hazards which can provide negative effects on ground water. The main sources of pollution include a lack of sanitation to deal with sewage, leaking sewers, sewage land discharges, leaking refuse pumps, leaking industrial storage tanks and pipelines, industrial water effluent lagoons and land discharges, leaking industrial waste disposal sites, and agro-chemicals and drainage water and other discharges from the mineral extraction industries.

In Manica, despite the legal provisions obliging the mining companies to undertake some environmental protection measures, there are still some problems, because the mining companies are damaging the environment. There are two large mining companies, one in gold and another in bauxite, which are not fully complying with their obligations for environmental conservation, involving the deviation of rivers and also creating some pollution to surface and ground water. The exploitation of gold in Manica causes serious problems in the Revue river valley, an excellent farming area which could be destroyed by alluvial dredging upsetting the hydrological balance.

Surface water is used without treatment in most of the non-urban areas. There are currently 122 urban water supply systems, one-third of which use ground water. A monitoring system must be set up for the use of this water, at least in the densely populated areas. Water management is desirable for hydropower production, irrigation, flood control, the provision of safe drinking water, stock watering and fish farming. Clearly, improved water management could be the key to development in several sectors of the economy and could make a positive impact on economic activity, the quality of the environment and sustainability. Water affected by mining in Manica should be treated using alternating sequence dams to decant the water, so that it can be used for further applications in mining processing or for drinking with prior treatment.

Industrial activity is very limited in Mozambique for historical reasons. Apart from mining, all industry is located in the urban centres, most notably Maputo and Beira. Thus, in general terms, the environmental problems resulting from industrial production in Mozambique can still be regarded as minor. In the case of the mining sector, the local impact on human living and agricultural resources is beginning to be significant in Manica, although there is a scarcity of data and scientific work on this topic. The key dimensions of the effects of pollution can be characterized as follows: sewage land discharges; industrial water effluent lagoons; and land discharges.

Added to these specific effects of pollution, a general picture of environmental damage can be summarized as follows, taking into account the activities of the small-scale miners: sewage land discharges; deviation of rivers from their normal courses; deforestation; soil damage without conservation; changes in river flows; pollution of surface and ground water due to mining processing; displacement of the population with its effects on farming; air pollution in populated areas; and changes in the equilibrium of different animal/plant ecosystems.

Currently, mining activities in Manica do not involve any satisfactory soil management and conservation, and there is no scientific study being undertaken in this field. The degradation of the land is a fact. Its conservation is meant to be enforced by mining legislation via the state authorities but this is not happening. The lack of comprehensive studies on the environmental impact of mining activities in Manica region means that a satisfactory report on the extent of the land degradation and its consequences for future agricultural productivity cannot be drawn up. A lack of environmental awareness amongst government authorities has led to a lack of planning, monitoring and research in the areas of intensive land use in different parts of Manica.

Recommendations
i)   Soil management and conservation practices are needed in Manica, to avoid soil degradation and to enhance its productivity.
ii)   On the other side of the border in Zimbabwe there is also mining of gold and bauxite and extensive agricultural activity, so cross-border environmental information on soil management and conservation should be shared in an institutionalized way.
iii) Since Manica is also traditionally a fertile agricultural region, it is worthwhile balancing the effects of agriculture as well as mining in terms of land use, in view of the conflicts of interest, given that in some areas agriculture and mining compete.

The Government of Mozambique needs to establish some legislation on the 'polluter-pays-principle'. Industry itself has to cover most of the costs of new technology and production processes and the safe discharge of waste. This principle involves internalizing the external costs to ensure that the full cost of pollution control or prevention measures is reflected in the cost of the goods produced and marketed. The principle works best when coupled with public financial incentives such as cheaper establishment loans to industries which incorporate anti-pollution measures in the production process, or which comply with discouraging the public to use scarce resources at particular times or locations.

Mining activity in Manica affects the environment in different ways, constraining the sustainable development of the region. Water treatment and soil management and conservation are required. The environmental, mining and administrative authorities need to reinforce their role in environmental management and to establish the clear principle of penalizing the polluters and those who create environmental damage more generally.

References
Francisco, C. (1995) *Policy and Strategies for the Development of the Energy and Mines Sectors.* Ministry of Mineral Resources and Energy, Maputo.
Ministry of Mineral Resources and Energy (1995) *Mineral Resources Development and Investment Opportunities.* Ministry of Mineral Resources and Energy, Maputo.
Munasinghe, M. (no date) *Environmental Economics and Valuation in Decision-making.* World Bank, Washington, DC.

8 Can International Co-operation Help Create Sustainable Development?

TERESA NETO
& ALEXANDRO DOS SANTOS MONTEIRO

Introduction

Mozambique is one of the poorest countries in the world with a GDP per capita of about US$80, and with 60% of the population living in absolute poverty. The economy is heavily dependent on external resources and there is little prospect of the country being able to end its dependence on international assistance in the near future. Current theories suggest that, unless there is greater co-operation between all countries, the divisions between 'wealth and poverty', 'industrialised and underdeveloped' countries will continue to pose threats to the environment and to sustainable development. Global co-operation is necessary, with all nations being willing to accept their responsibilities and contribute in a manner commensurate with their resources. This co-operation or global alliance will also necessitate properly funded international institutions, both non-governmental and inter-governmental. In short, the less developed countries (with lower incomes) must be helped to develop in a sustainable manner and to protect their environment.

This chapter will focus on Mozambique's experience and will put forward various ways of helping to build sustainable development with the help of external co-operation, more specifically via a case study of the United Nations Development Programme (UNDP). Funding comes through bilateral and multilateral co-operation channels, with very different funding modalities, in the form of credits, loans and grants. The choice of UNDP to provide a case study of good practice on the part of a multilateral agency is based on its relative impartiality and the facility it offers of negotiating the preparation of Country Programmes.

National development objectives and strategies

The civil war which began in Mozambique in 1977 and lasted until the signing of the Rome Agreements in1992, coupled with severe droughts, took the country into an emergency situation. In addition to provoking massive and on-going population movements inside the country and across its borders, the war caused tremendous devastation in the form of huge population increases in the urban areas, the virtual extinction of many species through poaching, the disappearance of forests, a shortage of firewood and a depletion of water resources. The war also had a profound influence on the orientation of all development programmes and projects.

The lack of security meant that most donors concentrated their activities in the capital city or in the provincial capitals. Logically, this meant that most of the programmes and projects were implemented in the urban areas, thus failing to correspond to the country's long-term development needs and contributing to the distorted pattern of development across the country.

Within this context of civil war and natural disasters, from the 1980s onwards Mozambique implemented an Emergency Programme, the Humanitarian Assistance Programme. The war forced it to apply its limited resources to the more immediate and urgent concerns within the Emergency Programme: firstly, health-related relief, followed by agriculture (food aid), transport and communications and primary-level education.

Given its size, scope and duration, the Emergency Programme distorted normal economic activity. The fundamental economic circumstances had deteriorated significantly between 1980 and 1986. Real GDP fell by 21% and merchandise exports by 72%. This deterioration in the economy led to the introduction of reforms, leading, in 1987, to an Economic Rehabilitation Programme (ERP) supported by the World Bank and the International Monetary Fund. Some time later and in order to lay a greater emphasis on alleviating the increasing poverty resulting from the harsh consequences of stabilization for the vulnerable social groups, the ERP was converted in 1980 into the Economic and Social Rehabilitation Programme (ESRP). Although substantial progress was achieved by means of the ERP, with an average real GDP growth of 5.2% in 1987–9 stimulated by increased agricultural production and light industry activity, an underlying incongruence persisted. This incongruence arose from the attempt to implement a strategy based on increasing agricultural production in a situation of severe insecurity in the countryside, such that, in 1990–92, real GDP only rose by 0.9%, and consumption per capita declined.

The ESRP has provided the guidelines for national development strategies. Following the signing of the Rome Agreements in October 1992, the government drew up the National Reconstruction Plan (NRP), its strategy for post-war reconstruction and the transition from the Emergency Programme to a Development Programme. The NRP is integrated with the ESRP, the Priority Districts Programme (PDP) and the Emergency Programme. It is guided by the major long-term objective of achieving self-sustainable economic development in order to resolve the problem of the extreme poverty afflicting more than three-quarters of the population.

The role of external co-operation

According to the UNDP's *Development Cooperation Report*, development assistance including humanitarian assistance to Mozambique totalled US$1,118 million in 1990, equivalent to about 78% of GDP and four times the value of government revenue. During the period 1988–90 6 multilateral agencies outside the United Nations system, 26 UN agencies, 44 bilateral donors and agencies representing 35 countries and 143 NGOs from 23 countries were operating in Mozambique. Bilateral donors furnished 72% of the external assistance contributed in 1990, the remainder being provided by non-UN multilaterals (11%), the UN system (11%) and NGOs (6%). Within the UN system the main donor was the World Bank (53%) followed by the World Food Programme (14%), UNDP (10%) and UNICEF (4%).

In 1990 a broader sectoral classification revealed that 69% of external assistance disbursements went to the economic sectors compared with 31% for the social sectors. The five most important sectors accounted for 71% of total disbursements: industry (18%), humanitarian assistance (16%), international trade (15%), agriculture (13%) and transport (10%). Technical co-operation accounted for 16% and technical co-operation for investment a further 8% of total disbursements in 1990.

Free Standing Technical Co-operation disbursements were highest for human resources (28%) and transport (23%), while Investment Technical Co-operation was highest in international trade, industry and transport and communications. The social sectors received 95% of NGO disbursements (31% for all donors), with humanitarian assistance the most important subsector comprising 72% of all NGO-financed external assistance.

UNDP activities

Immediately after independence, on 16 September 1976, Mozambique signed a basic Co-operation Agreement with the UNDP. This programme has since been translated into Five-Year programmes known as 'Country Programmes'. The Country Programme is the result of detailed negotiations between UNDP and the Ministry of Foreign Affairs and Co-operation involving the various technical assistance programmes.

An analysis of these cyclical UNDP/Mozambique programmes shows that, even before the 1992 Rio Conference, UNDP was in the vanguard amongst donor agencies in the promotion of environmental issues. This organization has offered continuing support in environmental initiatives and in the management of natural resources. The following list illustrates some of the salient UNDP programmes and projects initiated as far back as 1986 which relate to natural resource management and environmental questions: Forestry Development; Housing Policy; Agricultural Planning; Rural Training Centres; Agricultural Research; Land Resource Evaluation; Water and Sanitation; Water Management; Mineral Resources and Fisheries Training.

Much later in 1991 a crucially targeted level of support was provided to help establish what was eventually to become a Ministry for the Environment. This was a project to provide the core institutional funding to set up a more powerful environmental division within government.

The June 1992 UN Conference on the Environment and Development, and the signing of the Peace Agreement in October that same year, provided two major inputs for the 1993–7 Country Programme (the Fourth UNDP Programme). This focused on three thematic areas: poverty alleviation and post-war rehabilitation; economic and financial management; and management of the environment and natural resources. In this last area, although Mozambique has abundant unexploited natural resources, some parts of the country have suffered serious environmental deterioration owing to the concentration of large numbers of displaced people round towns and along the transport corridors and the coastal strip. Millions of people have also been resettled. In this context, the Fourth Programme asked for UNDP help in preparing policies and programmes for sustainable development and strategies for the management of natural resources (Support for the Pre-Programmes for the Management of Forest Resources and Wildlife, for Agriculture, for Water Resource Management, and for Fisheries). In addition, there was assistance for the *Katina P* oil spill.

Other organizations such as the World Bank and the United Nations Environment Programme have also played a role in environmental issues. With regard to the management of natural resources, other important donors include the Global Environmental Facility, the European Union and the International Union for the Conservation of Nature in the forestry and wildlife sector; UNICEF, AFDB, the Netherlands, France and the EU in the development of water resources and environmental impact studies; and DANIDA, the EU, the FAO, France, Japan, NORAD and the United Kingdom in fisheries.

Problems and possible policy options

Whilst external co-operation, in the specific case of the UNDP, has not distanced itself from environmental issues and natural resource management, a detailed assessment of the social and economic impact of these programmes and projects, in terms of creating sustainable development, would show that this objective has not yet been achieved. What is the problem? Essentially it is the absence of an ethic of sustainable development and concern for the environment on the part of both nationals and the donor community, as well as the country's extreme poverty. Together these have meant that:

(a) Policies and strategies have not been sufficiently clear, either on the part of the government or of the donor community, with the result that everyone has followed their own agendas, often to the detriment of a co-ordinated national response.
(b) Programmes and projects have been formulated separately within each programme objective and have failed to provide a coherent programme of interlinked actions with a strong impact.
(c) The environmental impact of development programmes, projects and policies has not been evaluated.
(d) The country's heavy external debt does not permit sustained economic growth.
(e) The extreme poverty of Mozambicans forces them to degrade the environment involuntarily through deforestation using fire to clear the land for cultivation, etc., combined with the fact that they do not always possess knowledge of the best techniques for managing natural resources.

Finding solutions requires adopting ways of life and development paths which respect nature and operate within its limits. This new approach must respect two fundamental requirements. Firstly, there is a need to ensure a broad and profound commitment to a new sustainable ethic and to translate its principles into practice through changes in behaviour and life styles, and into attitudes and strategies which are mutually dependent at the local, national and international levels. The survival or the disappearance of modern civilization will depend on our capacity radically to change our culture concerning our relationship with the environment. This means moving from a relationship based on exploitation to one based on sustainability.

Secondly, it is necessary to integrate conservation and development: conservation, in order to adjust our attitudes about the capacity of the Earth to withstand human impact; and development, to enable people to live long, healthy and fulfilling lives everywhere.

This will be possible if:

(a) The developed countries assume responsibility for both transferring resources to promote development and establishing an effective global response commensurate with the efforts made by developing countries themselves. This is the essence of co-operation for sustainability.
(b) Development assistance is increased to help countries to improve their knowledge and techniques and to strengthen institutions, thus stimulating the economic growth of developing countries so that their people can advance towards sustainable livelihoods.
(c) The United Nations mechanism continues to be reformulated and strengthened so that it can work in improved ways to build sustainable development.
(d) Mozambique's multilateral and bilateral external debt is rescheduled over the long term and a large part of it is forgiven, so that economic progress can be re-

established. This move is urgently needed to improve the quality of life and alleviate the extreme poverty of the majority of Mozambicans.

(e) The government makes the development process and responsibility for it the responsibility of the national authorities – ensuring linkages between programmes and projects with common objectives, and encouraging co-ordination within and between the various levels of government. In accordance with national development needs, international co-operation should be directed to where there are no resources. International aid should be used efficiently.

(f) The government defines national development policies and strategies. Policies and strategies can be better sustained when they emerge from the grassroots, and national, provincial and local plans should fit in with initiatives driven from the bottom up. National Development Plans should be handled in an integrated and realistic manner.

(g) All development projects, programmes and policies are subject to an assessment of their environmental impact in addition to the economic calculations.

(h) A global alliance is established between the state, civil society and the donor community to create sustainable development.

Since 1991, the Mozambican state has committed itself to this new environmental culture, as can be seen by the inclusion in the Constitution of eleven articles on the environment. In June 1992, the country was represented at the UN Conference on the Environment and Development in Rio de Janeiro by a high-level delegation led by the President. Given the importance Mozambique assigns to environmental and sustainable development questions, following the democratic elections in 1994 the Ministry for the Co-ordination of Environmental Action was created to ensure that the government has a co-ordinating body for environmental questions. This involved an institutional upgrading from the National Environment Commission. Its main functions are to work with other ministries in preparing the policies of each government institution, to harmonize them with the environment and to help establish a culture of environmental awareness and sustainability with the major objective of 'placing the country on a healthy and balanced development path, improving the quality of human life, and respecting the supportive capacity of the eco-systems which maintain us'. This new environmental culture also means more investment. The government is already investing budget funds and international co-operation has given its support.

9 Institutional Co-ordination & Harmonizing Formal & Customary Law in the Management of Natural Resources

ALDA SALAMÃO

Introduction

The National Environment Management Programme captures the first part of the problem contained in the title of this chapter in the following passage which reflects upon the past order:

... each sector was responsible for planning the use of natural resources in accordance with its own interests. Consequently, there was no single institution responsible for the integrated management and supervision of natural resources. On the whole, the country's institutional mechanisms tend to reflect options of a politico-economic and administrative nature, not the resources' real management needs or their optimal use. In other words, the foundations of sectoral programmes are based more on political and economic rather than technical, scientific and multi-sectoral grounds.

Once the government recognized the importance for sustainable development of institutional co-ordination and the participation of the general public in natural resource management, whether it be co-ordination between state institutions themselves, between state and private institutions or between state institutions and traditional authorities, various new initiatives began to be taken. However, measures taken to date have not explicitly included mechanisms for involving traditional authorities. Although they are not part of the state apparatus, the government programme clearly recognizes traditional authorities as being an extremely important institution having a decisive role to play locally in the administration of the public good and certainly in the management of natural resources. There has been no consideration of the customary law by which such authorities operate in their communities. This chapter addresses these important but hitherto neglected questions.

Although it does not claim to make great progress towards defining what should be the effective role of traditional authorities and hence customary law in the management of natural resources, this chapter aims to take a first step towards reflecting on these issues. This is a necessity in the context of improving effective natural resource management and the implementation of a sustainable development process for the country.

Intra-governmental institutional co-ordination and the involvement of the private sector

Once state structures began to recognize the importance of adopting institutional co-ordination mechanisms, this led to changes in the *status quo* of government behaviour in the natural resource management field. A major step forward occurred with the creation of the Ministry for the Co-ordination of Environmental Action (MICOA) and the proposed creation of a National Council for Sustainable Development (NCSD) under the draft Framework Law on the Environment. The prime vocation of these two institutions is precisely intended to guarantee harmonization and co-ordination among the various sectors involved in preparing and implementing natural resource management policies, strategies and activities. This marks an early attempt to establish a permanent system of co-ordinated institutional endeavour.

This new model of institutional organization has ramifications in a number of areas of natural resource management, including, of course, the legal field. The existing compartmentalized sectoral management model was reflected in the way the respective legal texts used to be prepared, with each sector individually and in isolation preparing its legislative proposals, without any prior consultation or harmonization with other sectors or even with existing laws on the subject.

In order to change this situation in the legal field, the Intersectoral Group on Environmental Legislation (IGEL) was created in MICOA, comprising representatives of various ministries, higher education institutions and non-governmental organizations. In addition, the principle was adopted of consulting the public during the drafting of environmental legislation. Although still embryonic, the efforts by government institutions and especially MICOA to co-ordinate and harmonize legislative initiatives can be seen in the way legislation is now being drafted or revised. Good examples include the preparation of the Environment Framework Law, the revision of the Land Law and the preparation of the Regulations for Environmental Impact Assessment. All these processes involved widespread participation by various sectors of society, and this is growing in both a qualitative and a quantitative sense.

The role of traditional authorities and customary law

The government has been moving towards the adoption of a decentralized public administration model. The first important step was Law 3/94, the Municipalities Law, giving municipalities a major role in the management of local resources, to enable them to become development centres promoting improved living conditions for their communities.

This new policy direction expressly anticipated the involvement of traditional authorities. The Government Programme stated:

The decentralization programme is governed by the following principles: the establishment of institutional mechanisms for involving traditional authorities and other forms of local community social organization which, although they are not part of the state administrative and municipal system, exercise relevant influence in civil society.

The initial principle of the decentralization of public administration advanced by the government, and which anticipated the involvement of traditional authorities, provided no indication as to the real role reserved for these authorities and traditional law in the management of natural resources in Mozambique, including the role of customary law. This still needs to be identified, or the application of one of the fundamental principles of sustainable environmental management will be overlooked: the principle of community participation, of benefitting from the resources and knowledge of local communities in the environment management process.

The National Environment Management Programme, as well as the Environment

Framework Law, assign great importance to community participation in managing the country's resources. However, at the same time they do not provide any indication as to how these communities, their authorities, their knowledge and their customs can be integrated into the overall process to ensure the country's sustainable development. This chapter inevitably raises more questions than it answers. However, the first step towards finding answers is to raise the important questions.

Institutional co-ordination in the preparation of environmental legislation in a way which brings public administration bodies face to face with traditional authorities, necessarily means comparing formal laws and traditional or customary laws, two parallel realities which co-exist in Mozambique's juridical order and which play an extremely important role in the management of the country's natural resources. On the one hand, the juridical order contains written laws emanating from, and applied by and for, its state institutions, essentially in the urban areas. On the other hand, there exist the norms of customary law applied by the agents of traditional authority and rural communities in the daily management of local resources.

Consequently, in the daily and effective management of resources we have the following formats:

FORMAL LAW – STATE INSTITUTIONS – URBAN POPULATION
CUSTOMARY LAW – TRADITIONAL AUTHORITIES – RURAL POPULATION

Given the country's demographic distribution, with approximately 25% of the population living in urban areas and 75% in rural areas, it is clear that the tensions existing between these two systems need to be seriously considered if the following objectives are to be achieved:

1. to confer authority and legitimacy on formal law as an instrument for creating greater homogeneity in Mozambican society;
2. to ensure that traditional, deeply rooted and duly recognized resource management practices are not lost with the expansion of the formal juridical order, which frequently has no connection with the social base for which it is intended.

To achieve these objectives, a good starting point would be to examine the existing principle of not recognizing custom as an autonomous source of law for the country's juridical order. Article 3 of the Civil Code states the following: 'Usage which is not contrary to the principles of good faith is judicially acceptable when the law so determines.' In other words, the rule is that customary law, or the usage and customs which govern the lives of the majority of the population, the relations between members of a community and between them and the natural environment in which they live, which have for years guaranteed the livelihoods of the individual and the group, are not recognized by formal authority and so cannot be invoked in law. The existing rule is that custom is not an autonomous source of law, but can only be a point of reference when the law determines it expressly.

The government began to reflect on this principle of the national juridical order in the context of natural resource management, when considering the National Land Policy, approved by the Council of Ministers in September 1995, and the Bill on the Revision of the Land Law. Recognizing the predominant role of traditional authorities and customary law in the management of the country's main natural resource, land, and providing important back-up for the formal law and authorities in this field, the National Land Policy states the following:

The main land policy decision relating to this system [the family system] is the land law's recognition of customary rights of access to land. This system includes the various systems of transfer and inheritance rights, as well as the role of local leaders in preventing and resolving conflicts and in legitimizing and legalizing the occupation and use of a given area.

These customary systems are an unquestionable resource and offer a public service in the administration and management of land in rural areas at virtually no cost to the state budget. For example, they worked effectively in reintegrating people displaced within the country and people returning from neighbouring countries. So these political systems which are operating in the vast majority of cases of land occupation and use should be considered in land legislation. In this context, it should be noted that there is a need for a flexible law which does not specify what to do in each different cultural situation, but which admits the principle that in each region the respective system of customary rights can function according to the local reality. Although the details should be investigated later, there is a need to assure the rights of the majority of producers who occupy areas judicially allocated by the customary laws of their areas and cultural patterns.

Further on, and in relation to the need to revise the Land Law, the policy adds:

The revision of the current land law in order to eliminate aspects which conflict with the country's new socio-economic situation and the constitution of the republic ... should introduce the following elements:
(a)   recognition of customary rights and the customary system of adjudicating/managing land.

Albeit timidly, the draft land bill makes progress towards granting customary law a more important role in the management of land, when it states the following:

Article 23 (Traditional Authorities)
1.   In the authorization of land concessions, traditional authorities can be requested to:
(a)   contribute on land occupied by communities in accordance with the respective customary law system and local reality;
(b)   collaborate, on the basis of customary law, in resolving land conflicts in their area.

Recommendations

Given the issues raised in order to clarify and determine the role of traditional power and authorities in the management of the country's resources and because the principles underlying this integration are extremely vague, there is an urgent need to begin analyzing some preliminary questions, so as to be able subsequently to integrate traditional institutions into the sustainable environmental management process by creating the necessary co-ordination mechanisms.

This chapter recommends that the following fundamental issues need to be researched. Although they apply to the system in general, they will certainly constitute an important starting point for finding a way forward:

i)   The factual and judicial foundations of Article 3 of the Civil Code: their relevance and applicability to the socio-cultural and economic reality of Mozambique.

ii)   The problem of national cultural diversity: the compatibilization of differences and the systematization of convergence between the various customary systems.

iii)   Analysis of and solutions to the constraints related to the unwritten nature of customary law.

Once these issues have been researched and on the basis of the data collected, there should follow experimentation on the closer integration of customary law into the national juridical order, specifically in the field of natural resource management.

The judicial norms prepared, whether on environmental management or on any other topic, will only be authentic and have the intended impact if they always take into account the socio-cultural and economic realities of the people at whom they are aimed. The people must identify with the content of the laws if they are to apply and defend them as citizens.

Update (by the editors)

Since this chapter was written the debates outlined continue to rumble on. In March 1996 the draft legislation proposing formal recognition of traditional authority was submitted to the Council of Ministers but was rejected. Later in September that same year, the Council of Ministers also removed references to customary law and traditional leaders from the draft Land Law (*Mozambique Peace Process Bulletin*, No. 19, September 1997).

In July 1997, the National Assembly finally passed the new Land Law. But it provoked bitter opposition and debate from Renamo, who argued that the bill marginalized traditional authorities. In Renamo's view, land distribution should be handed over to the chiefs (*AIM Bulletin*, No. 253, August 1997). The final bill represented a series of compromises in recognizing the role of custom. The whole process reflected not only a struggle between the parties in the Assembly but also a struggle between the Assembly and the Council of Ministers. The law passed by the Assembly reversed the decisions taken the previous year by the Council of Ministers, who wanted to remove the role for the traditional leaders. Strong lobbying by two important peasant organizations had helped swing the debate back in the other direction. These organizations were the National Peasants Union and the Rural Organization for Mutual Help, and they were supportive of the law finally passed, which also increased the rights of women and restricted to some degree the power of the Council of Ministers to determine land use.

Whilst land remains state property, use rights in the form of leases can be gained by occupancy or by the grant of a lease by the state. Communities or individuals occupying land for over a decade acquire permanent land-use rights and do not require title documents. The courts must accept verbal evidence of occupancy from community members.

The law presents a compromise between formal and customary law, stating that occupancy rights are given to groups and individuals occupying land 'according to customary norms and practices that are not contrary to the constitution' (*Mozambique Peace Process Bulletin*, No. 19, September 1997). Specifically, the law states that rules on land inheritance must not discriminate on gender grounds. The fundamental issues raised in this chapter will continue to roll on for many years. The law does not specify who represents the community nor does it prevent possible demarcation disputes between communities. These represent on-going areas of tension and challenge for the future.

10 Institutional Development for Community-Based Resource Management Research

ANTÓNIO RIBEIRO

The Forestry Research Department (CEF) is located within the National Directorate of Forestry and Wildlife (DNFFB) of the Ministry of Agriculture. Its role is to undertake applied research in forest and wildlife management issues from a social and institutional perspective, in collaboration with the technical units of the DNFFB. The CEF is charged with developing policy and identifying appropriate management and technical solutions for natural resource management activities.

The CEF was created in 1985, with a principal orientation towards industrial forestry for woodfuel and timber production through state plantations. It originally had three divisions: silviculture, wood technologies and forest economics. The objective of the programme in forest economics was to define methodologies for improving the efficiency of state plantations and forest industries. Since its foundation the CEF has collaborated closely with the Forestry Department at the Eduardo Mondlane University (UEM). Together they run a joint laboratory for work in wood technologies and are also collaborating on topics ranging from tree breeding to economic and project analysis.

In 1988 agroforestry was introduced into the silviculture division with the intention of complementing the DNFFB forest extension unit launched that year to work with the agricultural extension services in the provinces. Under stimulus from the International Centre for Research in Agroforestry (ICRAF), trials of *Leucaena* and *Sesbania* were established in stations and on farmers' fields, alongside experiments with several indigenous leguminous trees such as *Cassia siamea*. Once an awareness of agroforestry spread, staff began to report that farmers had their own existing agroforestry systems. For example, in Manica Province it was found that farmers managed *Albizia* in their fields to increase crop yields. This led the CEF to reflect that it could perhaps also rely on farmers' existing discoveries to develop agroforestry in Mozambique, alongside international technologies.

A second experience at this time was important in enabling the CEF to reconceive its role. In 1989 Manica Province Forestry and Wildlife Service (SPFFB) identified a peasant who had seen montane terraced agriculture combined with forestry in Tanzania. Staff worked with him to develop a system of terraces with *Leucaena* on half of his land, leaving the other half under the existing system of cultivation. The enhanced production from the modified plot was so substantial that in the second year four farmers adopted similar practices and in the third year over twenty farmers were involved. This took place in the context of war, displacement and tremendous rural poverty and enabled producers to graduate from semi-subsistence to becoming wealthy smallholders. It taught the CEF the lesson that developing new and more productive systems involved combining the state's operations with key members of communities who were themselves innovators.

On the basis of these kinds of experience the CEF began in 1991 to re-orientate itself towards meeting the needs of rural people. In 1992 a new institutional structure and research plan were established that gave key priority to carrying out research with rural communities, with the aim of making them the principal beneficiaries and enabling their knowledge and experience to become the basis of policy formulation and technology development. This national research plan was developed with other relevant institutions, including in the provinces, and involved the production of short- and long-term objectives. Welcomed by the government, this plan was part of a SADC initiative to strengthen forestry research capacity.

In 1992 the CEF initiated three new divisions to address the needs of rural communities: Woodland and Forest Management, Community Forestry and Ecology and Environmental Protection. The following year the Community Forestry and Economic Policy divisions were combined into a single development division because it was intended to orientate community work towards meeting peasant livelihood needs. The CEF also started a Wildlife Management unit, in response to a request from the DNFFB Department of Wildlife, in order to identify how best to link wildlife management with community development and wider ecosystem management. Until a suitable candidate is identified and trained, the unit is currently staffed by the CEF ecologist who is also the head of the Ecology and Environmental Protection Division. It is currently supporting four UEM students in biological sciences who are doing research in the Maputo Elephant Reserve.

The CEF also planned to start an Animal and Plant Disease and Protection Division, oriented towards meeting the needs of communities and the commercial sector in regard to the disease problems of key wildlife and forestry resources. It is engaged in discussions with staff at the UEM and with the strong Pathology Unit of the Forestry Commission of Zimbabwe to assist with this.

Concurrent with the desire to address the needs of the peasant sector, the CEF also intends to develop capacity to assist with the technical problems of the emergent private sector. This is because these enterprises are also very important for rural development, employment and the national economy. Furthermore, the new DNFFB initiatives intend to build up collaboration between the private sector and rural communities geared to managing the exploitation of natural resources. If these commercial enterprises are not efficient, this collaboration will not be profitable for the local communities. Finally, the CEF sees the private sector as potentially a useful client that will be able to pay for its services and thereby provide much needed additional resources.

In order to secure this institutional transformation into a socio-environmental applied research and policy unit that can really address the needs of rural people, the CEF needs to start by learning the existing techniques and management strategies of rural communities in relation to their wildlife and forest resources. Once something is known about these, it will then be possible to start to assess and try to improve these techniques in partnership with communities. The CEF can use its scientific research capacity to complement what is believed to be the substantial existing knowledge and practice of local communities.

It is not the intention that the CEF should become a large institution at national level. It intends to remain with about 15 professionals in Maputo, but with an increase in the current facility at the Marracuene headquarters in Maputo Province and the research station in Manica Province, to perhaps three or four field research stations. The way it will expand its activities is essentially to upgrade the training and experience of its existing core professionals and to mobilize and support field investigation by existing forestry and wildlife staff at the provincial level, alongside members of rural communities and the local authorities. In terms of building existing capacity, it is hoped to upgrade from the current situation of 2 MScs, 9 BScs and a number of diploma-level personnel to a goal of 2 D.Phils and 6 MScs. The Ford Foundation is assisting here in relation to the social and institutional aspects of natural resource use by rural communities.

Current constraints

There are several serious problems facing the CEF in switching its attention to rural communities and using participatory research to address their needs. Historically the CEF's development policies have been decided at the central level and imposed on the local people. This has led to failures at both a local and a national level. In Mozambique there are hardly any channels through which the state can discover and respond to local realities and needs. At the same time, local communities are isolated from useful ideas and small financial inputs from outside their own resources that could facilitate their development. Due to top-down government, local institutions have lost the power necessary for the management of natural resources and the rights to benefit from their exploitation. The central problem remains the lack of communication between rural people and the government and between the central, provincial and district government institutions, and this generates conflicts and contradictions and leads to missed opportunities.

There are currently hardly any Mozambicans with training in the social and institutional aspects of natural resources management. The few Mozambican professionals with technical training in these fields now recognize from personal experience that unless they can re-orientate their work towards rural communities they will not be successful. The CEF has been under-resourced, the only guarantee being for staff salaries, which are very low. The amount available for training, field work and other research is both small and too irregular for viable systematic and participatory studies to be undertaken. This reflects the general financial problems of the country and the fact that applied research in natural resource issues has not yet proved to the government, the commercial sector, or the general population that it can really help solve their problems. Now that provincial and local government bodies are acknowledging with enthusiasm the need for these kinds of activities, the CEF is being frustrated by the lack of financial resources to respond to their requests. Without an adequate input of resources it will not be possible to establish the credibility of the CEF's work.

Working in a participatory way with rural communities may prove difficult. With the end of the war so recent, the majority of Mozambican rural communities are extremely poor. There is also much population displacement and a sense of disruption and dislocation, with people often feeling they are not part of a functioning community. Furthermore, the population in general does not have much faith in the capacity of outsiders to solve their problems other than simply by distributing relief. All these factors therefore make it difficult to facilitate effective community-based initiatives.

The rural population generally only benefits from the subsistence use of its natural resources and historically is excluded from benefitting from the marketing of these resources, which is normally carried out by safari operators, private hunters, commercial loggers, etc. who reap these benefits. A consequence is that rural people are unable to develop economically and environmental degradation occurs in certain areas because the local people lack the interest or the institutional mechanisms to protect their natural resource base. Meanwhile, in other areas, individuals exploit firewood or charcoal production in an unsustainable fashion because of a lack of management mechanisms to facilitate more sustainable use. It will take prolonged efforts to transform this situation, since it requires changes in laws and in the attitudes and institutional behaviour of government officials, commercial companies and peasant communities.

Current opportunities for CEF initiatives

Despite the major problems faced in Mozambique, there are currently significant opportunities for the CEF to achieve its transition to an institution that works with rural communities to meet their development needs. These include the following:

(a) With the end of the war and the changes in the way the government conceives the role of the state in development, it has become possible to reformulate government extension programmes to address questions of poverty and the flow of information between government and rural communities. The 'Pre-Programmes' of both the Ministry of Agriculture and the DNFFB emphasize community management and participation as the foundation for rural reconstruction. The latter states explicitly: 'Community participation in sustainable forest management and an increased role for the family sector in agroforestry will be promoted'. The objective of the Pre-Programmes is to lay a foundation, in this period of transition from war, for future rural development policies. Furthermore, there is a general desire to change the roles of extension agents away from being passive carriers of classical agricultural technology towards becoming two-way change and information-flow agents.

(b) Major changes in local administration are being introduced by the decentralization programme of the Ministry of State Administration which will provide opportunities for local participation in development. The transfer of rights to the benefits from managing natural resources from the central government to the local municipalities will make these local government bodies allies in the search for sources of revenue for new approaches to the sustainable management and exploitation of natural resources. The CEF has already established good relations with the provincial authorities in Manica Province.

(c) Mozambicans recognize the failures of past rural development policies and many are now looking to research as a means of identifying new approaches to rural development that might work. Participatory approaches are needed, but in Mozambique little experience of this exists in agricultural development and natural resource management. If the CEF can manage to develop effective approaches in this area it could find many partners.

(d) An intensive interaction in recent years with the CEF's sister institutions in Zimbabwe has indicated that there is much that can be learned from, and shared with, colleagues there. They can be involved in Mozambique's own learning experience, and their experience can be adapted to the needs of Mozambique. The research and training capacity of the Centre for Applied Social Sciences (CASS) of the University of Zimbabwe, for example, is being used to help build up Mozambique's capacity.

Challenges of institutional transformation

One of the most critical challenges for the CEF staff as they initiate this programme is to learn how to start a process of consultation with the rural communities and to actually start to find out from them what they know. This is both a personal and an institutional challenge.

A related challenge is for the CEF to learn how to bring staff and officials of the forestry and wildlife departments to sit with and learn from local communities, so that a new dynamic can be initiated in the relationship between people and the state in the management of their natural resources. This is the key to the transformation that the CEF is seeking to achieve.

The biggest difficulty for the CEF will be taking the first steps towards this new approach to research and learning. The CEF knows how to 'talk and plan' but does not have the experience of actually implementing policy. It is confident, however, that once the work is started the process itself will drive the institution forward.

The challenge is to identify how the state and other external institutions can actually improve the livelihoods of rural people, and to identify policies that can link local development through people's participation with national development. This requires the involvement of local government structures.

Working with such a participatory social approach poses a major challenge to the CEF's staff who are scientists. Rural people have extensive existing knowledge of their environment, their society and their problems, and the challenges that they present to the CEF will be highly complex. Therefore to be able to assist them, the CEF will need to have not only a solid scientific capacity but also social scientific knowledge.

Short- and medium-term goals

There are short-term and medium-term goals established for the CEF's institutional development initiative for community-based resource management research. The immediate aim is to create a new dynamic in the development of rural communities based on the sustainable use of natural resources with the local community's participation in their management. The specific objectives envisaged are:

(a) to investigate the cultural, social and institutional aspects of the rural community;
(b) to investigate the ways of involving the community in the development process;
(c) to study the traditional ways and techniques for natural resources use and management;
(d) to analyze the benefits and revenues of natural resource use and management;
(e) to investigate the legal aspects of the community's land and resources rights, such as land tenure, customary rights, etc.

Major goals for the CEF to achieve over the space of five years include:

(a) the CEF should have the institutional capacity to provide practical policy advice and technical back-up in each of the divisions in support of rural development and natural resource management.
(b) the CEF should really know what it means to sit and consult with people in rural communities and to be able to work with them to identify the means to enhance their livelihoods.
(c) the demands of the people and the institutions with which the CEF works should start to drive the change in institutional development and thinking.
(d) National and provincial authorities, and increasingly ordinary Mozambicans, should start to see that the new way the CEF conducts research actually does contribute to concrete and sustainable development.
(e) the CEF should have established a small dedicated team of well trained researchers with different specialities in the social and natural sciences.
(f) the staff of the CEF should have developed the capacity to carry out high quality scientifically sound research that meets the needs of different sectors of Mozambican society.

(g) the CEF staff should also be able to channel the research capacity of field staff in the different divisions of the DNFFB and in other organizations, and be able to support their research activities with training, supervision and modest funding.

Activities and output

Proposed activities are as follows:

(a) Defining criteria for selecting the community, involving meetings and discussions with the local authorities.
(b) Selection and localization of the community based on the features defined.
(c) Elaboration of a development plan or strategy for the community, based on discussions and surveys, in order to know its wants and needs.
(d) Research and studies to support the above.

The aim of this initiative is to attain the following outputs:

(a) Sustainable development of the targeted community to facilitate its control of the development and management of its natural resources.
(b) More understanding of indigenous knowledge.
(c) Better understanding of the legal implications in order to formulate policy and legislative proposals related to land tenure and natural resources.
(d) Training of technicians in related subjects such as social and natural resources, ecology and management.

To achieve these goals, the strategy is to select two or three communities as pilot research communities in Manica Province. The aim is to install a multidisciplinary research team which will work together with the local people in order to act as a catalyst for the development of these rural communities, based on the sustainable use of the natural resources with the local communities participating in the resource management. This entire project can be characterized as a capacity building effort for the CEF to perform its mandate. CEF staff have identified the following four main categories of activities to achieve this:

(a) formal training for CEF staff;
(b) community-based research to be implemented by the CEF;
(c) institutional support for the CEF;
(d) strengthening and supporting local field investigation throughout the country, and mobilizing potential researchers from rural communities, government and other institutions.

In 1985, when the CEF started, it had only 2 BScs and 4 diploma-level staff. Now there are 15 scientific staff at the CEF. At present no staff are trained at the doctoral level. Only two members have masters level training, one with a degree in silviculture and tree breeding and the other in forest economics.

The absence of formal training is only one side of the training problem facing the CEF. The other critical need is for field research experience. Aside from 7 research sites for silviculture, CEF staff are not engaged in any field research. The CEF's strategic plan explicitly recognizes that formal academic training is not the only way to build staff capacity, although this is being pursued. Field research is seen as the other half of the capacity-building strategy. The CEF can only achieve its staff development goals by giving all staff opportunities for field research and staggering their academic training programmes.

Field research in Manica

Because of war and the lack of resources, CEF staff have only been able to carry out very limited field research. For the CEF to have any impact on the welfare of rural Mozambicans it is essential that staff should move out of their offices and start field research. The staff decided to start pilot research activities in Manica Province for a number of reasons.

(a) It is important for CEF research staff to work closely with provincial-level agricultural, forestry and wildlife staff. Of the ten provinces in Mozambique, the CEF found that Manica SPFFB was the most active in working with communities in participatory resource management activities. This provided CEF staff with a firm foundation on which to build their research effort. Also, CEF researchers would work closely with provincial staff and this would make it easier for research results to be applied in development programmes.

(b) The CEF's first research station, which began to be re-developed after the neglect of the post-independence period, is located in Sussundenga District, in Manica Province. This station possesses indigenous species woodlots for research purposes. Using this infrastructure, the pilot project could more easily be implemented by field support staff.

(c) Manica is historically one of the most important provinces with respect to forestry and has a major forest product industry. One of the questions to be addressed is how formal forest-based industry can be linked positively to peasant farmers.

(d) Manica Province borders Zimbabwe, close to Harare, making it easy for staff to establish and maintain academic and research links with staff at the University of Zimbabwe and the Research Division of Zimbabwe's Forestry Commission. This will enable CEF staff to benefit from the experiences of Zimbabwe institutions.

(e) The only diploma level college for forestry, IAC, is in Manica Province. This will enable the CEF to provide on-the-job training/research experience in its pilot research activities for the students at this college. Students at IAC will be employed in the forestry sector and their involvement in the CEF research activities may have a positive influence on how they carry out their jobs.

(f) Staff of Manica SPFFB and of the Provincial Directorate of Agriculture were the first people to start work with community resources management in Mozambique. They have made progress in this field but were obliged to stop their activities because of a lack of funds. By working with staff who initiated this work it will be possible to strengthen their capacity and benefit from what they have learned.

(g) Some areas of the Province suffer from extreme population pressures on natural resources, while in other areas there are very low population densities with an abundance of resources. The CEF's research should help explain the causes and effects of population movements and their pressure on resources. It should also contribute to identifying and testing alternative resource management strategies that would improve the economic welfare of these people and the quality of the resource base. In resource-rich areas, the CEF's research should be able to identify alternative resource-based livelihood strategies that might encourage people to settle more evenly across the less densely populated areas of the Province.

(h) Manica Province is one of the highest potential agricultural areas in the country.

At the same time, it also has great potential for the sustainable management of the natural resource base. The CEF's research should be able to identify strategies for using this wealth of resources in a harmonious and sustainable way that improves the economic well-being of poor rural Mozambicans.

(i)   The Chimanimani area on the western border of Manica Province is to be designated as one of the three trans-border national parks in Mozambique. A critical issue in this process is what will happen to the communities living in this area. It is hoped that the CEF's research in Manica will help identify strategies that will enable communities to be engaged in deciding their future and in benefitting from the sustainable use of this national heritage.

(j)   The Forestry Department at the UEM has its field research training station in Manica. This gives CEF staff an opportunity to share research work with students and hopefully influence their understanding of community-based resource management.

(k)   Manica Province is rich in different forest ecosystems, ranging from montane and plantation forests in the west and southwest and the central plateau, to miombo woodlands in the centre and mopane woodlands in the north. Mozambican institutions have little knowledge of the ecology and management of these and other natural forest types. Carrying out research in Manica will enable the CEF to start learning about these important ecosystems and how they can be sustainably managed to benefit local people.

A focal point of this field research effort will be to learn about the existing practices that rural people use to manage and utilize natural resources in different parts of Manica Province, and to learn about the local people's perceptions of the different components of their environments, their problems and their ideas for possible solutions. It will also be important to investigate local perceptions of land and resource tenure.

It is also important to seek to understand the local economic value of resources and how this value can be enhanced by changing the way resources are used, and to learn who controls decision-making about their use. Staff need to understand how the environment influences people's lives and how local communities influence the environment. It is of critical importance to learn how changes in resource management and use can have a positive impact on the economic welfare of local people.

The CEF's new research strategy will also enable the institution to identify and refine research methods and approaches that can be used by Mozambican institutions to involve rural people effectively in the research and the formulation of policy. Through this participatory research process, Mozambican scientists will learn a great deal about the diversity of species in Mozambique, the dynamic ecologies of this vast country and the great potential of its natural resources.

The staff of the CEF believe that community-level research cannot be complete without considering all facets of a community. This definitely includes gender, social rank and age. These are critical research variables in understanding the dynamic interactions between rural people, their environment and the process of development.

The CEF is fortunate in having a high percentage of women scientists on its staff and thus the capacity to work effectively with men and women of rural communities. To be truly effective in their research, however, CEF scientists will need to learn to use methods for analyzing scientifically the role of gender in resource use and management. This pilot research project should provide opportunities for them to learn how to use gender analysis research methods.

The CEF will never have enough researchers to work in all the districts of Mozambique. To be effective in their proposed new approach, therefore, CEF scientists continue to engage the field staff of the Provincial Directorates of Agriculture and are beginning to engage members of rural communities and the local authorities. To achieve this goal, the CEF will need to create an open and helpful approach to field staff and rural people and to seek them out and learn from these 'local experts'.

More important, however, is the contribution the CEF can make to the capacity of participatory extension programmes in Mozambique by changing the approach of extension staff toward local knowledge. The CEF plans to use this pilot field research programme to train capable staff, to sharpen their skills and enhance their research capacity.

Staff at the CEF will also seek to act as a catalyst to stimulate curiosity among all staff and to support those individuals who show research talent and interest in expanding the understanding of local knowledge and existing practices. Through engagement with field staff, it is hoped that the CEF will be able to decentralize research capacity to the district level. In time, senior CEF staff could be 'supervising' the research of extension officers, game scouts and other Directorate officials at the provincial level. Doing this can help the CEF to achieve its research goals. The CEF would therefore like to be able to provide modest funding to enable the most capable field staff to realize their research dreams.

C MECHANISMS

11 National Environment Management Programme

BERNARDO FERRAZ
& BARRY MUNSLOW

Introduction

The National Environment Management Programme developed in Mozambique was the culmination of an enormous collective effort stretching over a long period of time. Its central feature is that it was developed by Mozambicans themselves, determined to identify their own experience and understanding of the problems that faced their country and to devise solutions to these problems which were equally well rooted inside the country. On this basis, more effective forms of outside assistance could be called upon to boost domestic efforts.

Various international institutions had developed their own formulas for the elaboration of national strategies in this regard. The IUCN had its National Conservation Strategies (NCS), the World Bank, its National Environment Action Programmes (NEAP) and the United Nations Environment Programme, its National Environment Management Programme (NEMP). Mozambique chose to call its own initiative a NEMP, but this acronym did not reflect a choice of one of these existing models. Rather it reflected a determination to make this a *national* exercise that would stress the *management* aspects of the programme, and avoid any potential criticism that it was an externally motivated initiative. Hence it would be incorrect to read too much into the name and acronym chosen for the programme, other than that there was a clear determination that it should be driven by Mozambicans rather than by outside donor agencies and consultants, and this still remains the case. Outside donor agencies do have a vitally important role to play, however, in supporting this national effort. Indeed, most donors are very supportive of the fact that this is a domestically driven initiative. Donor support has helped to develop and sustain the momentum of the NEMP, although at times the slowness of the aid bureaucracies in channelling the actual funding has been a constraint.

Overview

Mozambique is facing the challenge of building a future of sustainable development in the context of a recently ended war, and is confronting the massive task of national reconstruction not only with a fragile, newly established democracy but also with the complexities of moving both from a centrally planned to a market-based economy and from a highly centralized political system to one which is more participatory and decentralized. With all of these momentous changes occurring simultaneously, the time is ripe to reshape a more effective approach to improving the human resource management of the natural resource base, which is what a sustainable development approach is all about. This is the essential aim of the NEMP.

Mozambique possesses potentially rich land, marine and mineral resources. Almost 70% of the territory is covered by savannah and secondary forests. Approximately 45% of it has potential for agriculture, although not all of it is arable. Nine major river systems cross the country. Mozambique's coastline, stretching for 2,700 km, is ranked as the third longest in Africa. There are extensive wetland systems along the coast and coral reefs offshore in the north and south. Important reserves of sub-surface resources include minerals, coal and natural gas.

The current population in Mozambique is estimated at more than 16.5 million and is expected to grow at an annual rate of 3%. Approximately two-thirds of the population live along the coastal strip. Nampula and Zambezia Provinces, which constitute about a quarter of the territory, are home to more than 40% of the country's population. About one-quarter of the population live in urban areas and no substantial reversal of the extensive migratory movement to the coastal urban areas is expected. The big environmental problems in the cities are the lack of sanitation systems and the low quality of potable water. Biomass is still the primary source of fuel in Mozambique and deforestation is accelerating around the cities.

Most of Mozambique's natural resources are currently in a reasonable state of preservation. The exceptions are the national parks and game and forest reserves, which together cover approximately 11.5% of the territory but which have long been abandoned. However, there are some acute problems in the urban areas and in parts of the coastal zone, in addition to the wildlife sector, mainly as a result of the war. The abundance of natural resources contributes little, however, to the well-being of the population. This is primarily because of a limited management capacity and the unbalanced distribution of benefits arising from natural resource use.

Existing legislation and institutions that deal with the environment and natural resources are compartmentalized along sectoral lines. Mozambique's current state of flux and transition demands effective intersectoral responses. While some institutional reforms have been undertaken, others are still needed, including completing the review of the environmental legislation.

The government continues to debate the complex question of land tenure reform. It set up an inter-ministerial co-ordinating body for land-use planning, and some guidelines have been completed. Several field projects looking at land tenure have also been undertaken.

Co-ordination of efforts and sharing of information and experience on environmental management are essential. Field work and research need to be expanded and the results assessed and integrated into comprehensive recommendations for reform. This needs to be done quickly, as measures to mitigate the demographic pressures caused by wartime migrations and to encourage rural productivity are already being taken. Such an effort will require multi-donor support and a strong focal point that can co-ordinate the process.

A change in public attitudes will be necessary so that all sectors of society consciously begin to manage the resources available for development in an appropriate manner. But cultural change is a lengthy process and must be carefully oriented to limit the possibility of losing existing positive moral and cultural values. The traditional culture's knowledge and good practices in replenishing natural resources must be used to the fullest extent possible.

The NEMP

The National Environment Management Programme provides an overview plan for the environment in Mozambique. It contains a national environment policy, umbrella environment legislation and an environmental strategy. It is also a programme of sectoral plans, containing projections for the medium and the long term, and aiming to help lead the country towards sustainable socio-economic development.

The NEMP strategy is to set out a clear environmental policy, establish a legal framework that supports the policy and provides the institutional base to implement it and apply and enforce the laws. The goal of the NEMP is sustainable development for Mozambique. The NEMP proposes to achieve this by introducing an environmental culture into Mozambican society, with particular emphasis on sustainable production and consumption processes. The approach adopted in the NEMP is to decentralize the existing vertical governmental structures, to democratize and to introduce participatory processes that involve all sectors of society.

The components of the NEMP include the following:

- institutional capacity building and empowerment within the Ministry for the Co-ordination of Environmental Action (MICOA);
- policy analysis, review and development;
- legislation, implementation of policy through the revision of existing laws and regulations and the drafting of new legal instruments;
- research and information, on-going data collection and monitoring and the organization and publication of findings;
- priority issues of immediate concern involving management of the coastal zone and urban environmental management.

The overall objective of the programme is to address environmental management as an important component of the five-year government programme aimed at poverty alleviation and the promotion of sustainable development. The programme addresses capacity-building issues primarily within the Ministry for the Co-ordination of Environmental Action, which has the mandate to co-ordinate national policies towards sustainable development and to implement the national objectives formulated in the NEMP. Other relevant sectors dealing with environmental management, including government departments, NGOs, civic groups and the community in general, are involved in this programme and their active participation is encouraged.

The NEMP examines the country's principal environmental problems and their causes. The following problems were identified by the Mozambican team led by MICOA, and these determine the current agenda of debate.

Policy
There has been a gradual evolution of policy. The 1990 Constitution was for the first time explicit in relation to the environment. Article 39 states that the state will promote initiatives to guarantee ecological equilibrium and the conservation and preservation of the environment with a view to improving the quality of life of its citizens. Article 72 goes further and states that all citizens have both a right to live in a balanced environment and a duty to defend this principle. The government took further steps to develop its policy framework with its production of the national report to the Rio Earth summit of 1992 and later with the finalization of its NEMP document in 1995.

This document speaks very frankly about the limited extent to which environmental concerns are linked to development in practice, and how the importance of these relationships is not properly understood. Given the extreme poverty of the country, the fundamental policy emphasis is on economic development *per se*. By implication, the importance of environmental concerns in ensuring successful and sustainable long-term development has been ignored. This lack of awareness of the issues has been reinforced by a relative lack of environmental degradation and of hard information concerning the state of the environment, and of environmental management capacity and experience inside the country.

We would add to the list of reasons why environmental issues have not been properly integrated into development thinking, the historical compartmentalization of training in individual academic disciplines which rarely ever included environmental or interdisciplinary training. There has also been a poor level of training in public administration and development management and in the skills to apply academic learning to real world contexts. Given the preponderance of donor financing in the Mozambican economy, donors have also not always been entirely clear about how their stated policy commitments to sustainable development would be translated into their programmes and projects in Mozambique.

A fundamental misconception concerns the perceived notion that environmental concerns are an irrelevance in the push for economic growth and that environmental issues are just one more instance of Western concerns being forced upon the agendas of developing countries along with such issues as gender awareness and democratization, say. Environmental considerations are in fact of vital concern if development initiatives are to be managed wisely and to maximum effect. The broader perspective gained by key actors and interests involved in adopting a sustainable development approach will permit synergies and value added to the development process if a more integrated policy approach emerges.

The NEMP document begins to wrestle with the central problem facing most of the poorer developing countries. Rapid mining of their renewable and non-renewable natural resource base appears to offer the easiest short-term solution to achieving economic growth. Economic sectors particularly dependent upon renewable resources include agriculture, fishing, forestry and tourism (based primarily on the coastal and wildlife resource). Mining is by its nature concerned with non-renewable resources. Because of its history and current situation, Mozambique is often regarded as a high-risk investment; hence quick profit-taking rather than longer-term sustainable development concerns can predominate, with all the risks this entails. The NEMP document calls for a realistic compromise to be made between socio-economic progress and conservation of the environment.

Institutional context
There is weak institutional capacity for the rational management of the natural resource base. Not until the 1990s did the government begin to develop an institutional capacity for environmental management. This still remains weak and will need support into the medium to long term. A National Environment Commission (CNA) was set up in 1992 and a Ministry for the Co-ordination of Environmental Action (MICOA) at the end of 1994, yet still in the final years of the 1990s it remains unclear how well top-level intersectoral co-ordination will operate, not only at the level of government ministries, but in the increasingly important arena of the interface between state institutions, the private sector and non-governmental organizations.

The CNA never had the status to co-ordinate the various ministerial efforts effectively. Later MICOA, as its formal title suggested, was created precisely with the aim of co-ordinating environmental action. This marked an enormous step forward, not least with the decision to give the environment ministerial status. Without this, it could remain a voice crying in the wilderness.

The mandate of MICOA is to co-ordinate, supervise and monitor environmental management in Mozambique. Sectoral ministries will continue to execute projects. As MICOA is in its early stages of institution building, it has been negotiating its mandate and areas of competence with the sectoral ministries and determining the roles and functions it has to perform.

In general terms, co-ordination implies bringing together actors engaged in separate but complementary activities aiming at a common objective, and providing the means to facilitate co-operation between the co-ordinated parties. As sustainable development is a stated principle of government policy, the responsibility for environmental management has to be shared by all ministries. Sectoral policies must integrate environmental dimensions. MICOA has a supportive task in this respect in identifying 'policy gaps' within and between sectoral competencies. It insists on the respective responsibilities of each government entity being upheld with regard to national objectives.

Within its mandate, MICOA can execute certain types of projects, for example pilot projects where new approaches are developed or tested and for which no other Ministry has yet taken the initiative. MICOA may also execute and implement projects serving the major objective of the 'capacity building' of its staff.

Within its mandate, MICOA has a right jointly to assess the capacity of other actors to realize environmental objectives and to support them in building up their institutional and human resource capacities. Furthermore, it makes sense that MICOA could be instrumental in avoiding duplication of efforts, given its oversight role.

MICOA has also been given the authority to address the degradation of Mozambique's natural environment, as formulated in the NEMP. To this effect, environmental rules and regulations have to be devised and enforced. This obliges MICOA to monitor the degree to which other ministries promote and implement sound environmental policy, thereby reinforcing its co-ordination mandate. Public awareness-raising and promotion of social control through community participation in resource use and conservation are indispensable instruments to achieve this objective.

The legislation gives the following functions to MICOA. MICOA should, as far as possible, and in close co-ordination with other ministries and private and civil groups, work towards:

(a) the development of intersectoral policies for sustainable development;
(b) the development and promotion of integrated resource-use planning;
(c) the promotion of awareness-raising among the general public;
(d) the fostering of formal environmental education for sustainable environmental management;
(e) the preparation of general environmental legislation, the promotion of sectoral legislation and the establishment of norms and criteria for the sustainable use of the country's natural resources;
(f) the creation of preconditions for law enforcement and environmental monitoring; and
(g) the establishment of a database on the state of the environment, sufficient for the determination of policy priorities.

The Ministry is positioned at the centre of a network of relationships with both governmental and non-governmental institutions. These linkages have been developing over the past decade as the environment began to be established as a serious policy issue. Of particular significance has been the Capacity 21 initiative which has permitted MICOA to avail itself of the resources to carry out intensive training courses in sustainable development for the Council of Ministers, Provincial Governors, national and provincial civil servants, key indigenous NGOs and grassroots agents of change. The next phase will be characterized by a strengthening and diversification of the network. More importantly, the institutional arrangements governing environmental management policies will need further formalization and *de facto* support in implementation.

A fundamental weakness remains, however. There is an absence of sufficiently effective intersectoral co-ordination. What is the power of MICOA or any other higher government structure to insist upon a co-ordinated approach? The answer is still, very little. The Council of Ministers and the Ministry of Finance and Planning are the key co-ordinating agencies of government. This problem continues to be wrestled with. Furthermore, existing ministries covering the major sectors of production – Agriculture, Mining, Fisheries, etc. – have remained both autonomous and powerful. There had been little clarity within state structures concerning the institutional mandate of the environment in the process of government until MICOA was set up. Whilst the formation of MICOA was in itself an important statement of policy commitment, its creation was far from resolving the problems of attaining a co-ordinated government response. The actual position and competency of MICOA in relation to other organizations involved in the utilization of the country's natural resource base remains at best uncertain.

Weak technical capacity is a further constraint. This problem is well-known, especially in relation to the environment and sustainable development. Few people have technical skills in this area and, of these, some have been trained outside the country and face difficulties in applying the concepts they have learnt to Mozambican realities.

Excessive centralization is acknowledged to be a problem in most developing countries. Mozambique is no exception and, given its particular legacy, can be regarded as facing even greater challenges than most in this regard. Elsewhere in this volume some of the efforts being made to build a more decentralized approach are outlined in detail. The NEMP is fully supportive of such an approach. The aim is to tackle the whole array of problems on the most appropriate scale.

Legal aspects
The existing sectoral legislation identifies certain key aspects of sustainable development and environmental concerns under the following laws:

Land law: The state owns all land but people can obtain 50 year land-use rights. Critics argue that there is no incentive to invest for sustainability in land; and as peasants do not have to obtain a legal land title, there are conflicts over who actually has rights to land, as two systems exist concurrently – a formal and a customary land use system. Alda Salamão in Chapter 9 discusses these issues in more detail.
Mining law: Under this law the Ministry of Mines is obliged to consult MICOA over the granting of mining licences.
Fishing law: Capacity for taxation and control is extremely weak.
Water law: Major water works require an EIA.
Investment law: Investment projects have to be screened to see if an EIA is required.
Municipalities law: This will be progressively implemented and under the law the municipalities will become the main managers and co-ordinators responsible for the environment. MICOA and the Ministry of State Administration will have to work together to prepare complementary legislation to facilitate this.

International Conventions have been signed and Mozambique is well integrated into the international framework of laws on the environment.

Environmental education
In the formal education sector significant rebuilding is required. Between 1983 and 1992 3,402 out of 5,886 schools were either closed or destroyed. The closure of

schools plus the increase in population has put the educational system under great stress. This is in the context of poor national indices for literacy and an unacceptably low educational level for the population as a whole. The educational system in primary schools is in a desperate state. Only a third of seven year-olds pass the first grade of primary education. In the schools which continue to function, there is no equipment, massive overcrowding, with various shifts in a day to cope with the numbers, hence reduced teaching contact. Given poor salaries and working conditions, there is a shortage of teachers willing to teach and a high rate of absenteeism. Teacher training, syllabus reform and teaching methods are areas in urgent need of attention. There is no coherent, all-encompassing approach to environmental education in the system.

In the non-formal sector, problems include: the lack of a government policy to stimulate environmental education; environmental issues do not command the public's attention to the extent required and are scarcely considered; a high level of illiteracy means teaching methods will have to be adapted to people's culture and traditions; there is a lack of coherence in seminar and short course programmes, and a lack of institutional co-ordination mechanisms.

Yet in traditional communities people have a close relationship with nature and a knowledge base does exist. But there is little hard information about it and about how the war may have affected this potentially important resource. Mario Souto's chapter in this volume explores MICOA's strategy for environmental education in both the formal and the non-formal sectors. The NEMP also highlights the importance of environmental documentation and research and these will feed into the other outputs.

Rural coastal problems

Given the importance of the coastal zone and the fact that little has been done to improve the management of this vital area, we shall spend some time highlighting a number of the critical areas of concern.

Population concentrations, particularly in the principal urban centres, and intensive economic activities create serious problems of conflicting demands upon the natural resource base of the coastal zone. People settled in these environmentally sensitive areas to escape from the war in the interior and to avail themselves of the limited services, commercialization and aid disbursement networks available. A particular problem concerns deforestation along the coastal zone, including destruction of the mangroves. Livelihood-sustaining activities and economic development more generally in agriculture, industry and settlements are having a negative effect on the coastal and marine environments. In the coastal cities, urban and industrial pollution of the bays is a growing problem.

Problems exist in the fishing sector, where it is necessary to: establish the size of the resource and catch limits; feed the people; and improve the situation of artisanal fishermen who lack all but the minimum resources. Finally, there is a weak institutional set-up in the sector. Some species such as prawns have reached or exceeded their maximum sustainable off-take limit, whilst there is room for a larger catch to be taken amongst some other species. Nationally, there are about 90,000 artisanal fishermen. The artisanal sector faces various problems: lack of fishing equipment and its high cost for dispersed fishing communities; a weak commercial network; high losses; lack of infrastructure and credit; and weak government support.

Problems in the industrial sector include: weak technical and financial management for the sustainable use of the fish resource, a particular challenge for prawns (the principal export); shortage of skilled labour and dependence on foreign technical assistance with little value added to export products; poor knowledge of alternative resources to be exploited; weak monitoring, taxation and control, hygiene monitoring and research capacity; and finally a degraded infrastructure.

Other problems in the coastal zone involve creating incentives and a framework to develop marine aquaculture, and more seriously the degradation of the coastal and marine ecosystem. Population concentration is putting great pressure on the coastal resources. Uncertainties about the economic future mean that there is no rush back to the interior for displaced people living along the coastal zone. There is a lack of policy, institutional capacity and legislation to undertake coastal planning, plus the necessary information base is missing. New economic initiatives are taking place without any order or planning, and degradation of the coastal environment is occurring. There is a lack of qualified people to deal with the complex issues involved in coastal zone management. Some pilot schemes have begun but it is very early days.

Mangroves, seagrass beds and corals are essential parts of marine ecosystems. In some areas these are being degraded through the use of industrial fishing techniques. Coastal erosion affects a number of places along the 2,700 km coastline and can cause damage to the infrastructure and loss of soil fertility, and disturb sensitive ecosystems, corals, etc. There is no institution with the mandate to deal with this.

Marine pollution results from a number of sources. The domestic use of agrochemicals is a future potential problem as the economy picks up. It is also a problem imported in the river flow from more developed neighbouring countries. Industrial waste is a problem mainly in Maputo and Beira. The Texlom factory in Maputo uses 1,000 tons of caustic soda a month plus other chemicals. The treatment of residues is inadequate, with a high alkaline content discharged into Matola River and the sea. Municipal waste is a more widespread problem. Only Maputo has a water treatment process for waste water, but it does not operate efficiently. Strong indications of faecal contamination exist in the Bay of Maputo, Beira and Nacala. None of the nine main ports has facilities to receive, store and treat shipping wastes, nor to deal with any emergency.

There is no adequate management of marine parks. There is neither the information available nor the legislation, norms and regulations to enable these parks to be managed properly. More generally, there is weak institutional capacity in the tourist sector. Enormous potential exists for tourism along the coast. The underdevelopment of the tourist industry accounts for the existing absence of negative environmental aspects in the main. A free-for-all has been occurring with proposals for tourism development, without due concern for the potential negative environmental impacts which may undermine long-term potential.

There is a serious lack of inter-sectoral co-ordination and effective liaison between central and local authorities and also inadequate legislation. A limited capacity for undertaking Environmental Impact Assessments is available amongst existing structures dealing with tourism initiatives. Problems of uncontrolled and inadequately managed tourism soon became apparent in the 1990s in Bilene, Ponta D'Ouro, Xai-Xai and Maputo, involving the unnecessary felling of trees, destruction of dunes, litter, and general degradation of the coastal and marine ecosystems.

Degradation of the land operates at two levels. Firstly, in some areas there are too many peasant farmers trying to cultivate marginal land with inadequate management techniques based on traditional slash-and-burn methods. Secondly, for commercial farmers using irrigation systems, again inadequate land-use management techniques are being employed which can lead to salinization, alkalinization and erosion of soils.

Deterioration of forestry and wildlife resources is a further concern. Much of the country is covered by savanna which has a low commercial value but provides the rural population with fuelwood, building materials, fruit, medicinal plants, pasture for cattle, etc. In areas of localized population concentrations, the tree resource has come under pressure. Slash-and-burn cultivation means that between 35% and 45% of the country's forested areas are estimated to be subject to annual burnings. Mangroves are particularly affected in some areas.

Finally, challenges in the coastal zone include a degradation of the water resource and mineral resource exploitation. The chapter by Sitoe in this book explores the problems of the coastal zone in greater depth.

Urban environment

Degradation of sanitation systems and low quality of drinking water are the critical environmental issues. Specifically this entails:

- deficient and obsolete sanitation systems;
- population pressure and demand in excess of the system's capacity;
- poor usage and maintenance of the system;
- lack of finance from Municipal Councils.

Hence water pipes burst, stagnant and polluted pools of water form, surface and sub-terranean pollution of water occurs and these flow into the sea and rivers.

Lack of drainage systems in the suburbs of cities and in small and medium-sized towns contributes to the contamination of the urban environment and the spread of disease. People are forced to use waste water for their domestic needs. Many of the population do not have access to a toilet and defecate in the open air, others use toilets incorrectly. This is a serious problem in Beira.

A majority of the coastal cities face problems of flooding with the attendant creation of areas of stagnant water, with negative effects on public health including the incidence of malaria, cholera and diarrhoea. A serious cholera outbreak began in August 1997 and only ended in June 1998, with over 700 deaths recorded. Maputo and Beira were most seriously affected. A 1992 survey concluded that 81% of towns had no water treatment system for human consumption; 64% of people obtained their water needs from surface water (rivers, lakes and springs) vulnerable to contamination; 22% of the population relied upon wells to some extent.

Main problems include inadequate maintenance of the existing system and a failure to expand the provisioning system, tariff receipts are very low, there is weak financial management and a low level of technical capacity amongst the human resource base. A fundamental cause of these problems is a lack of autonomy and failure to integrate these water companies in local government. The chapter by Chutumia in this volume handles these issues in detail. Soil erosion and deforestation are further results of the excessive pressure on the natural resource base in urban areas.

Conclusion

The NEMP is intended to be a flexible policy instrument and a catalyst for institutional and human resource building, along with being an initiator of legislative change and improved co-ordination. This is no easy task. Ensuring these advances requires real material resources being made available to create the human and institutional incentives to promote the goodwill and effective action necessary for success.

Let us look into the abyss. The dominant wisdom in political science is that in Africa the 'politics of the belly' rules (Bayart, 1993). This has its resonance in popular culture throughout the continent. In Mozambique, there is talk of 'cabritismo' and 'tubarões': the goats and the sharks consume everything. This is not untypical of talk in most countries in the continent. Given a get-rich-quick mentality in a context of poverty, mining the existing natural resource base is the most readily available and obvious route to riches, and occupying state power is a main avenue for accumulation in Africa. Is it really possible therefore to achieve long-term success in adhering to a set of high-sounding sustainable development principles, as elaborated at the Rio Earth Summit and elsewhere, when the 'politics of the belly' is said to be the determinant force in Africa? The only way to cope with these two potentially contradictory sets of forces is to ensure that consumers, producers, electorates and aid donors really do have the environment and sustainability on their own agendas. The move towards market-based economics and a democratically based political system could thus begin to counteract the 'politics of the belly', creating a positive upward spiral of sustainable development rather than a negative downward spiral of mining the resource base for the benefit of the few and ignoring the needs of the poor who are the majority.

Reference
Bayart, J.F. (1993) *The State in Africa. The Politics of the Belly*, Longman, London.

12 Rapid Appraisal

BIE NIO ONG
& BARRY MUNSLOW

Rapid appraisal: the method

Rapid Appraisal is a method aimed at understanding the needs of deprived communities and as such is intended to strengthen the principles of equity, participation and multi-sectoral co-operation. This chapter will outline the general principles of the methodology, and provide a brief Mozambique case study. A more detailed applied study to demonstrate its relevance in practice is given in the chapter by Lorna Gujral specifically on the health sector.

Rapid Appraisal actually began as Rapid Rural Appraisal, a user-friendly methodology developed primarily in Africa and Asia. Its usefulness is such that its derivative Rapid Appraisal is used not only in developing countries but in industrialized countries as well. It is a system developed as a reaction to complicated, time-consuming and expensive research conducted by external consultants. Whilst it is called Rapid Appraisal it could equally well be called Relaxed Appraisal.

The fundamental idea is that the people who are experiencing the problems of development have considerable knowledge within themselves and within their community of what needs to be done to help solve their problems. The methodology is a way not only of eliciting bottom-up problem identifications but also of mobilizing the great untapped development potential of the latent capacity of individuals and communities.

The main strength of the approach is that it is based on the idea that we need to go out and talk with the target communities; it is a field-based rather than a desk-based approach. Researchers need to adopt a modest and functional approach. Given limited resources, it is very easy to spend these on detailed studies of development problems rather than supporting actual community-based development initiatives. Rapid Appraisal is a semi-structured process of learning from the target population. It recognizes the limitations of research budgets and tries to obtain, in an ethically honest, but functional, efficient and effective way, the best available data from the bottom up to inform management decisions.

Rapid Appraisal aims to gain an insight into a community's own perspective on its priority needs and therefore provides a picture of what the strength of feeling is, rather than how many people are affected by a particular issue. In this sense it is concerned with a qualitative rather than a quantitative understanding of the problems. Secondly, Rapid Appraisal uses methods of a community development type, but instead of appointing separate researchers/community development workers who are feeding results back to managers, ideally the managers themselves are the researchers.

This is a key characteristic of RA, because the emphasis is placed on translating research findings into managerial action, or more specifically into redefining resource allocation in line with the identification of priority needs. Thirdly, the method can be applied to a whole variety of problem areas in needs assessment, such as rural development, natural resource management, agriculture, credit programmes, etc. If the emphasis is on the assessment of health needs this means understanding health in all its physical, psychological and social dimensions. There has to be a multi-disciplinary and multi-agency approach to needs assessment. The multi-disciplinary nature of the assessment requires broad participation from various organizations. To prevent this from becoming too dispersed and ineffective it is essential to provide a tight focus on a specific community in order to counterbalance the potential negative effects.

Part of the strength of this approach is that it gathers the information from the intended beneficiaries who are also participants, whilst they are in their own setting; it is not abstract research on the drawing board or in the ivory tower of academia. An important component is seeking out diversity, discovering the different groups and sets of interests that exist within a target community, and identifying mini-stakeholder groups. In particular, care has to be taken to discover the needs of the weakest, poorest and least vocal elements.

If this methodology is to achieve maximum benefits for the development process, then the attitudes adopted by the outsiders have to be appropriate. It is important not to arrive as the big, important outsider who knows everything and delivers judgements from on high. Rather, this is where the process of facilitating development and creating new partnerships really has to take off. Those undertaking the Rapid Appraisal need to demonstrate from the outset their respect for the people they are interviewing and their knowledge and contribution, and a degree of humility about their own expertise in relation to the highly specific target group and the local circumstances. Patience and the ability to listen and encourage people to talk about the issues involved are important for the Rapid Appraisal team.

There are a number of obvious potential weaknesses in such an approach; key influential informants can lead the appraisal astray. Cross-checking and verification of sources of information are therefore essential. A multi-disciplinary approach, employing a range of different information-gathering tools and different types of information, can help to guard against being led astray.

When gathering the various sources of information, the key considerations are veracity, relevance and usefulness. Tough decisions constantly need to be made to ensure that best use is being made of the time and resources in this investigative phase. Rapid Appraisal is an appraisal in that it provides a qualitative picture of the priorities of a community in terms of the variety of human needs. It is rapid in that the whole exercise can be done in approximately 10 working days.

Typically the stages of the research are as follows:

i)   A two-day workshop for a multi-disciplinary, multi-agency team of development workers and managers examining the scope of the method, generating the key questions for the research, determining the target population and respondents, and setting out the work schedule.

ii) Fieldwork, consisting of open-ended interviews with the selected respondents. This is generally done by small multi-disciplinary teams, who also do an initial rough analysis of their data. Secondary data collection also takes place and observations are recorded.

iii) Half-day workshop of the whole team to distil the qualitative data into a list of needs as defined by the community.

iv) Return to the respondents to ask them to put the list of needs into order of priority.
v) Analysis (computer assisted or manual) of the individual priority listings and formulation of a composite priority list in a half-day workshop.
vi) Open meeting with the community to decide the first set of priorities for action and agree specific action plans.
vii) Regular evaluation of progress and revision of action plans.

The main skill needed for this approach is the willingness to work across disciplines and organizations in order to focus on need rather than supply. This means that good listening is a fundamental requirement, as well as developing imaginative solutions that do not always fall within established patterns of provision. It also means that development workers and managers have to be willing to engage in uncomfortable discussions with communities about the different perceptions of priorities. However, it does not mean that one always has to do what the community says, because they, of course, can be wrong as well. For example, in one of the communities where RA was used, people said they did not think immunization and vaccination should be continued. This is a suggestion that needs to be discussed but it has to be pointed out that it is not a good idea.

More formal skills involve some basic understanding of open-ended interviewing (and in particular the distinction from 'having a chat') and how one analyzes qualitative data. Computer skills in SPSS (Statistical Package for Social Scientists) are helpful but not essential.

What kind of knowledge does rapid appraisal generate?
The method focuses on the subjective elements of a community's definitions of priorities. It is able to complement quantitative knowledge, for example demographic and service utilization data, with information about the experiences and perceptions of a community.

Thus, it is important to understand the strengths and limitations of this method. Its strength is that it can provide insights into a community's experience and sense of need which, ultimately, are the determining factors in generating the active involvement of people. Having a 'feel' of what communities consider important issues will aid serious collaborative action, rather than telling people that statistically they have a particular problem. For example, with regard to a particular community, statistical data may suggest that there is a fuelwood shortage but people consider a shortage of water as being the most important issue since this affects food, health and indeed the capacity to grow and nurture trees.

The limitations of the method are that it tells development workers and managers what the strength of feeling is in a community but not how many people are affected. Therefore, the data need to be augmented with quantitative data in order to understand relative magnitudes, before priority setting in resource allocation can take place. A particular difficulty is that local elites and local political processes will co-opt whatever outside initiative occurs. It would be naive to think that it could be otherwise. The art is to know this and build the initiative accordingly, to maximize the end result desired.

Rapid Appraisal defines a community primarily as a social entity and attempts to understand it by means of interviewing so-called key informants. This approach is based on the premise that there is not one 'truth' about a community and that an understanding can be built up through a variety of perspectives. Thus, information is collected from different categories of people, who are knowledgeable about how a community lives and operates.

Firstly, people who work as professionals in the community have a knowledge that is specific and focused. These are, for example, teachers, health workers, policemen, etc. Secondly, each community may have traditional, elected or self-elected leaders who have insight with respect to particular interests. Thirdly, there are people who occupy a central position in the community because of their location or particular function, for example, the shopkeeper, traditional healer or priest. By eliciting information from these sets of informants, one can build up a multi-faceted picture and, by comparing and contrasting, gain an 'intersubjective' understanding of the complexity of community life. It is important, of course, in building up a valid picture, to scrutinize the choice of informants carefully. In order to achieve in-depth intersubjectivity, one has to be sure that all (or most) perspectives have been covered. Using a 'snowball' approach to constructing the sample of key informants is a useful approach. Also, ensuring that contrasting views are sought ensures the multi-faceted perspective.

The findings are typical of the selected community and cannot be seen as capable of being generalized. Rapid Appraisal is a snapshot in time and does not aim to provide a stable picture over time. But this is precisely the strength of the method, in that it reinforces the action-oriented approach, i.e. it demonstrates current concerns, formulates action plans and moves on to a changed reality as a result of (hopefully successful) interventions. In order to evaluate the success of the planned joint action, a new Rapid Appraisal can help refocus the agenda and stimulate an on-going programme of work.

Rapid Appraisal attempts to combine two aims: first, to involve resource holders, i.e. managers and development workers, in the research process so that they can formulate actions with a community; secondly, to develop relationships with a community based on joint working and continuing assessment. It has proved difficult, however, to pursue both objectives with equal success, because senior managers, for example, tend to move at regular intervals or to be very busy and cannot always maintain continuity with a community. If middle managers are chosen, stability of relationships can often be achieved but this cadre tends to have less decision-making power and the action-oriented aspects do not move as rapidly as they should. The choice of managers/development workers/researchers has to be made carefully, in order to pursue both objectives equally.

Needs assessment
There has been a lot of debate about involving users in assessing needs. Rapid Appraisal addresses the heart of the matter: it asks people to formulate needs and priorities, which means that they are involved in the planning of development projects and services. This is most important if development agencies are to be seen to be serious about user input. The debate about how communities formulate their needs and how they do or do not match up to professional outside assessment, has to be engaged in if development agencies are to champion the people's cause. A needs assessment exercise endeavours to integrate the views of the experts with the lay view which is grounded in the cultural experience of needs. It is important to realize that RA focuses on community needs in the widest sense and some priorities will fall outside the remit of the particular development agency. Therefore, a dialogue has to be set up with the community which defines the parameters of the agency's operations in order not to raise false expectations of what can be done. Once people are involved in decisions about resource allocation, it makes sense for them also to be asked whether they feel satisfied with the delivery. They can evaluate both the content, i.e. are resources allocated in such a way as to address their need, and the form, are services delivered in a user-friendly manner? The RA methodology mobilizes professionals across

different sectors and organizations. It combines strategic planning with direct feed-back on development initiatives and provision, and it should productively combine the efforts of funders, providers and recipients from a range of organizations in the study of a community.

Doing rapid appraisal

Setting up an RA study requires external input from people who are familiar with the methodology and who preferably have some experience in applying it. As the method is still relatively new and continues to be further developed, training is required.

The product from a Rapid Appraisal is a clear action plan (or plans) for joint work-ing between a community and the development organization, based on an agreed understanding of priority needs in the specific community. Progress can be moni-tored jointly by assessing whether the objectives of the various plans have been achieved. Plans therefore have to be defined as realistic, with the participation of all parties and within a relatively short time frame, e.g. six months. Regular meetings will be necessary to monitor implementation and progress.

Rapid Appraisal is a method which works well with small, clearly defined commu-nities and provides in-depth insight into the community's own perspective on prior-ity needs. It has to be used alongside more quantitative methods in order to produce a wider context for the findings. RA can only be successful if there is a genuine com-mitment from development agencies (i.e. managers) to translate findings into action.

This raises the important question of how to define a community. In some cases it may be relatively easy to define and at other times it may be more difficult. Generally with Rapid Appraisal a qualitative approach is adopted by choosing individuals or groups which appear to be representative of the various perspectives within the sam-ple population. If some knowledge exists about a particular community a list can be drawn up of the important sub-groups and individuals who may need to be con-sulted. Care has to be taken to include all significant perspectives, especially those of the most disadvantaged.

From rural roots to urban applicability

Whilst Rapid Appraisal was developed in relation to rural areas, it has potentially equal usage in urban areas. Apart from providing an analysis of poverty, the method-ology can help to build the strength of urban communities *vis-à-vis* local and national government structures in terms of negotiating improved service delivery. This will involve identifying and establishing mechanisms to include key stakeholders in the development process and developing appropriate partnership initiatives.

Livelihood strategies take different forms in urban and rural areas. Yet at the same time there are important interconnections between rural and urban sources of liveli-hood for many individuals, families and networks. The rural areas provide greater opportunities for gaining a livelihood by directly utilizing natural resources. The food, water and fuel which people obtain from the environment themselves by their own labours in the rural areas, become commodities which have to be purchased with cash in the towns. In urban areas formal and informal sector employment is far more important. People work to earn the cash to purchase their basic needs; in the rural areas people directly utilize the natural resource base to extract their basic needs.

Risk minimization in rural areas means employing a diversity of agricultural prac-tices. In urban areas where there is limited access to the use of the natural resource base, diversity of employment and income generation is the risk-minimizing strategy.

Commerce – buying and selling – and living off the margin of the price difference, is the key survival strategy for many in urban areas.

There is a great diversity of social and cultural structures amongst urban communities, as the old rural clan and lineage networks may no longer be the key survival mechanisms. New networks are created based on a variety of new structures and relationships formed through work, the church or other avenues.

In applying RA techniques there is sufficient which is similar to make its application across urban and rural areas beneficial. In Mozambique there is a measure of uncertainty about land tenure in both rural and urban areas. A second problem concerns the cohesiveness of communities. In many areas of Mozambique both rural and urban communities have been tossed into uncertainty as a result of the social disruptions and population movements engendered by a protracted period of war and emergency. Defining communities can be a problem both in the rural and the urban areas.

Whilst there may well be environmental, social and economic differences between low-income urban and rural households they still have much in common. In addition, many families and networks depend on having a foot in both camps. When development agencies individually or in combination, state – NGOs – private sector, address both the urban and the rural spheres they need to start from an understanding of *how* people survive and obtain the various ingredients necessary for their livelihoods. At the barest minimum the state, NGOs and the private sector should do all in their power to reconcile their own agendas with letting people get on with their own survival strategies, and facilitating these in every way possible. Importantly, the specialists in both urban and rural areas have much to learn from each other by trying out these participatory techniques and sharing information about what does and does not work.

Rapid Appraisal has many variants. An important one is Participatory Rural Appraisal (PRA). As the name suggests, the emphasis here is on an inclusive process of appraisal, with the stress on participation. PRA is most applicable when the emphasis is on a continuing process of participation, with the target beneficiaries being involved not only in producing the information but also in analyzing it, defining their needs and monitoring progress. RA is much more of a functional management tool. PRA is a somewhat more ambitious social project. The crucial issue here is the extent to which it is intended that power be transferred from the various forms of development agencies, state, NGO and private sector, to communities.

Table 12.1 indicates the potential strengths and weaknesses of RA and PRA.

Why the emphasis on participation?

The basic answer has to be that it is very difficult for one person to develop another unless he/she wants that development to occur and actively engages in the process. People and communities need to be proactive in their own self-development. At the same time, outside development agencies have a great deal to contribute. Both the target group and the development agents have the task of analyzing and minimizing the constraints and vulnerabilities and maximizing the opportunities and the capacities at the individual and community level to respond to these opportunities in the most effective way possible. Unless people build up their own capacities they fall victim to the vulnerabilities of the circumstances in which they find themselves.

Participatory methodologies exist to address a variety of problem situations. Capacities and Vulnerabilities Analysis exists to encourage participatory approaches in emergency situations, helping to build up people's capacity to overcome vulnerability. Gender Framework Analysis can help redress gender bias in development initiatives and increase women's participatory role. There are several variants on this

Table 12.1   *Strengths and weaknesses of RA/PRA*

Strengths

1. *Access to less literate people within groups*

The flexibility and range of techniques enable illiterate or semi-literate people to share in the systematic collection, and viewpoints of women and men who are otherwise marginalized may be articulated and taken into account

2. *Reveals differences within communities, groups and households*

RA/PRA is better able than traditional methods to draw out sensitive information, since the techniques rank rather than measure the power and resources which different people enjoy. This can help to expose and differentiate between the perspectives of women and men at community level and within the household

3. *Good basis for planning*

The qualitative and detailed assessment of local realities which RA/PRA provides is a good basis for sensitive project planning. The social mapping technique provides baseline data as perceived by individuals within the group in question: it gives their starting point and so reveals their priorities as indicators for qualitative change

4. *Relatively low cost*

RA/PRA tends to use local materials, relies on only a small number of outsiders and takes less time than conventional academic methods to produce a comprehensive set of data, in a form accessible to the people directly involved

5. *Flexible*

RA/PRA can be combined with formal appraisal, planning, monitoring and evaluation methods and can often enhance them. It is more culturally adaptable than most other approaches.

Weaknesses

1. *High level of expertise required*

Whilst RA/PRA techniques appear simple, the approach needs to be learned, cannot be improvised and is difficult to do well. The right attitudes and behaviour are crucial to its success. Practitioners need to start out with an understanding of the particular culture, in order to tease out sensitive information in a non-conflictual way: it can, therefore, be difficult to assemble a strong team for a specific project

2. *Site-specific data*

Focusing on the particular, RA/PRA is site-specific and unless it is thoroughly integrated into the working methods of a project, may also be time-bound. The data it produces offer only limited opportunities for comparison between different situations. This is not a problem for the women and men directly involved but may constitute a weakness for NGOs which need to make comparisons in order to monitor and evaluate their own work

3. *Exposes, but does not deal with, conflicts*

The purpose of RA/PRA is to reveal and explore differences and inequalities within communities, groups or households, through techniques which rely on people working together in an open way. This may not be possible in situations of extreme social distrust, in particular for the people who are most vulnerable to reprisals or discrimination. Even in relatively stable settings, information about individuals which is made public, e.g. wealth ranking, could generate far-reaching conflicts which neither the RA/PRA practitioners nor the development NGO are competent to handle approach which can be applied according to the specific circumstances and requirements.

The aim with participation is to release the knowledge base that exists within communities to fuel the development effort. This approach therefore acknowledges the limitations of the knowledge base and its applicability and relevance for developing local communities amongst the various state, NGO and private sector development agencies. There is not one single truth, but there are multiple truths based upon relevance, acceptability, applicability and an unwillingness to experiment too far beyond the limits of existing world views and always with due regard to the minimization of risk, as people live on the boundaries of survival.

In RA special attention is given to listening to the views of people who are not normally heard by decision-makers. For the participation to be genuine, it is necessary that, during the research stage, interviews should be semi-structured, thus allowing the interviewee to raise his or her own concerns. The aim is to elicit the community's own perspective on need in order to facilitate their voice being heard in policy-making and policy implementation structures.

Planning a programme
The first stage involves preliminary planning where the assessment is made. At this stage the target community has to get to know what the development agency can offer it and the nature of the contribution that it will be expected to make in the form of labour inputs, say. The assessment is intended to locate and specify the problems and gather the information to plan the overall programme. The second stage involves the detailed planning, which provides the overall programme framework within which particular projects will be instituted.

Whether the initiative is stimulated by the community itself or by a development agency, the important point is that there has to be an open process of dialogue and communication. Whatever happens, the target community has to be highly motivated, and encouraging an active process of participation and ownership is essential. Care is needed here to sustain community motivation. Long time periods may elapse between the initial phase of community discussions and the actual process of starting work. On other occasions a project may be started and then the funding dries up and this demotivates, or there may be a long gap in the funding which has a similar effect. It is essential that both sides make every effort to follow through on the commitments that they make so that trust and partnership are maintained.

The steps within a Rapid Appraisal can be broadly defined, but have to be understood in a flexible manner, as local circumstances can dictate alterations to the sequence. An outline pattern can be offered:

Step 1   Defining purpose, target community and agencies involved
Step 2   Project leader or team to prepare RA
Step 3   Workshop with multi-agency, multi-disciplinary team
Step 4   Fieldwork: observation, secondary data collection, interviews
Step 5   Collation and analysis of data – formulation of needs list
Step 6   Prioritization of needs
Step 7   Feedback to community, discussion of action
Step 8   Programme of change
Step 9   Evaluation and redefinition of priorities
Step 10   Second RA? Envisioning the future?

Holloway and Lindsey (1996) in a case study of refugee returnees in Tete Province, Mozambique have shown how PRA can be a useful tool for assessing the hazards, vulnerabilities and capacities of disaster-prone communities, for empowering them to reduce their vulnerability to known threats and for improving programme planning. We let the authors explain their findings in their own words below:

Background and methods used

The community in Tete is in the process of re-establishing itself after several years in refugee camps in neighbouring countries. As part of the rehabilitation process, a number of outside organisations have developed programmes to put these communities back on their feet. However, it seems that many of these programmes were carried out without a complete picture of the area's risk profile (especially the fact that it is drought-prone). Moreover, there appeared to be little understanding of the community's capacity to deal with drought in the past and how this capacity needed to be supported and strengthened as the returnee communities re-established themselves.

As a result the programmes, although well-intended, have not been as effective as they might have been in reducing the vulnerability of the communities. For example, while returnees did receive seeds, these were non-drought-tolerant maize seeds and were delivered late for planting. Thus the crop failed because of the prevailing drought conditions.

We spent three days working with several communities, followed by a review of the information gathered. Information for programme-planning that was risk-sensitive and specially drought-sensitive was generated. They were also of help to outsiders trying to understand the drought-related vulnerability and capacity of the refugee returnees. Box 1 describes the type of information generated using a variety of PRA methods.

Box 1
METHODS FOR UNDERSTANDING COPING STRATEGIES

Time-line
From the time-line, events that had occurred in the community were tracked over many years. This revealed that the hazard of drought was a recurrent event in the community's past. We also learned that the community had been able to cope with these droughts in the past. For example, the 'Kansale' drought in 1973 got its name from the particular wild fruit that the community ate to survive. At this time, the community was also cultivating drought-tolerant crops, such as sorghum. So although people were drought-affected, they were fully able to manage without external assistance.

Time trend
This helped us understand the rain patterns during a good harvest year, compared with those during a bad one. This way we were also able to understand the drought's impact on crop production. The time trends were also useful for knowing when the demands are for work in the fields. This was key for planning community meetings or other gatherings that would take time away from cultivation.

Seasonality mapping
This revealed the times when people collect wild foods such as fruit, nuts, roots, etc.

Community mapping
This showed where the water sources were located, allowing a better understanding of drought-related vulnerabilities.

Needs matrix
This helped to prioritize the community's most urgent needs: food, water and medicine.

Alisa Holloway and Diane Lindsey: c/o Regional Delegation, International Federation of the Red Cross and Red Crescent Societies, 11 Phillips Avenue, Belgravia, Harare, Zimbabwe

From PRA to disaster reduction planning

The key findings generated by the PRA methods allowed us to begin planning a programme to build on existing capacity amongst the community and address their vulnerabilities in order to reduce the impact of recurrent drought. Some of the capacities and vulnerabilities revealed during the PRA exercises include:

- The fact that the area is drought-prone.
- Hunger/food insecurity is perceived as the most important risk facing the community.
- Lack of safe and accessible water as well as essential medicines are perceived as key vulnerabilities by the community.
- Older members of the community have good knowledge of and openness to using drought-tolerant crops.
- Older members of the community are knowledgeable about the availabilities and use of wild foods.
- The community indicated when they would be fully committed to preparing and cultivating their fields, highlighting a capacity to protect household food security, which any outside intervention should not undermine.

Building on some of the capacities identified above (such as the awareness amongst older community members of the importance of drought-tolerant seed and the clear commitment by the community to cultivate fields actively, due to their desire to not remain passive recipients of food aid), a programme to reduce drought-related vulnerability could have three components:

- Start up distribution of drought-tolerant seeds such as sorghum, as well as maize and groundnut.
- Start a community-managed seed bank.
- Provide training for young people in local cultivation methods by involving the older members of the community. It should be remembered that most of the young people have spent much of their formative years in refugee camps, where food was delivered by relief agencies and not cultivated by the household.

Conclusions

As shown here, it is important that from a disaster-reduction perspective, PRA can be used to assess key vulnerabilities and capabilities, as these relate to the risk faced by disaster-prone communities. Compared with other assessment methods, PRA is particularly powerful since it:

- actively involves the community;
- empowers the community to identify the risks and priorities as well as its capacities to reduce these risks;
- provides a picture of the community's perceptions of the risks it faces;
- allows both community insiders and outsiders to jointly identify risk reduction measures;
- is both time- and cost-effective.

In this example, PRA provided a wealth of information directly relevant to the risks affecting returnee communities and the capacities which could be strengthened to reduce these. This type of information is critical if outside agencies are to develop programmes which lower both disaster risk and community vulnerability in the long term.

Note

More details of ways in which PRA can be applied to disaster mitigation are also described in *Reducing Risk: Participatory Learning Activities for Disaster Mitigation in Southern Africa*, jointly published by and available from the Southern African Delegation of the International Federation of the Red Cross and Red Crescent Societies and the Department of Adult and Community Education at the University of Natal.

Sustainability and change

The purpose of Rapid Appraisal and its specific use has to be clear from the outset if both change and sustainability are to be on the agenda. Moreover, the scope of the Rapid Appraisal must be defined in order to set realistic bounds on what it can achieve. Both are important in determining the participants, thus paying due attention to the level of seniority, the range of skills and the extent of the responsibilities of institutional team members. The range of people to be interviewed from the community and to be involved in a programme of change requires equally careful consideration in terms of their scope of knowledge and influence, their credibility and representativeness, and their ability and willingness to engage in a dialogue with policy-makers. In order to secure the commitment from both sides, one has to return to the foundations of Rapid Appraisal;

- it has to be rapid, ensuring that findings and recommendations are timely and quickly available to decision-makers. This is particularly important in relation to the rapport and credibility that can be built up between institutions and communities through quick action;
- it has to be an appraisal which reflects the concerns of communities and the diversity within those communities;
- it has to be flexible, allowing the exploration of new ideas and options, tapping the creativity of all stakeholders and creating long-term and sustainable relationships which facilitate the exploitation of this creativity;
- emphasis on low costs. It can be argued that Rapid Appraisals are cheap in comparison with sample surveys and in terms of actual money being paid out. They are not cheap when opportunity costs are calculated, that is, managerial and community time during and following the appraisals. However, without a proper cost-effectiveness analysis the true cost and benefits of Rapid Appraisals cannot be established with certainty, but they appear to be good value for money in instituting rapid change and building capacity.

There is no set approach to offering feedback to the respondents and the community at large. The only rule is that meaningful feedback has to be given, both about the process and the outcome, in order to make the Rapid Appraisal transparent and to be accountable for the results of the exercise and its recommendations.

In most Rapid Appraisals a report is written about the process and the priority listings. This can be accompanied by a short summary or letter to be distributed to the whole community and backed up by an article in the local newspaper or a feature on the local radio. Public meetings have been used to discuss the findings or smaller meetings with specific interest groups. Again, the range of possibilities is endless and depends very much on the level of local interest and organizational structures.

The feedback process is often directly tied into the programme of change, especially when the medium of public meetings is used. Through these meetings discussions can take place between the Rapid Appraisal team and community groups about translating the findings into action. In many Rapid Appraisals a small number of actions are agreed, which can be achieved over a short time frame (usually six months) with clearly defined objectives, which involve both the community and one (or more) agencies and which are at or near the top of the priority listing. Some key priorities cannot be addressed because of their being too large-scale, beyond the scope of the organizations involved, taking too much time and so on. Agreement has to be reached about the timing and order of priority actions, the way in which they are planned and carried out and the involvement of individuals, groups and organizations. A clear division of labour also has to be agreed.

Some action plans are aimed at the community as a whole, others are for the benefit of particular groupings. It is advisable to find an acceptable balance between general and specific actions in order to maintain credibility with the community, and also to discuss the reasons behind the selection.

As the action plans all operate within a limited time frame, regular evaluation of progress is possible. A mechanism has to be found or devised to carry out such evaluations, which can be through established community groups or a specially created RA implementation group. Agreement has to be reached about the criteria for success and the way in which certain actions are brought to an end. Furthermore, there has to be an accepted approach to moving new priorities up the agenda and perhaps redefining priorities in the light of earlier achievements. It is essential to involve the community in the evaluation and re-ordering of priorities so that a sustained programme of action can be instigated and supported by both the community and the relevant organizations.

Reference
Holloway, A. and Lindsey, D. (1996) 'PRA for Risk Reduction: lessons from Mozambique', *PLA Notes 25*. IIED Sustainable Agriculture Programme, IIED, London, February.

13 Improving Coastal Zone Management

JOÃO SITÕE

The coastal zone of Mozambique stretches over 2,700 km from the Rovuma river mouth southwards to Ponta d'Ouro on the South African border. It contains rich ecosystems and considerable biodiversity and possesses enormous economic potential including tourism, transport, fishing and agriculture. Increasingly it is recognized that the coastal zone is under growing pressures which can undermine the sustainable use of its abundant natural resources, placing at risk its ecosystems and biodiversity.

This chapter will identify the main problems affecting this coastal zone and will endeavour to indicate some of the available opportunities for overcoming these constraints. The overall aim is to ensure sustainable development, by creating the necessary human resource capability both to conserve biodiversity and to improve the economic utilization of the natural resource base of the zone. Strategic planning for the coastal zone and an outline for an action plan will be set within the framework of the Government Programme for 1995 to 1999 and the National Environment Management Programme (NEMP). This chapter represents a modest contribution to what must be an inclusive, multi-disciplinary, on-going long-term initiative.

Mozambique lies between latitudes 10° 20'S and 26° 50'S on the east coast of Africa. It is separated from the island of Madagascar by the Mozambique Channel which at its narrowest point is 400 km wide. Whilst the continental shelf is generally narrow, it widens in the central part of the country to 130 km off the port of Beira. The coastline is deeply indented from the Rovuma River south to Maputo Bay and is generally lower-lying than in other East African countries, with 90% of the low coastal plain consisting of sand and mud stabilized by vegetation. The remaining 10% of the coast, mainly in the north, is formed from coral rock.

Twenty-five rivers discharge their flow into the Indian Ocean, each in an estuary with mangrove swamps. Dwarfing all other rivers is the mighty Zambezi in the centre of the country, discharging in the rainy season 15,000 to 20,000 cu m./s. of fresh water into the sea from January to March each year. Three rivers enter both the Bay of Maputo, the Limpopo, Incomati and Maputo, and the Bight of Sofala, the Buzi, Gorongosa and Save.

The climate is tropical humid to sub-humid with a dry winter season. North of the Zambezi, precipitation is strongly influenced by the southern end of the East African monsoon system. South of the Zambezi it is influenced by the Indian Ocean subtropical Anticyclone System of the south-east trade wind zone. Both systems overlap on the central coast between Beira and Pebane. Rainfall is highest in this central section of the coast – in Beira for instance it is 1,418 mm/annum – and is lowest along the southern sector – in Maputo it is 775 mm/annum. The coast as a whole is subject to the effects of high velocity storm winds which can create major changes in the shoreline over relatively short periods of time.

Currents with the greatest coastal influence are the Equatorial Current, the Mozambique Current and further south the Agulhas. The Mozambique Current passes close to the shore near Mossuril and Cabo das Corrents, attaining a velocity of more than 6 km/hour in October and November when the north-east monsoon is blowing. Large counter currents occur in the Bights of Sofala and Maputo. These form the north-facing peninsulas of Machangulo, Inhambane and Sao Sebastiao (Bazaruto). The Bazaruto Archipelago and Inhaca were once peninsula headlands of the mainland until, severed by wind and sea action, they became islands. The coast remains relatively well protected from open Indian Ocean wave action by the proximity of Madagascar; as a result there is considerable deposition and longshore transportation of river-derived sediments.

Tides are semi-diurnal to mixed, but mainly semi-diurnal. One of the highest ranges along the entire African coast is found at Beira (6.3 m) which is above average for coral reef shores and is influenced by the broad but shallow continental shelf at this point.

The coastal zone in relation to the national development strategy

Following the General Peace Agreement of 1992 and the multi-party democratic elections of 1994, the future effectiveness of the country's economic policies will depend crucially upon its ability to ensure the prevalence of a stable, predictable and supportive political and economic climate. Such a climate is a prerequisite for restoring productive activities, attracting foreign investment, turning the country's potentially rich natural resource endowment into a positive force for economic development and generally ensuring a more sustainable development future.

Rapid, sustained and equitable economic growth based on the private sector, agriculture, labour-intensive activities and increasing exports as a source of foreign exchange will in turn help reduce poverty, restore macroeconomic balances, regain external viability, strengthen the market economy and generally establish a firm foundation for national reconstruction, sustainable development and the consolidation of democracy. Traditional exports such as prawns and cashews are products of the coastal zone. Most of the population lives in the coastal zone. Hence the overall strategy for development is ultimately dependent on improving the management of the coastal zone. Itemized below are those aspects of government strategy which will have a particular impact on the coastal zone and any specific strategy that has been devised.

The general development objectives and priorities for the present government's period of office (1995–9) include:

- poverty alleviation and the promotion of sustainable human and economic development;
- improving human development indicators, with special attention being given to education, health, rural development, restoring essential services and rehabilitating social infrastructure and employment;
- decentralizing decision-making, and facilitating greater participation and freedom within institutions;
- ensuring a more balanced development of the different regions;
- encouraging and supporting foreign and national investment;
- increasing domestic production and reducing reliance on external aid;

- fostering growth in the private sector, reducing external imbalances by stimulating export activities and raising public sector efficiency

No less important than the definition of the overall development strategy is the reorganization of the state institutions to ensure that the institutional capacity exists to implement such a strategy. Such initiatives should include:

- professionalization of the public service within the framework of the Constitution;
- modernizing the state administration through: the creation of an adequate regulatory structure for the new institutional framework; instituting the necessary training components; clarifying administrative procedures and producing a code to enforce transparency and efficiency; debureaucratizing administrative procedures and encouraging a change in the approach and attitudes of civil servants; and promoting the participation of citizens in public administration;
- decentralization of the public administration by: substituting the former local government agencies with new municipal districts exercising administrative, financial, ownership and decision-making autonomy; and establishing mechanisms to create a better regional balance and inter-municipal solidarity to reduce the existing asymmetry between different regions of the country, namely, the interior and the coastal zone, rural and urban areas, and the north and the south.

In terms of the country's environment policy a serious step forward has been taken with the NEMP. Some of the most salient features for coastal zone management are the following:

- a national policy for the management of natural resources aiming to improve the quality of life of present and future generations in a sustainable manner requires: establishing environmental management capacity in all state sectors; incorporating environmental principles in all economic policies and development programmes; ensuring improved co-ordination at all levels, between the different sectors and between the national, provincial and local levels; decentralizing and democratizing the management of natural resources (i.e. through stakeholder consultations); implementing a widespread environmental consciousness-raising programme; establishing mechanisms for the surveillance and control of environmental changes and degradation.
- to achieve the government's objectives: the NEMP needs to be formally ratified and implemented in practice; the overall Environment Law needs to be passed and it has to be ensured that all the necessary sectoral legislation is passed and is compatible with the overall law; a contingency plan is required to meet any natural and man-made disasters.

In terms of the fisheries sector, the relevant strategy involves:

- ensuring an increasing supply for the internal market;
- ensuring increasing foreign-exchange-earning exports;
- improving the quality of life of the fishing community;
- the government's role to support the above objectives will be: to encourage the rational exploitation of fish resources and ensure sustainable utilization; to promote training; to ensure that quality control programmes are in place; to establish a surveillance system to promote conservation; to promote efficiency of the ship repair and shipbuilding industry and to create land infrastructure to ensure that activities supporting fisheries are operational; to promote artisanal fishery; to

promote the development of aquaculture; and to encourage the participation of the private sector in fishery production activities.

Tourism was in the past a major source of foreign exchange (in the 1960–74 period). The intention of the government is that a national tourism policy will help to maximize the economic and the social benefits from tourism. The government will aim to:

- improve the quality of the hotel industry;
- turn tourism into a significant foreign-exchange-earning industry;
- strengthen regional development based on the local tourist industry;
- promote internal tourism;
- contribute towards conservation by promoting national parks with a particular ecological and historical value;
- ensure adequate legislation to make Mozambique an attractive place for tourists.

The transport sector has a crucial role to play in the modernization of the country. Government policy includes:

- encouraging an improvement in road, rail, maritime and air transport;
- improving the infrastructure and conditions for the circulation of goods, particularly maritime coastal transport;
- transforming the Nacala, Beira and Maputo corridors into centres for national development;
- developing port infrastructure.

Concerning mineral resources, the government has undertaken to revise mining legislation, in particular as it relates to the small-scale sector, and is actively encouraging private sector investment. Proposed activities include:

- surveying and issuing geological charts of the country and of the continental platforms, and creating a mines inventory in the northern part of the country;
- geological surveys and feasibility studies of heavy sands in the coastal zones of Pebane-Moabase, Micaúne-Deia and Angoche;
- developing Pande natural gas;
- continuing studies in the Limpopo River area to determine resource potential;
- organizing promotional campaigns to attract on-shore and off-shore petroleum research investment.

Constraints and opportunities

Defining the terrain
Improving the management of the coastal zone, in whichever country in the world it is undertaken, is always going to be difficult, as this is where the competing sectoral demands upon the ecological systems and the natural resource base are at their most intense. A critical first step involves actually defining what is the coastal zone. Currently there is no clear legal definition of this in Mozambique. On the ocean side and based on the principles of the UN Convention on the Law of the Sea, Mozambique has claimed 12 km for its territorial waters and 200 nautical miles for an exclusive economic zone. Following the country's independence this was passed first through Decree Law No. 31/76 and later by Law No. 04/96, known as the 'Law of the Sea', as approved by the National Assembly. This provides a jurisdictional definition of Mozambique's coastal waters.

In addition, there exists a definition of the public domain maritime lane or zone (*orla marítima*), comprising a 100-meter wide shoreline strip, as measured from the maximum hightide level horizontally inland. This definition is enshrined in Law of the Land No. 16/87 and in the Law of the Sea No. 04/96.

Beyond these existing legal definitions and instruments, there is a far more complex situation on the landward side. The broader littoral area contains the country's two major cities and the majority of the population, thus exerting a massive impact upon coastal zone activities, both directly and indirectly. What happens in the coastal zone significantly affects the livelihoods of Mozambique's population.

The coastal zone is the site of rich renewable natural resources, it produces potentially the highest foreign-exchange earnings from fishing, tourism, and transit trade port and shipping activity. At the same time, there is non-renewable natural resource potential in mining which can also be exploited. There is an uncomfortable juxtaposition of rich biodiversity (fauna and fisheries), population density and intensity of social and economic activities. Inevitably the overlapping of interests can create potential conflicts. The coastal ecosystems are also particularly fragile and vulnerable. In addition, there is a multiplicity of state administrative structures including district administrations, municipal councils, maritime administrations and of course provincial and central government ministries and agencies.

Given the complexity of the situation outlined above, it is clearly no easy task to arrive at a functional definition of the coastal zone within which an effective management strategy could be put into operation. To arrive at a more operational definition, the following elements are put forward for consideration. The coastal zone is that area where the land, sea and atmosphere interact. It includes the land area from the shoreline up to the jurisdictional boundaries of the administrative coastal districts. On the oceanic side it extends to the jurisdictional boundaries of the ocean waters of the Republic of Mozambique. It is quintessentially the interface zone between the ocean and the land. This includes the fragile but essential coastal dunes, mangroves, coral reefs and sea-grass beds.

Identifying the stakeholders
Multiple activities take place in the coastal zone. Most people have their homes there, with all the attendant needs for water, sanitation, transport, health care, education, job opportunities and so on. Economic activities include: fishing; tourism; shipping, with the ports and shipyards; mining; salt production; construction; agriculture; and hunting and gathering. Stakeholder groups are multiple and exhibit various levels of organization and articulation of their interests. The following list is indicative rather than exhaustive: fishermen, fishing companies, tourism enterprises from the large to the smallest scale, shipping enterprises again from the mega to the minute, mining companies, salters, builders, farmers, hunters, commercial traders, and so it goes on.

Government institutions involved in coastal zone management, planning, surveillance and research, and with other responsibilities are the following:

i)   Ministry of Transport and Communications
  - SAFMAR (Maritime Administration)
  - National Institute of Hydrography and Navigation (Navigation Aids)
  - National Meteorological Institute
  - National Institute of Teleco
  - National Maritime Directorate
ii) Ministry of Agriculture and Fisheries
  - National Directorate of Forestry and Wildlife
  - National Directorate of Geography and Cadastre and National Institute for Physical Planning
  - Fisheries Research Institute

- National Directorate for Fishery Administration
iii) Ministry of Commerce, Industry and Tourism
  - National Directorate of Tourism
  - Department of Commerce
iv) Ministry for the Co-ordination of Environmental Action
v) Eduardo Mondlane University (Inhaca Island coastal reserve)
vi) Ministry of Health
vii) Ministry of State Administration
  - District administrations
  - Municipal Councils of the coastal zone
viii) Ministry of Mineral Resources and Energy
ix) Ministry of National Defence
x) Ministry of Planning and Finance
xi) Ministry of Co-operation and Foreign Affairs
xii) Ministry of Housing and Public Construction

Finally there are also the various local authorities: district administrations, municipal councils, the maritime administration and local representatives of the central and provincial organs of government. There are, in other words, multiple stakeholders involved in any coastal zone management exercise.

Aquatic habitats, biodiversity and fishing
Mozambique's coast can be divided into three zones. The northern third, stretching from Rovuma to Angoche, comprises a relatively narrow rocky or coral line continental shelf. The central third, from Angoche to Bazaruto, is where the outflow of the Zambezi, Pungue and Save rivers has created a muddy or sandy shelf. The southern third, from Bazaruto to Ponta d'Ouro, has a rocky bottom.

Marine habitats can be classified as offshore or coastal. There are five major offshore habitats. First, there is the deep ocean outside the slopes of the continental shelf which includes the ocean waters of the Mozambique Channel and contains important tuna and pelagic fish resources. Secondly, there are the hard bottoms of the continental slopes, yielding fish and lobsters, mainly in the southern and northern thirds of the country. Thirdly, the soft bottoms of the continental shelf provide the valuable deep-water shrimp, crayfish and crab resources, principally in the area stretching from Angoche to Ponta d'Ouro. Fourthly, there are the rocky bottoms and reef systems of the continental shelf which contain under-exploited stocks of prime fish, mainly in the northern and southern thirds of the country. Finally, the soft bottoms of the continental shelf are heavily exploited for shrimp and small demersal fish, mainly from Angoche to Chiloane.

There are four distinct coastal habitats. Enclosed bays, lagoons and estuaries provide the first category. These areas possess crustacean and finfish resources and also include coastal swamps and wetlands which serve as important breeding grounds for fish and bird life. Secondly, there are the sandy beaches yielding harvests of small demersal fish and of penaeide and non-penaeide shrimp and bivalves. This area has the relatively fragile sand dunes which are so important for the prevention of coastal erosion. Thirdly, there are the mangrove swamps, essential breeding grounds for many species. They also provide the mangrove crab and a timber resource which is heavily overused in some locations. Mangroves form an important barrier against coastal erosion but offer a tempting target for the fast growing shrimp aquaculture industry. Finally, there are the atolls and coral reefs which in all probability have a greater potential as a tourist resource than for commercial fisheries.

Inland water bodies include rivers and associated flood plains containing stocks of cichlids, carp and catfish and lakes and swamps with important resources of kapenta (Cabora Bass) and ornamental fish (Niassa).

Coastal conservation areas
Considering the diversity of habitats along the length of the Mozambican coastline and the economic importance of the littoral waters, remarkably few coastal areas are under protection status. The largest proclaimed area, the Marromeu Reserve (150,000 ha) located in the Zambezi deltaic system, comprises mangrove swamps, freshwater swamps and flood plains. The large populations of buffalo that once inhabited the flood plain system in this reserve have been significantly reduced. The Maputo Elephant Reserve (70,000 ha) was proclaimed a reserve in 1960 in order to protect the elephant population; again this was severely reduced during the recent armed conflict.

The only other coastal areas with conservation status are the Bazaruto National Park (8,000 ha), the Pomene Reserve (20,000 ha) and the Inhaca and Portuguese Island Reserves. The first and only true marine national park in Mozambique was proclaimed in 1971, namely, the two islands of the Bazaruto Archipelago, Benguera and Margaruque Islands, with a peripheral 5 km marine zone. The largest island of the Archipelago, Bazaruto Island, is not included in the park.

Tinley *et al.* (1976) have usefully proposed several conservation areas along the Mozambique coast including:

i) the Primeira and Segundo Archipelago. These islands are considered a top priority to receive conservation status.

ii) the mainland area opposite the Primeira Islands, between Moebase and Ponta Lipobane. These have evergreen moist forest, dunes, mangrove estuaries and coast savanna.

iii) between Ibo Island and the point opposite Pemba on the north side of the Bay, including the islands and the mainland with bays, coral, and rock cliffs with coast thicket of *Guiabourtia schliebenni*.

iv) between Nacala and Mossuril, the mainland coast between Ponta Melano and Matibane Village including the islands, fringing reefs and Quitangonha Island. The latter island is an important bird nesting site. Part of the area is already Forestry Reserve (Reserva Florestal de Matibane).

v) between Missangage River and Ponta Mituasi, which has an undisturbed forest and sand dune coast.

vi) the peninsula stub of the greater peninsula which gave rise to the Bazaruto Islands. This possesses sea turtle nesting beaches, flamingo nesting areas, cycad populations, undisturbed brachystegia coast savanna and dune thicket.

vii) between Cape Correntes and the Limpopo Mouth, there is a large freshwater barrier lake, high forest covering parabolic dune systems, and dune rock outcrops. The area should include one of the sites containing endemic freshwater fish.

viii) important coral reefs such as the Pinda Coral Reef (fringing coral), the fringing reefs off the peninsula south of the Lurio River Mouth (Ponta Metacua and Serisse) and between Pemba and Mecufi.

In addition to these sites suggested by Tinley and his colleagues, the possibility of extending the conservation status of the mainland area in (iv) above to include Ilha de Mozambique, currently a Cultural World Heritage site, has also been recommended.

Fisheries: constraints and opportunities

The coast is a complex and fragile ecological zone that faces the most profound environmental problems in the country. There are multiple demands upon the resource base and inevitable conflicts over resource use which act to the detriment of sustainable development. Approximately 100,000 people are directly or indirectly employed in the fisheries sector. Assuming that each employed person is a member of a household of 6.7 people, a total of 670,000 people, or approximately 4% of the Mozambique population, are in some way dependent on the living aquatic resources of the country to sustain their livelihoods. An even greater proportion of the population rely on the catch for an important part of their protein input. There has been a steady decrease year by year from 1986 to 1994 in the total catch, mainly for those products contributing most to foreign-exchange earnings.

Let us first examine the potential constraints to improving the management of the fishery resource. The living aquatic resources of Mozambique are common-property resources with multiple competing users. Conflicts of interest frequently arise between the different user groups, as between sporting and commercial fishermen, say, and require a degree of management to minimize these conflicts. There is considerable local resentment against foreign fishermen who, under the cover of 'tourism', remove a considerable quantity of fish for commercial purposes, taking advantage of the weak institutional capacity for control and surveillance of all fishing activities.

Near the major cities, disposal of untreated sewage is already causing problems regarding the quality of fish for human consumption. Future economic development may worsen the situation with additional industrial waste being added to the existing pollution of the coastal city waters.

Commercial fishing, shell hunting and harvesting of corals and ornamental fish can cause long-term damage to coral reefs and reduce their value as tourist attractions. Rare and vulnerable marine species and communities, such as the dugong and five species of marine turtles, are under threat. Corals are damaged by irresponsible scuba divers who take advantage of the existing institutional weaknesses concerning control and surveillance.

Overfishing is a major problem, as artisanal fishermen are obliged by their poverty to stay in the inshore waters. They have neither the boats nor the engines to venture further out to sea. There is both overfishing and non-sustainable shellfish collection along many parts of the shoreline. Commercial exploitation of the crustacean resource is reaching its limits. Destruction of the mangroves for timber and firewood extraction destroys nurseries both for fish and for the most important of the country's exports, prawns.

Land-based activities causing pollution in coastal ecosystems include the use of agricultural pesticides and agrochemicals, dams and untreated domestic and industrial waste, all of which pour into the inshore waters of the coastal cities with negative effects on health, the fishing industry and tourist potential.

The exploitation both of petroleum resources off the continental shelf and of the mineral sands of the Pebane/Moma area could have a potentially negative environmental impact with consequences for the shrimp industry. There also appears to be an ill-defined relationship between the outflow of the Zambezi (with water release from the Cabora Bassa hydropower plant) and the shrimp stocks. Similarly the exploitation of undersea gas and oil in the Bazaruto area could have a deleterious effect on the fishing and tourist industries. Development of shrimp aquaculture could destroy large expanses of mangrove, reduce biodiversity and deprive communities of important firewood resources and natural barriers to erosion.

The real potential of the existing aquatic resources and ecosystems is unknown.

The necessary qualified human and financial resources to carry out a proper resource assessment are lacking. There is weak institutional capacity to implement a proposed Master Plan if approved.

Let us turn now to the opportunities. As we saw in Chapter 11, the 1990 Constitution is very explicit about the environment. The NEMP document outlines the environmental measures necessary to ensure successful and sustainable long-term development. To date these have been neglected. The financial benefit of Mozambique's living aquatic resources in the mid-1990s can be summarized as follows: industrial fishing, US$70 million per year; artisanal and subsistence fishing $40m. per year; leisure activities and tourism, $5–10m. per year. Potential for economic expansion in the sector will depend upon the creation of investment and marketing opportunities for the small-scale fishermen, as defined in the Fisheries Master Plan. In that Plan, no major expansion in the industrial harvest of crustacea is envisaged and development is likely to occur through the export of value-added products, rather than of raw materials, as is currently the case. A gradual expansion in shrimp and freshwater aquaculture is likely.

Tourism

A number of constraints operate against a more sustainable development of the tourism sector. There is a lack of institutional capacity to guide tourist activities sensibly in the coastal zone, and indeed more generally. There is a lack of co-ordination between the central government and the local authorities, either with the municipalities or with the local Maritime Administration or Maritime Delegation, to ensure proper regulation of tourists' behaviour. Beaches are being degraded by tourists camping in places where they are not allowed, such as on the fragile dunes. As noted above, commercial fishing, shell hunting and harvesting of corals are being damaged by scuba-divers, and foreign fishermen, under the cover of sporting pursuits, remove fish for commercial purposes. Generally improvements are required both in legislation and in the capacity to enforce existing legislation, including having adequate and trained personnel.

In spite of these constraints, a considerable number of opportunities do exist. Tourist potential is excellent if the natural assets of the coastal zone and nature reserves can be conserved. Tourism offers a powerful source of foreign exchange. A policy is in place and there are growing signs of an expansion in the tourist industry. Continued affluence in South Africa could encourage a significant expansion of the tourist industry including underwater safaris, sailing and other water-based leisure activities.

The NEMP indicates the outline of a strategy to make tourism a sustainable activity. A Tourism Facilitation Commission, created by Decree No. 32/95, could contribute to improved intersectoral co-ordination. To be effective it needs to involve the following ministries: Industry, Trade and Tourism (chairperson), Planning and Finance, Foreign Affairs and Co-operation, Home Affairs, Agriculture and Fisheries, Co-ordination of Environmental Action, Transport and Communications, and Culture, Youth and Sports.

Under the Commission there is a Technical Council chaired by the Vice-Minister of Industry, Trade and Tourism. Representatives of the following national directorates are involved: Tourism; Customs; Civil Aviation: Road Transport; Maritime Affairs; Wildlife and Forestry; Geography and Land Use Planning; Co-ordination of Environmental Action; Culture; Migration, plus representatives of the General Police Command, the Tourism Fund, tourist operators, hotels and transport services.

Marine pollution

During the last thirty years the pollution of the world's oceans has become a matter of increasing international concern. Most of it comes from land-based sources and includes industrial by-products, run-off from agricultural pesticides and herbicides and effluents discharged from urban areas.

A series of problems will have to be overcome in order to allow coastal land and water resources to fulfil their sustainable development potential. Discharge of untreated industrial and domestic wastes will have to be dealt with, along with inadequate design standards for projects located within fragile coastal environments. Environmental assessments are needed to provide information on the most appropriate locations for development initiatives and the combinations of use best suited to them. Greater emphasis is required on opportunities for multiple use in coastal and marine resource systems. There is an obvious need to improve co-ordination between agencies, which currently tend to concentrate individually on single-purpose exclusive use. There is a shortage of technical and administrative skills amongst the people responsible for managing the diverse aspects of the coastal zone. Legislation needs to be properly elaborated. Public awareness also needs to be raised concerning the important role of marine and coastal resources in supporting national economic and social objectives.

Use of pesticides, herbicides and synthetic organic chemicals should be rigorously controlled and the adoption of integrated pest management accelerated. Sedimentation needs to be reduced by controlling land clearance and limiting deforestation. The flow of nutrients to coastal waters should be maintained by careful control of existing or future initiatives to impound river flows, notably by the creation of dams. The direct discharge of industrial and municipal wastes into the ocean is a significant threat to the local coastal and marine environment adjacent to the main urban centres, in particular Maputo, Inhambane, Beira, Quelimane, Nacala and Pemba. The environmental risks will increase considerably if the Matola refinery near Maputo comes into operation, both as a result of the operations of the plant itself and of the increase in tanker traffic in the Matola Channel. Attention must be paid to the provision of anti-pollution measures and traffic control in any plan to re-establish the refinery.

Domestic sewage is an important source of pollution in coastal waters adjacent to major population centres. Discharges into the surf zone are not dispersed but tend to spread in the shallow water along the coast and may give rise to serious contamination problems along bathing beaches. In most coast cities part of the drainage system, including the sewage system, leads directly into the sea without any adequate treatment. There is no precise indication of the quantities involved but sewage is one of the major sources of organic and bacteriological pollution in the port areas. In the absence of arrangements to monitor sewage and drainage effluents, it is impossible to construct reliable estimates of pathogenic organisms or toxic leachates.

Agriculture may also represent a significant source of pollution in the coastal waters. Any agricultural chemicals used within river drainage systems may enter the coastal and marine environment adjacent to the mouth of the rivers. Despite the widespread use of pesticides, there is no policy to prevent or control the use of hazardous agricultural materials.

Siltation also results from beach sand mining and from quarrying for limestone adjacent to the coast. Such disturbance to coastal landforms also poses the threat of erosion and further destabilization of the coastal sand dunes. The main problem along most of the coast is erosion. The impact of increased silt load upon the coral systems can be very severe and can significantly reduce their ability to support fish stocks.

The main current constraint is that legislation is not being enforced and also needs updating. Those employed to implement the rules that do exist have not been properly trained and motivated and they lack transportation and other means to make their work effective.

Opportunities do exist, however. The Montreal Guidelines for the Protection of the Marine Environment against Pollution from land-based sources, drafted by UNEP, could provide the basis for Southern African regional conventions as well as for the development of national policy and legislation. The NEMP, supported by an effective legislative framework, could have an important impact if it was properly disseminated down to the district and municipality levels. Polluting industries need to pay a higher levy, with the funds raised thereby being made available to local authorities for the installation of treatment facilities.

Pollution from ships
To date coastal pollution from ships has been limited. However, there is the notable exception of the *Katina P* oil tanker spill of 1992, when about 3,000 tons of heavy fuel oil polluted parts of the coast around Maputo Bay. Whilst being the most serious recorded occurrence in recent history, this is by no means an isolated incident. Reported accidents include M/T *Dimini I* and M/V *Shin Kakogawa Maru* in 1994, M/V *Maine* in 1981, M/T *Ryoyoshi*, *Matchedji* and *Amazena* in 1980, M/V *Churabe* and M/T *Regis Trade* in 1979 and M/T *Edinburgh* in 1978.

In addition to these accidents, a significant amount of pollution is caused by shipping and maritime activities generally. In tonnage terms, the most important pollutant resulting from shipping operations is oil. The most common pollution incidents occur during terminal operations when oil is being loaded or discharged – perhaps as much as 92% of oil spills, according to figures published by the International Tanker Owners Pollution Federation (ITOPF). A much greater quantity of oil enters the sea as a result of normal tanker operations, usually associated with the cleaning of cargo residues (clingage) which takes place when the ship is returning from the port of discharge to take on another cargo of oil. Other causes of marine oil pollution include tank cleaning in connection with dry docking, bilge and fuel oil (from dry cargo ships as well as tankers) and non-tanker accidents.

Many of the chemicals transported by sea are far more dangerous to the marine environment than the pollution by oil which has been the most public concern. Chemical substances may constitute an environmental threat which bears no relation to the size of the unit in which they are carried. As an example, polychlorinated biphenyls (PCBs) are potentially so harmful that the International Maritime Organization (IMO) has recommended that their bulk carriage should be banned, not only because they are a pollution threat but because they can be extremely hazardous to ships and equipment and, most importantly, to people. The amount of noxious substances carried at sea is only a fraction of the amount of oil transported each year. Many are carried in bulk form in tankers specially designed for the purpose.

Garbage and sewage from ships have traditionally been dumped into the sea and in relation to the amount of similar wastes poured into the sea each year from the land, the quantities in the past were not considered excessive. Today, however, the situation is very different because of the growing everyday use of substances like plastic which are non-biodegradable. Once thrown into the sea they can stay there for years.

Dumping in any circumstances, of certain highly dangerous substances such as mercury, cadmium, high level radioactive waste and substances produced for biological or chemical warfare, should be prohibited.

The Mozambique Channel is a well established ocean route which is compulsory for laden tankers. As far back as 1981, 70,000 million ton-miles of crude oil traffic was crossing Mozambique's waters. A mean of 450 million tons of hydrocarbon products pass through the channel, representing one third of the world's tanker traffic (1.3 billion tons). Every year about 5,000 tankers pass through the Mozambique Channel, including 1,200 Very Large Crude Carrier tankers (VLCC) of 200,000 tons or more.

Given this high level of ocean traffic there is a clear vulnerability to potential accidents. The extent of the impact of any significant oil spillage will depend on the pattern of ocean currents and the predominant winds. The possibility of an oil tanker disaster as a result of a collision, hurricanes or human error is very high. The *Katina P* accident which spilled substantial amounts of oil into Maputo Bay in April 1992 caused significant environmental damage and losses to the public and private sectors of the economy including: fisheries, salt pans, tourism, the power station, government agencies, the costs of the clean-up, etc.

No contingency plan for a marine pollution accident is in place. There is as yet no National Programme for Management of the Coastal Zone (NPMCZ). Nor is there adequate compensation legislation for oil spill damage.

Nevertheless, a number of opportunities exist in spite of the constraints. The National Administration and Maritime Surveillance Authority (SAFMAR) was created by Decree No. 34/94, replacing the old 'capitanias dos portos'. It is administratively autonomous in its exercise of maritime authority, and aims to enforce maritime safety regulations, ensure surveillance, and prevent and combat marine pollution in waters under the jurisdiction of the Republic of Mozambique.

The NEMP lists nine international conventions to which Mozambique adheres. Under Resolutions 23 to 26/94 the government approved the following additional international conventions: the Civil Liability Convention (1971) for hydrocarbon spill compensation; the Fund Convention (1969), also for hydrocarbon spills; the International Convention on Search and Rescue at Sea (1979); and the International Conventions on Safety of Life at Sea (1974 and 1978). There is still an on-going process of finalizing the acceding instruments with the International Maritime Organization (IMO) in London. The legal framework to develop maritime legislation in Mozambique is contained in the Maritime Law Decree No. 04/96, the 'Law of the Sea'.

It has been recognized for many years that marine pollution from ships, which affects so many nations, can only be satisfactorily tackled through an international marine forum like the IMO. IMO international Conventions tackle the problem of marine pollution in a number of ways, including the following:

(a) **Preventing operational pollution**. This can result, for example, from the discharge of oil-water mixtures resulting from tank cleaning directly into the sea. Anti-pollution measures have been introduced into the design, equipment and operation of ships.

(b) **Reducing accidents**. This is principally achieved by enforcing strict standards and navigational procedures on a world-wide basis. While principally aimed at making shipping safer, these measures have a secondary advantage in that they also help cut pollution resulting from accidents.

(c) **Reducing the consequences of accidents**. Measures have been introduced which are designed to lessen the amount of pollution resulting from an accident, e.g. by limiting the size of tanks and thereby limiting the amount of oil entering the sea in the event of a tanker going aground or being involved in a collision.

(d) **Providing compensation**. The costs of pollution can be enormous. A series of measures have been adopted to enable victims of pollution to be compensated for their losses.

(e) **Helping implementation.** The IMO has provided technical and other assistance to governments in developing contingency plans for countering pollution.

Agriculture
The primary constraints are the consequence of the population concentration in the coastal zone. This population pressure has a number of negative environmental effects. There is depletion of the mangroves, clearing of vegetation cover more generally, increased river sedimentation, and erosion, and some traditional agricultural practices such as burning reduce soil fertility. Given that the key constraint is the population concentration, there are insufficient incentives to encourage people to return to their homes in the interior now that peace has been restored. There is also a lack of institutional capacity to monitor and alleviate the situation. The key opportunity here lies in involving local communities in improving resource management, in the many ways discussed elsewhere in this book.

Coastal erosion Mangrove destruction causes reduced coastal protection. Mozambique is one of ten countries most at risk from rising sea water levels as a result of global warming, with extensive low-lying coastal plains subject to storms and extremely high tidal rises. The majority of the coast is of the soft type, vulnerable to erosion. Shifting cultivation leads to deforestation and destabilizes sand dunes, increasing the risks of dune encroachment along the coastline. Inadequate management of dams exacerbates the problems, along with inadequate management of mining activities. Further causes of coastal erosion include the practice of agriculture on marginal land and allowing four-wheel-drive cars on beaches or dunes: the erosion occurs mainly in Maputo, Xai-Xai, Beira, Nacala and Pemba.

Constraints in tackling these problems involve the usual combination of a lack of skilled personnel and of institutional co-ordination. Opportunities lie in training, improving co-ordination, effective decentralization and involvement of local communities in erosion control.

Mining
Uncontrolled mining can contribute to coastal erosion with all the attendant consequences, permanently altering ecosystems. Particular caution will need to be exercised as mining for the exploitation of heavy metal sands is planned to take place in the coastal zone at Congolone, Nampula, Moebase-Mecalonga, Zambezia and at Xai-Xai-Chonguene, Gaza.

Key constraints involve a lack of updated legislation and enforcement capacity but opportunities exist to tackle both problems (see the chapters on mining in this book).

Coastal engineering management
Coastal engineering is a branch of civil engineering established in co-operation with scientists of other related fields such as oceanography, meteorology, geography and geology, and it leans heavily on fluid mechanics, electronics, structural mechanics, and other disciplines. Previously this type of work was considered to be marine civil engineering port and harbour engineering. Novices in the field should proceed with caution. Along the coastlines of the world, numerous engineering works in various stages of disintegration testify to the futility and wastefulness of disregarding the tremendous destructive forces of the sea. Far worse than the destruction of insubstantial coastal works has been the damage to adjacent shorelines caused by structures planned in ignorance of, and occasionally in disregard of, the shoreline processes operative in the area.

Research fields within coastal engineering may be classified as coastal hydraulics, coastal sediments and coastal structures. The coastal hydraulics field includes work on: understanding waves and currents, coastal and estuary phenomena and the processes of circulation of water and pollutants in the near shore environment. The coastal sediments and coastal structures field includes work on understanding the mechanisms of coastal sediment movement and finding solutions to the related engineering problems in the coastal zone. The coastal structure field includes establishing guidance for the effective design and construction practices of coastal structures and determining the impact of the construction of coastal structures on the littoral zone.

The subjects treated in coastal engineering have expanded to include not only harbour and coastal protection works but also the development and environmental preservation of the coastal zones. In related coastal zone engineering and management works, the impact on the biological environment as well as on the physical aspects of the shoreline is now being taken seriously. Therefore coastal engineering, given its intrinsic interdisciplinary nature, benefits from inputs from other related fields such as chemistry, biology, fisheries science and environmental engineering.

The problems dealt with in coastal engineering are generally complicated. An approach based on site-specific case studies is therefore the most effective means of determining the on-going natural processes and furthering an understanding of both the natural laws and possible sustainable solutions.

Along Mozambique's coastal zone, mainly in the urban areas, there is considerable barrier destruction, for example in Maputo, Xai-Xai, Beira, Nacala and Pemba. Barriers to littoral transport can be either natural, e.g. rocky headlands or sediment sinks, or man-made, e.g. harbour piers. The natural barriers have been in existence for thousands of years. Man-made structures have been in place only for the last hundred years or less and they will in all likelihood disappear within the next few hundred years, although new structures will undoubtedly be constructed. However, while the man-made structures exist, these 'artificial' barriers – harbour piers and dredged navigational channels, for example – may alter the natural transport patterns. Dredging and mining can have significant impacts on sedimentation and littoral processes. Material is lost to the littoral zone when it is dredged from navigable waters (channels and harbour entrances) within a littoral cell and dumped outside the cell, such as at landfill areas or in deep water.

Given the desire of much of humanity to live as close to the sea as possible, coastal protection works are sometimes carried out with the objective of protecting property or shore lands from coastal erosion, or at least postponing further erosion for a generation or two. Coastal protection may be carried out in the nearshore, backshore, and onshore locations on the shore zone, as well as in the dune fields.

Generally, protection works are engineered methods, either structural or non-structural, and are called in the literature 'hard' or 'soft'. Structural protection methods involve the construction and placement of additional materials or structures on the eroding shoreline, such as revetments, seawalls, dykes, groynes, detached breakwaters, headlands, beach nourishment and/or a combination of these. All structural protection works may be considered 'hard' solutions, apart from beach nourishment (or beach fill), which is considered 'soft' protection. Non-structural protection methods include: relocation (inland), floodproofing, dune enhancement, bluff grading and vegetation.

Structural protection works are commonly associated with impacts on the natural physical environment. Proper attention must therefore be paid during the early phases of a project to ensuring that the effects of the proposed works on the coastline are taken into account. In contrast, non-structural methods tend to have little or no impact on the existing shore processes.

Constraints on coastal protection include the non-existence of a coastal engineering management policy, lack of national expertise in coastal engineering management, and a lack of the necessary instruments and institutional co-ordination to insist on effective EIAs in project approval processes.

Opportunities do exist. Mozambican civil engineers can obtain top-up qualifications in coastal engineering management abroad. The Ministry of Housing and Public Construction can co-ordinate efforts through its provincial directorates.

Institutional issues
Government institutions with functions related to the coastal zone include the following:

Ministry of Transport and Communications

- SAFMAR
- National Institute of Hydrography and Navigation, which functions to facilitate the operation and maintenance of navigational aids (charts, tide tables, navigation warnings, hydrography surveys, and other scientific research)
- National Meteorological Institute for research and weather forecasts
- National Institute of Telecommunications which grants licences to all radio stations and all vessels registered under the Mozambique flag.

Ministry of Agriculture and Fisheries

- National Directorate of Forestry and Wildlife is meant, through its provincial directorates, to carry out the planning, management and surveillance of coastal reserves and mangroves, with responsibility for the flora and fauna
- National Agronomic Research Institute
- Fisheries Research Institute
- National Directorate for Fishery Administration
- National Directorate of Geography and Cadastre undertakes, through its provincial directorates, planning and surveillance of the coastal land.

Ministry of Commerce, Industry and Tourism

- National Directorate of Tourism

Ministry of State Administration

- District Administrations of the coastal zone (around 43) and the Municipal Councils of the coastal cities grant authorizations for land use.

Ministry for the Co-ordination of Environmental Action

- The Ministry is playing a growing role in trying to initiate more co-ordinated coastal zone management nationwide. It has a coastal zone management unit.

Ministry of Housing and Public Works

- Management and planning of housing, roads, bridges and public infrastructure

Eduardo Mondlane University

- Through its Maritime Biology station it runs the maritime reserve on Inhaca island.

Institutional difficulties are a central feature of the country's coastal zone management problems. There is no co-ordinated intervention by the various government agencies in the research, management, planning, or surveillance of coastal resources or with enforcement of existing legislation. Intervention takes place in a disorganized manner which encourages disturbances in the coastal ecosystems and inappropriate exploitation of the natural resources. Integrated sustainable management of the coastal zone is currently conspicuous by its absence.

No authority exists to co-ordinate management of the coastal zone. It is true that there are a number of government functions, i.e. management, economic or physical planning, surveillance and research on the different and specific activities in the coastal zone. Yet these initiatives exist in parallel rather than being co-ordinated, and all too often they are not being carried out in the manner required. A clearer geographical definition of the coastal zone is necessary in order to set some spatial parameters to facilitate improved co-ordination.

Another pressing concern is the granting of land-use concessions for the different activities in the coastal zone. There are no clearly established procedures for who should do what. One example of this is land-use authorization in the maritime zone of the public domain. Confusion over authority can exist between the Municipal Council, the district administrations, the Maritime Administrations and sometimes with the central level of some government agencies.

Given the absence of adequate research, there is much uncertainty concerning the actual natural resource potential of the coastal zone, the exact requirements to protect the existing biodiversity, the extent to which any resources are 'under' or 'over' exploited. Several government agencies are involved in research into, and the management of, coastal resources. However, there is no mechanism for them to collaborate in research, management, planning, surveillance and enforcement.

Pollution, either from land-based activities or other disturbances like deforestation, erosion, tourism, mining, overfishing of certain species, etc., is undermining the sustainable environment of the coastal zone. Surveillance and enforcement of the existing legislation by different institutions are matters of great concern. Lack of means/equipment, financial resources, and qualified and motivated human resources are constraints common to all of Mozambique's institutions.

Lack of institutional capacity for improved natural resource conservation and sustainable development planning, insufficient qualified human resources, the absence of intersectoral co-ordination, and excessive centralization in planning and management summarize the main institutional problems and constraints in the coastal zone. Notwithstanding the zone's ecological and economic importance, no national policy for the integrated and sustainable management of the coastal resources is in place.

These problems and constraints call for improved management of the coastal zone in Mozambique. A programme and an action plan are recommended, which aim to establish a Coastal Zone Authority for the improved management and planning of the different activities taking place in the zone. Finally, there is a lack of co-ordination and of instruments to impose EIAs on coastal engineering projects.

Very little sectoral legislation demands EIAs before granting licences for activities. Most of the legislation needs to be updated:

- Maritime Oil Pollution law No. 495/73 needs updating and its content is poor. This instrument proposed a National Commission for Combating Oil Pollution at Sea, yet this Commission has never been established.
- Land Law. The state owns all land; people can obtain 50-year use rights but this situation limits any individual incentive to invest for sustainability. Peasants do not have to obtain a legal land title. Inevitably there are conflicts between the two systems, one formal and the other informal. There is no clear picture on who, what and when anyone can act in the granting of land use.
- The Fishing Law proclaims that surveillance of fishing activities is a function of the Fishery Authority. This surveillance capacity does not exist, however, and the

system being used is extremely weak. There is neither the equipment nor the human resources with the capacity to undertake such a function.

Other conventions related to maritime oil pollution need to be considered sooner rather than later. These are the following:

- MARPOL 1973 plus its Protocol of 1978. This regulates measures to prevent oil pollution from ships and to minimize oil pollution in case of an accident with a laden tanker.
- OPPRC 1990 Oil Pollution Preparedness, Response and Co-operation should facilitate international co-operation in the event of a major oil pollution disaster.

A considerable number of opportunities do exist. The NEMP is not sufficiently well known and needs dissemination at all levels amongst planners and managers. There can be implementation of the NEMP Capacity 21 Project at all levels. The National Council for Sustainable Development should begin to function effectively. The coastal zone management unit (CZMU) of MICOA can be developed, involving representatives of all government institutions involved in the coastal zone. A levy should be collected from all economic activities taking place in the coastal zone in order to secure a budget for the CZMU and for financing research. Training at university level abroad in coastal engineering can be explored. With regard to the Investment Law, investment projects are required to pass an EIA. Under the Municipal Law the municipalities will be the main environment managers and co-ordinators. According to the Water Law, major water projects require EIAs. Under the Mining Law the Ministry of Mines is obliged to consult MICOA on EIAs before issuing any licence. In addition to the nine international conventions listed in the NEMP, four others have been acceded to.

A series of legislative measures discussed previously are in train. The Fisheries Research Institute is currently upgrading academic staff training and recruiting newly graduated fisheries biologists, reflecting the importance of the fisheries sector to the national economy. Several Mozambican scientists at the UEM are currently carrying out research into coastal systems for their M.Sc. and/or PhD degrees. Research areas include marine mammal ecology, crustacean biology, phytoplankton zooplankton dynamics, sea grass ecology, marine pollution and coastal forest ecology. Most of the UEM higher degree-level research is supported by Swedish aid. Once they are qualified, expertise in coastal zone ecology, planning and management will be greatly enhanced.

A number of comprehensive environmental mapping and inventory activities and pilot projects have recently been undertaken in the coastal zone or are under way, the most important being:

(a) **The Mecufi Coastal Zone Management Project.** The implementing agency is MICOA. The long-term objective of the project is the establishment of sustainable socio-economic development through environmentally sound use of the region's coastal resources. The project is currently under way and resource inventories have been carried out and the vegetation mapped for Mecufi District, Cabo Delgade Province.

(b) **Integrated Coastal Area Management (Xai-Xai).** The implementing agency was MICOA, funded by UNEP/FAO. The goal of the project was to design a coastal profile for the Xai-Xai coastal district and to develop management plans for the area. Digital base maps for the project area were produced using GIS.

(c) **The Ecology of Inhaca Island Project,** being implemented by the

Department of Biological Sciences, Eduardo Mondlane University (components funded by several donors). Resource inventories and vegetation mapping have been carried out. Several Masters and PhD research projects are under way.

(d) **Mapping of forest cover** of the whole country (including the coastal zones) at 1:1 million scale, using satellite imagery, is currently being undertaken by the National Wildlife and Forestry Department.

Under the auspices of the office of marine projects within SAFMAR, action is proposed for Mozambique to:

i) accede to the MARPOL international convention 1973/1978 (see above);

ii) obtain financial resources for the installation of oil reception facilities in those major Mozambican ports not provided with adequate means to prevent operational oil spills, and for oil residues, slops, etc.;

iii) establish an oil spill contingency plan within SAFMAR.

Conclusions and recommendations

i) Development of a national coastal zone management policy is an urgent necessity. This would provide a means of reviewing each sector's benefits from and impacts on the coastal zone and help determine how the needs of each sector should be balanced and the demands of conservation and development should be combined. The policy should also set out procedures for dealing with man-made shoreline instability, including coastal erosion, coastal engineering, rise in sea level, subsidence, saltwater intrusion and settling of deltas during extraction of groundwater, mining or other activities, etc.

ii) There should be assessment of all policies, programmes and projects related to activities taking place in the coastal zone, to determine their impact on marine ecosystems. All activities must take full account of the coastal zone and marine ecosystems to ensure that they are properly protected.

iii) A Coastal Zone Authority or other institutional mechanism should be established to co-ordinate the planning and allocation of uses of the zone. It would be vested with overall budgetary authority and responsibility for co-ordination in a cabinet-level office and would use inter-agency committees systematically to ensure co-ordination and regulation of intersectoral interests.

iv) Local communities and the main stakeholders must be involved in the development of land-use plans for coastal zones and marine ecosystems, giving priority to drainage basins where pollution and land uses have a substantial impact on marine resources and ecosystems.

v) A detailed survey of the coastal zone should be undertaken, plus a mapping inventory of the zone's resources. Defining sensitive areas for comprehensive area-specific marine management and planning is essential for maintaining the productivity, diversity and economic benefits of coastal regions. This management must incorporate comprehensive planning of waste management, including recycling of wastes and treatment and disposal options that result in minimum harm to the environment and human health. It should also include local criteria, assessments, monitoring and research.

vi) EIAs should specifically consider impacts on maritime ecosystems in order to identify areas vulnerable to coastal zone changes and should act accordingly. Living marine resources should be protected from non-selective exploitation and consideration should be given to banning non-selective fishing methods, notably dynamiting, the use of long drift nets and the use of non-degradable fish traps. EIAs must include social impact assessment.

vii) Attention should be paid to coastal engineering policy and management and the special need for long-term coastal protection. Plans should cover not only specific locations but also major stretches of the coasts and whole river basins with the aim of controlling erosion and siltation, restricting excessive nutrient input and reducing chemical contamination.

viii) The best experience and technology available should be used to deal with areas that are vulnerable to rising sea levels, storm surges, coastal flooding or erosion. The main concern should be to maintain coastal habitats, such as mangroves and other wetlands, coral reefs and coastal barriers and lagoons, and natural coastal processes such as sedimentation and marsh growth that offer the best defences against adverse changes. In most cases, the best coastal protection will be achieved by establishing buffer zones where uses are compatible with natural nearshore processes. The width of the buffer zones will depend on the likelihood of coastal disaster and habitat alteration.

ix) An ecosystem approach should be used for the management of marine resources and to reconcile inshore and offshore fisheries. It is important to recognize that inshore and offshore fisheries are connected, since they rely on the same ecosystems and often exploit the same fish stocks but at different stages in their development.

x) Management of sporting fisheries should be integrated with that of other fisheries. Sporting fisheries often comprise a large portion of the take in certain areas or for certain species. The catches are often not quantified and are poorly regulated, making fisheries management difficult.

xi) Interdisciplinary research and exchange of information on marine ecosystems should be promoted.

xii) UNEP's Eastern Africa Regional Seas (EARS) Convention should be adopted and National Coastal Zone Management should be developed including national, regional and local management programmes. Items of particular interest to UNEP's EARS programmes are: protection of a unique coastal ecosystem, protection for regionally endangered species and habitats, and training of coastal specialists.

xiii) National legislation against marine pollution must be urgently devised. This legislation, in addition to preventative measures, should also consider restricting laden tankers to a certain distance from the coastal zone.

xiv) At regional and local levels Marine Pollution Control and Combating Units (MPCCU) should be created and a pollution contingency plan should be established. Local communities and all stakeholders should be integrated at all stages.

xv) Linkages between government offices responsible for physical planning, fisheries, agriculture, industry, mining, hydropower, tourism, marine transport (oil pollution), etc. must be clearly defined and procedures for the analysis and approval of projects which may have a major environmental impact (dams, mines, heavy industry) should be defined.

Reference
Tinley, K.L., Rosinha, A.J., Lobao Tellor, J.L.P. and Sutton, T.P. (1976) 'Wildlife and Wild Places in Mozambique', *Oryx* 13(4) pp. 344–350.

14 Strengthening Human Resource Capacity for Community-Based Sustainable Development

The historical evolution of social services in Mozambique

Social services appeared in Mozambique only at the turn of the twentieth century. Their development can be divided into four distinct stages, each of which had its own special characteristics.

Stage 1: 1908–50 – Simple assistance

The first kind of social work began in 1908 in the form of cash assistance to small, marginalized groups with social problems. This was simple social assistance which was the responsibility of officials of the colonial administration and the police force. There were no specialized staff to carry out this work. A further form of assistance, subsidized financially by the colonial state, was provided by religious organizations which established a link between the Church and the state.

Stage 2: 1950–75 – Social promotion

Faced with the political changes on the world scene after the Second World War, together with the movements for self-determination and for improvements in living standards and working conditions, the state was forced to shoulder a new range of obligations aimed at raising the social conditions of different classes and population groups.

Social work was initially developed by volunteers in hospitals and then within the communities. 'Popular suburbs' were organized and constructed by the Population Settlement Board. Firms set up social services (canteens and holiday camps) for their workers and their families. It was at this time that the first voluntary organizations, assisted financially by the colonial bourgeoisie, emerged. These included the 'Works of the Volunteers of Charity' and the 'Technical Research Institute'. At the same time, the Catholic Church expanded its social services, through homes and orphanages, under the terms of the *concordat* between the Vatican and the metropolitan power, while private interests administered profitable enterprises, such as creches and nurseries. This phase was generally characterized by the adoption of 'palliative' solutions or measures to alleviate social problems.

Stage 3: 1975–1986 – Social services centralized in the state

After independence, the government nationalized all institutions providing social services, following the socialist development model. A centralized sub-system of social services was designed within the National Health System. The state's objectives in the sphere of social welfare were as follows:

- To guarantee that all citizens had the best possible quality of life, as individuals, as members of a family and as a community.
- To allow citizens, both individually and collectively, to contribute towards their own welfare and that of their family, community and nation.
- In general terms, the whole economic and social system was designed to protect the great majority of the population who derived their livelihood from wage labour – the 'working masses' in the urban and rural areas.

Services were provided through nationalized state institutions and in the community by means of co-ordination between state-employed social workers and the mass organizations or by foreign non-governmental organizations.

Stage 4: 1987 to the present – Decentralization and de-institutionalization of social services
The combined effects of war, natural disasters and the introduction of a structural adjustment programme imposed a profound though evolutionary change, both in the design of social services and in the methods of delivery and the overall approach to social work. Several Mozambican associations dedicated to giving assistance to vulnerable groups were set up following a change in attitude on the part of some donors and with the development of greater freedom of association.

The sections of the population in need of material, moral and social assistance increased dramatically, including children, women, the disabled and the elderly, displaced people, refugees and the destitute living in the urban areas. The existing institutions were not equipped to deal with the growing number of social problems, and they did not provide effective solutions. The provision of social services became selective rather than universal, basically reaching only the extremely deprived social groups.

The complexity and scale of social problems were such that the state alone was unable to provide solutions. Space was created for the participation of other social forces from within civil society through NGOs and religious organizations. The state retained the role of deciding on policy and co-ordinating the process of implementation.

As a result of these changes in social work there was greater community and beneficiary participation in the resolution of social problems. This meant that social work no longer involved simply the provision of services by state institutions. Service delivery gradually became the task of social workers in the community, with the ultimate aim of giving communities themselves the capacity to resolve their own problems.

The State Secretariat for Social Welfare was established in 1990 with the responsibility to direct, co-ordinate and monitor the implementation of government policy on social welfare in support of underprivileged groups at risk. In this now defunct department, it was felt that its objectives and purpose should be tailored to the pace of development and the practice of social work carried out by both government institutions and private non-profit organizations. When a policy on social welfare was being drafted, it was recognized that the scope of activities would have to be expanded to include new target groups such as women and the family and that the activities of social workers in relation to children, the disabled and elderly, and drug addicts would have to be made more effective. In fact, children, the disabled and the elderly live within a family setting in which women play an important supportive role.

Thus, as soon as the Ministry for the Co-ordination of Social Action was established in December 1994, the previous discussion was resumed and a revision began of the government's objectives in the sphere of social welfare. These objectives would serve as the basis for determining the institution's responsibilities and functions. The Ministry was given the responsibility to intervene in the following areas: strengthening the role of the family; supporting and strengthening the role of women; assisting children, the elderly and the most underprivileged groups; and coordinating social reintegration. At the same time, it directs research activities in the sphere of social action and drafts policy papers on each target group. Moreover, it is required to monitor and evaluate the impact of implementing its policies.

Staff training is one of the Ministry's principal tools in performing its duties. The centralization of training activities for social workers will permit the harmonization and standardization of strategies and methods of work in both state institutions and NGOs involved in social work.

The problems

The situation in Mozambique today is influenced by the following factors. It was only relatively recently freed from colonial rule. It suffered a state of war almost continuously for 28 years. It is also suffering the social hardship of structural adjustment measures. It is frequently affected by natural disasters – drought which lasts several years and periodic floods. These factors contributed towards Mozambique's economic and social decline, along with the destruction of the economic and social infrastructure, the mass movement of the population, the mutilation of thousands of people, the disruption of the system of social values, unemployment, low rates of education and a range of diseases which raised the infant and maternal mortality rates. As a result of this situation, some 60 to 70% of the population suffer extreme poverty, with an annual income of only US$80 per capita. Malnutrition affects large numbers of families in both the urban and the rural areas.

The low level of development in Mozambique, with the predominance of subsistence agriculture and low levels of production and productivity, affects households that have labour power available but produce little because of a number of structural factors. Examples of such factors include:

- the high number of female-headed households (some 65% in the urban areas) also including high numbers of dependants, children and the elderly;
- the large number of people without any support from their families, including war orphans, street children, the disabled and the elderly;
- the groups of people unable to generate an adequate income because of lack of employment, land or access roads to markets.

In addition to war and natural disasters, the movement of people, including repatriated refugees and displaced people, disrupted productive activities and the satisfaction of basic needs. The structural adjustment measures have helped make the situation worse because of the rapid and steep rise in the price of basic products and other goods and the laying off of workers. At the same time, the deterioration of basic services such as health, water supply, education and housing has had serious consequences for human capital and social welfare.

Why sustainable community development

The aim of sustainable community development is to help to reduce poverty and improve people's living conditions, capitalizing on the development of human capacity in order to help meet the different needs of various groups.

The Ministry for the Co-ordination of Social Action has, among others, the following objectives:

(a) to co-ordinate and integrate the work of governmental and non-governmental institutions in the provision of assistance to population groups with the greatest need for material, social and moral support, namely, children, women, the elderly, the disabled, displaced people and returned refugees, by promoting welfare through raising living standards and creating opportunities for people to develop their skills.
(b) to alleviate the impact of structural adjustment measures on the most vulnerable groups.

The approach adopted is based on the premise that each individual in the target groups is a member of a family and each family is part of a community. Under the existing living conditions experienced by vulnerable groups in society, it is important to understand sustainable community development as being the principal vehicle for achieving the Ministry's objectives of meeting basic needs and improving the living conditions of the neediest families. Sustainable community development allows people in the community to develop their own knowledge about themselves, their environment, their needs and resources, which gives them a better chance to take more effective action, turning themselves into active agents of development. Sustainable community development is a process whereby the people of the community play a decisive and leadership role, together with the social workers representing government structures, specialists and others, who act as facilitators.

Strengthening capacity for community-based initiatives

Interventions by the government, religious organizations and NGOs in programmes and projects to eliminate poverty and raise the living standards of the vulnerable population are indispensable, provided the people themselves shoulder their share of the responsibility and participate in making decisions about what to do, how and when to do it and with whom to implement micro-projects. The Ministry for the Co-ordination of Social Action intends to play a facilitating role in this process throughout the country, training social workers in the districts to work with the communities involved.

It is very important that social workers and members of NGOs and other institutions involved in work to improve social welfare are introduced to this approach to sustainable community development, so that they understand its value and the advantages for community growth. This will prepare the project co-ordinators to adjust the administrative procedures so as to increase the utility and effectiveness of sustainable community development. The involvement of the community in the design, execution and evaluation is a key element for the success of this approach.

Another important question is how to facilitate the interchange of experience and publicize models of good practice in order to ensure that the whole process is dynamic. Moreover, training is essential to create a framework for intersectoral co-ordination that is functional and objective.

The overall objective of the Ministry for the Co-ordination of Social Action is the promotion of sustainable community development by means of this initiative with its strategy to eradicate poverty. The strategy includes:

* the formulation of sectoral policies for social action and of a global social policy;
* the development of community capacities to act and to shoulder responsibilities by providing appropriate training;

- the provision of human, technical and financial resources;
- public awareness of these activities.

The specific objectives of the initiative are to equip the participants to integrate the principles and practice of sustainable community development into their day-to-day activities. Thus training programmes should include:

- the design, principles and strategies of sustainable community development;
- skills in environmental and community management;
- methodologies and techniques for the identification of human, natural, manufactured and organizational resources, as well as for conflict resolution with community participation;
- skills to help members of the community develop their human capital and their self-confidence;
- approaches for the development of intersectoral and multi-disciplinary co-ordination.

The government programme has established the following strategic principles aimed at achieving its social goals:

(a) community participation in the identification and resolution of problems;
(b) the promotion of gender equity in all aspects of social, economic and political life;
(c) the sustainability of all programmed activities;
(d) the encouragement of civil society's participation through associations and religious and other organizations in the implementation of social action programmes.

To inspire confidence in these principles and in the aims of sustainable community development, the beneficiaries will be the communities covered by the project in different provinces in the country. The plan is to select two or three communities with large numbers of poor and needy people in each province. The communities will not be abstract notions, since they will also contain institutions and organized groups with whom the social workers should work. Priority will be given to: female-headed households; rural households affected by the war with returned refugees and displaced people, orphaned and abandoned children and war-disabled people; poor households, such as street children, the elderly and the disabled; women involved in the informal sector who can generate more work for other members of the community.

The target groups for training courses will be: social workers in various state institutions; workers in the National Institute for Social Action; social activists in the districts; members of community NGOs; members of religious organizations linked to the communities.

Implementing this strategy will involve:

(a) Preparing a group of 40 trainers in sustainable community development from among the social workers in different state institutions (the Ministry for the Co-ordination of Social Action, the National Institute for Social Action, the Ministry for the Co-ordination of Environmental Action, the Ministry of Agriculture and Fisheries, the National Institute for Rural Development, the Institute for the Development of Local Industry, the Ministry of Health, the Ministry of Education, etc.).
(b) The creation of a corps of 160 facilitators for sustainable community development from among the workers of the National Institute for Social Action and the

Ministry for the Co-ordination of Social Action in the provinces, social activists in the districts and members of religious organizations in the districts and the communities.

(c) The selection and training of 20 to 30 communities for sustainable community development.

(d) The preparation of public awareness campaigns on the work of the communities, with examples of models of good practice.

It is planned to implement this initiative in the period from 1997 to 1999. At the end of the programmed activities, it is hoped that the following outputs will be achieved:

(a) 40 trainers trained in the principles and practice of sustainable community development.

(b) A corps of 160 facilitators in sustainable community development created.

(c) 20 to 30 communities given the skills for sustainable community development.

(d) Action taken to improve inter-sectoral and multi-disciplinary co-ordination.

The initiative will be co-ordinated by the Ministry for the Co-ordination of Social Action and the executing agency will be the National Institute for Social Action.

15 Strategies for the Formulation of a National Population Policy

FONSECA MARIO MACHAULE

Under its five-year development programme the Mozambique government decided to elaborate a National Population Policy (NPP) as one of its economic and social development strategies. The decision was based on the fact that the country's population, currently about 17 million, is growing rapidly and the population structure is such that it may constrain per capita GDP growth and efforts to improve people's quality of life, particularly for the poorest households (Republic of Mozambique, 1995, 24).

Since independence, the government has recognized the close relationship that exists between population growth and social and economic development. It identifies the basis for resolving problems arising from this inter-relationship as resting primarily in economic and social transformation. This provides one important strand contributing towards a sustainable development approach overall. The government's position on population policy coincides with the consensus reached at the 1994 International Conference on Population and Development in Cairo (ICPD): namely, that population, poverty, development and the environment are strongly inter-related and thus cannot be considered in isolation (United Nations, 1995).

However, preparation of the NPP requires the implementation of a set of strategies which will vary according to the reality and needs of each country in terms of its specific population and development issues. Consequently, the Population and Planning Unit (PPU) where the present author works has prepared, and is implementing, a particular combination of strategies for the formulation of the NPP in Mozambique.

Strategies

The first strategy followed by the PPU, with donor assistance, was to prepare the document 'Guiding Elements for the Formulation of a National Population Policy in Mozambique'. An inter-sectoral working group was established comprising technicians from various sectors, including the National Directorate of Statistics, the Mother and Child Health and Family Planning Services (Ministry of Health), the Centre for African Studies (Eduardo Mondlane University), the National Institute for the Development of Education (Ministry of Education) and the Ministry for the Co-ordination of Environmental Action.

The document evaluates both the current status of population issues and the country's development situation. It aims to build a consensus on the nature of the future National Population Policy, its objectives and instruments, the role of the various sectors involved and their inter-linkages. It also sets out the steps to be followed for the final formulation of the policy. What follows offers both a synthesis of, and reflections upon, the 'Guiding Elements' document.

To be effective, a National Population Policy should provide a coherent set of government measures of a social and economic nature, involving, among others, such areas as education, health, employment, potable water supply, environmental sanitation and plumbing, which are intended to influence the country's demographic dynamics in keeping with its development objectives. As will be readily appreciated, this is no easy task.

Mozambique's population is growing fast. From a baseline of 6.5 million in 1950 it grew to 7.6 million in 1960, 9.4 million in 1970 and 12.1 million in 1980. The annual growth rate thus rose from 1.6% in the 1950s to 2.7% in the 1980s. New projections indicate that the 1995 Mozambican population is about 17 million, growing at an average annual rate of 2.7%. This is two-thirds higher than the rate in the 1950s, thus reducing the time for the population to double from 43 to 25 years. This rapid growth results from the combined effect of birth rates which have remained high and virtually constant, and declining death rates. According to the results of the 1991 National Demographic Survey (NDS), the country's fertility level is still high, about 6.2 children per woman, whereas mortality rates are tending to fall, even though life expectancy at birth has not altered significantly. Under-15s and those over 60 form a majority in the country, indicating a structure more oriented towards consumption than production.

Current levels of basic services, particularly education and health provision, are not adequate to cope with such population growth levels, combined with the fact that, as GDP is still far too low for the country to be self-sustainable, most of the population lives in poverty.

Population growth is also an indirect consequence of the mother's level of education, since the more educated a mother, the greater the probability that her fertility will be lower, in part because of the number of years it takes for her to complete a given level of education. Hence there is a significant difference in fertility between mothers who do not have any education and those who do. The fertility of educated mothers further differs according to their level of education. The evidence points markedly towards the importance of prioritizing educating girls and women.

The inherited pattern of spatial distribution has been altered profoundly by the population movements caused by the war, particularly in the interior of every province. The full extent of these alterations is still not sufficiently known, given the lack of up-to-date population statistics. Analysis of the urbanization process has been complicated by the different methodologies used in every census and in the 1991 NDS. On the whole, urban population growth in Mozambique used to be slow compared with many other African countries, but this has now changed.

Initial studies by the PPU have shown that the rapid population growth in Mozambique is a clear reality. This continuous rapid growth and the high percentage of children and young people in the overall population poses a serious challenge for the government and the country as a whole. Growth is particularly concentrated in the less developed provinces containing the vast majority of the population and where the economy is dominated by traditional agriculture. The limited expansion and development of the market economy explains the restricted availability of basic education in the country. The highest fertility and child mortality rates and the lowest life expectancy at birth are found in the less developed provinces and amongst the population groups with low productivity levels and thus low incomes.

The high level of urban population growth is due to high birth rates and the rural exodus, which was intensified by the recently terminated war. The subsequent return of people to the countryside has been somewhat selective, such that it will prove difficult for urban population growth rates to fall. The demographic dynamics of extremely poor households in urban areas (Maputo city and the provincial capitals) constitute an excessive burden in their fight to overcome poverty, since the number of dependent people within poor households continues to grow. The socio-economic, demographic and cultural characteristics of extremely poor households have a negative effect on their members, limiting their opportunities for education and training.

Contrary to the early post-independence years, the government's current position favours the global and sectoral integration of population activities into a single 'National Population Policy. Available indicators on population growth rates and the current development planning context provide favourable conditions for beginning to formulate such a policy. This formulation must be accompanied by the creation of greater awareness at all levels, particularly in the provinces, about the need for such a policy. One of the characteristics of this policy would be that its implementation would promote improvements in the collection, analysis and research on population topics for programming, implementation and training purposes, for the creation and/or strengthening of relevant institutions and for monitoring and evaluating population and development activities.

Some studies have argued that population growth does not always necessarily have to conflict with economic growth. Its negative effect is mainly on the environment in poor countries, as reflected in deforestation, soil erosion and in the deterioration of basic services. Inevitably over the long term this is a drain on the development effort.

As regards the poor, some studies claim that there is little direct evidence that rapid population growth necessarily causes poverty. But they do point significantly to indirect evidence that population growth can cause a continuation of poverty and its transmission to subsequent generations.

Given the proposed objectives of the National Population Policy, two kinds of nationwide programmes furnish its policy instruments. Firstly, there are general programmes of a normative nature to promote co-ordination and an improved management of the relationship between population, poverty, development and the environment. These programmes are the following: Population and Development; Gender, Population and Development; and Co-ordination, Supervision and Evaluation of Population Matters.

Secondly, there are specific programmes of an operational and supportive nature, carried out by public and private social sectors in close co-ordination with the productive sectors. These programmes are: Integrated Reproductive, Child and Adolescent Health; Education, Population, Communications and Development; Data Collection and Analysis; Research and Population and Environment.

Both the general and the specific programmes are executed by specialized institutions, in particular institutions dealing with health, education, communications and population information, the environment and certain non-governmental organizations. But in order to implement the NPP successfully, these institutions need to be strengthened institutionally and with technical staff. Other structures need to be created to co-ordinate and implement the policy, especially at the top administrative, technical and political levels, such as a National Council for Population and Development or perhaps even a Sustainable Development Council.

Other important strategies currently being implemented are the following:

(a) continuing awareness-raising at central, provincial and local levels and in different sectors, because population issues are still novel and need to be brought into the open, disseminated and dealt with;

(b) producing sectoral position papers on population issues, since these will be considered by sectors such as Health, Education, Environment and Labour, taking into account the question of sustainable development;

(c carrying out study visits to countries with strong population programmes, to get to know their experience in formulating an NPP and the institutions created to implement it;

(d) setting up workshops and seminars to collect sectoral and provincial proposals for the formulation of the NPP;

(e) preparing the draft NPP on the basis of contributions made in workshops and seminars and from other bodies;

(f) holding a National Conference on the NPP to enrich the final National Population Policy document.

References

Republic of Mozambique (1995) *Government Five Year Programme*, Maputo.

United Nations (1995) *Population and Development*, Department for Economic and Social Information and Policy Analysis, ST/ESA/SER.A/149, New York.

16 Developing a Capacity for Environmental Scrutiny

ROGÉRIO WAMUSSE

Environmental inspection

Environmental inspection is essential to ensure efficient environmental management. It is a mechanism for maintaining the quality of the environment at an acceptable level, according to standards which are set to protect natural processes from any form of change which could threaten the existence of higher and lower organisms alike.

The Ministry for the Co-ordination of Environmental Action (MICOA) is mandated to make regular and comprehensive reports on the state of the environment both to the government and to the general public. To do this, it needs to set up practical mechanisms which allow it to evaluate the well-being of the various components of the country's environment. Two processes are involved: environmental monitoring and environmental auditing. The first involves the systematic and regular monitoring of the various key indicators of the state of the environment. The second requires the periodic verification by the national authority responsible for environmental management that there is compliance with legally established standards for the maintenance of a healthy environment.

Environmental degradation can cost the country huge sums of money to counter the effects of severe water pollution in the rivers and the sea, air and soil pollution and a decline in the economic potential of various natural resources as a result of their misuse. Environmental inspection is a mechanism intended to permit the use of the environment and natural resources within limits established to guarantee their continued use. This means strict compliance with the upper and lower thresholds established by law for each specific case.

The main constraints on the system of environmental inspection in Mozambique are:

- the lack of adequate legislation (laws and regulations, established standards of environmental quality);
- a lack of the basic resources required to enforce the law;
- the absence of a uniform system of environmental inspection, which is currently fragmented and subject to the particular interests of the different sectors;
- the lack of incentives to reward good practice in the use of natural resources and of measures to penalize offenders.

Access to and use of natural resources and the environment operate in Mozambique at two main levels: public or community control and private control. The first category is found in the towns and cities and residential areas in the countryside, while the second refers to concessions granted by the state to private interests for the exercise of specific economic activities. In the latter case environmental management is carried out by means of a pre-emptive assessment of the environmental impact of the particular initiative, which indicates concrete measures to mitigate the negative and augment the positive effects. With regard to the first category, there is as yet no system of inspection or legislation for this purpose. The use and exploitation of resources under public or community control operate without any regulation. In the few cases where regulations do exist, they are not applied in practice on a regular basis. Thus, environmental inspection in Mozambique needs to take into consideration the specific conditions of each of the components mentioned above.

Environmental monitoring of natural resources and the environment under public or community control needs to be an on-going activity carried out by the institution responsible for environmental and natural resources management at the relevant levels in the administrative hierarchy. In the main urban areas, for example, this task will be the responsibility of the municipality, which will be required to correct any irregularities that may be found. Currently the national institution responsible for industrial activity is also charged with monitoring the quality of industrial effluent and emissions or other waste resulting from industrial production. Industrialists whose installations are located within cities should monitor the area for which they are responsible. Penalties may be imposed in the case of infringement of particular regulations. In general, monitoring is to be conducted at the sectoral level, notably in fisheries, forestry and wildlife, tourism, agriculture, urban sanitation and environmental health, among others. To put this into practice, the national institution responsible for environmental management should collaborate with all the various sectors in reviewing and assessing existing capacity and identifying the gaps, needs and assistance required in each case, giving priority to key sectors and locations. The National Council for Sustainable Development, the highest co-ordinating body for sustainable development, could play a prominent role in establishing a unified system of environmental inspection in Mozambique and making it operational. Priority should be given to sectors that already possess the basic conditions necessary to carry out such supervision.

The current system of supervision which operates only at the sectoral level needs to be revised. The role and responsibilities for sectoral inspection or supervision must be redefined, notably in forestry, wildlife and fisheries, among others. A new type of inspection is needed to go beyond the limits imposed by the specific situation in the different sectors, in order to achieve an integrated vision of the problems related to the use and exploitation of natural resources in the country as a whole. There are clear tensions at present between the need for a more holistic local control and the central sectoral control of local activities currently in operation.

The basic objective of environmental impact assessment (EIA) is to identify a set of measures aimed at containing or eliminating the direct and indirect negative environmental effects and alternatively at augmenting the positive effects of any development project. These measures as a whole constitute the environmental management programme of the project, and are formulated on the basis of information produced by the EIA on the various environmental components under the direct or indirect influence of the project, namely the ecological, economic and socio-cultural environments. The ultimate aim of the environmental monitoring of any given project is to check on its effects on the environmental systems within the area of the direct and indirect influence of the undertaking, so as to evaluate the effectiveness of the mitigation measures and take prompt corrective action should problems arise.

Before project implementation begins and a monitoring system goes into operation, variables must be selected to serve as indicators of change in the environment of the project area. Once the variables have been selected, laboratory measurements or observations need to be made to provide baseline data as benchmarks for comparison during the implementation of the project. It will thus be possible to evaluate any changes in the environment, namely whether the environment is improving, deteriorating or remaining stable.

Environmental monitoring will consist of a regular programme of measurement, laboratory analysis or observation of the selected variable. The results of the measurement have to be matched against the threshold values established by law (standards of environmental quality), which set the quantity of residue, pressure or rate of exploitation that nature can sustain or tolerate without resulting in gradual environmental degradation.

In order to ensure that the measurements are reliable and can be compared with each other and with baseline standards of environmental quality, a common methodology needs to be adopted. For example, the method of analysis for BOD (biological oxygen demand) measurements should be the same for all projects. This would include the collection of samples and storage until laboratory analysis is undertaken in order to establish the first benchmark data measurements. If possible, the same laboratory and criteria should be used throughout.

The frequency with which samples and measurements are taken should be established according to the variable being monitored. It may be different for projects located in different areas, but never for projects in the same location, since the environment is the same. The variables in question should be graphed in order to show their behaviour over time, so as to give a better picture of any changes in the environment in the project area. The measurements for the benchmark data should be taken separately in both seasons: the dry and the rainy seasons. Subsequently measurements should be compared with the benchmark in the appropriate season.

The government body responsible for environmental management can never possess all the resources and capacity needed to monitor all the development projects subject to EIA. The monitoring programme should therefore be the entire responsibility of the project implementers. However, the department in charge of environmental management in the different tiers of government should provide the implementers with all the necessary back-up support so that they can monitor the effects on the environment of their own projects. This support includes providing standards of environmental quality, methodologies of analysis and recommendations on suitable laboratories.

Project implementers should, when requested, provide information to the body responsible for environmental management in the area of jurisdiction in which the project is located, the province or district for projects at this level, or the central government department for national-level projects. Development projects should therefore be organized in such a way that they have a unit or an individual dealing with environmental management and monitoring of the project. This unit or individual will handle all the day-to-day work, routine measurements, data processing, documentation, environmental education, for the environmental monitoring of projects subject to EIA and seek solutions to the problems which may arise.

Environmental auditing of development projects

The environmental auditing of development projects is the exclusive responsibility of the government body in charge of environmental management in the area of jurisdiction in which the project is located. For national (large-scale) projects, environmental auditing is carried out by the government body responsible for environmental management at the central level.

This process will consist of regular checks on how far the project implementers have introduced the mitigation measures included in the environmental management programme of the project. The auditing will be carried out by means of regular visits, both with and without prior notice, or through requests for relevant information.

Where there is any doubt as to the reliability of data relating to a particular variable, the body responsible for environmental auditing may request measurements or analyses from an independent laboratory with recognized capacity to produce reliable results in order to get at the truth. Any costs involved in this cross-checking will be borne by the project implementers.

The aim of environmental auditing is not to punish project implementers where a negative environmental impact is found. The purpose is rather to check on the environmental conditions in the area of the project so that, should any irregularity arise because of flaws in the mitigation measures adopted, the necessary action can be taken to correct the situation. However, project implementers may be penalized if it is shown that damage to the environment in the area of the project results from their neglect or failure to comply with measures included in the environmental management programme.

Environmental auditing of development projects will be carried out by officials of the government body responsible for the environmental management of the project, either at provincial or national level as appropriate. These officials should receive specific training in the basic subjects required to exercise this function. These subjects include the environmental legal framework and various environmental regulations, the basic principles of EIA and environmental auditing methodology, as well as the key features of public relations.

The environmental management of development projects will thus be in the hands of environmental inspectors, and this will require a rigorous selection process in order to avoid the risk of corruption. In the final analysis, corruption could endanger the basic objectives of EIA – environmental management and sustainable development.

The basic legal instruments governing environmental auditing will be the Environmental Framework Law and the sectoral regulations already in force or to be created, along with their respective standards of environmental quality. The definition and establishment of those standards is a long process, closely linked to the country's level of economic, technological and cultural development. All sectors should be capable of complying with these standards in the implementation of their development programmes and the body in charge of environmental management should have the laboratory and other technical capacity to check on this compliance. The standards therefore need to be set at an appropriate level.

The establishment of minimum acceptable levels of concentration of different substances implies a great deal of work with laboratory measurements to determine the degree of absorption by different parts of the environment of residues resulting from production processes, the application of agricultural chemicals or simply the release of certain wastes. Until it is possible to carry out this work, standards of environmental quality in other countries should be adopted, provided that they can be easily adapted for Mozambique, taking account of the specific conditions of the environmental component or the resources to be preserved, as well as their purpose.

Finally, all the legislation and procedures required for the rational use of natural resources should be widely publicized among the users. Specific regulations should be drawn up to cover environmental auditing, as well as rules of conduct and directives to govern the exercise of this activity.

How to carry out environmental auditing of development projects

Environmental auditing of development projects is the vital and dynamic part of the whole process of EIA. Without environmental auditing, EIA is completely devoid of any practical utility and is therefore of no interest as a tool for environmental management. The general process involved in the auditing of development projects is represented in the following flow chart.

FLOW CHART OF ENVIRONMENTAL AUDITING OF DEVELOPMENT PROJECTS
Definition of the scope and objectives of the audit
Collection of baseline data
Preparation of the protocol of the audit
Presentation of the members of the auditing team to the management of the firm
Visit to the factory/location to be audited
Collection of data on the various environmental indicators appropriate to the audit
Analysis of the data obtained
Preparation of recommendations
Debriefing with the management of the firm
Reporting the results of the audit

In the case of Mozambique, environmental auditing should not be restrictive from the outset. It should be an exercise aimed at gradually leading users of the environment and natural resources to cultivate an environmentalist approach by adopting environmentally sound activities, be they profit-making or subsistence, and observing the legally established norms.

Environmental auditing should not depend on the personal opinions of the team leader or any other member of the auditing team. A uniform framework should be established for the whole country against which the quality of the environment in the various sectors can be measured. The quality of the environment at the site to be inspected should be measured first by comparing the information obtained during the environmental monitoring programme with the benchmark data collected before the start of implementation, and then comparing the results with the established standards of environmental quality.

A team which plans to carry out environmental auditing at a production enterprise should organize in advance all the relevant baseline data on the enterprise to be visited. These data are usually contained in the environmental impact study for the project. The auditing protocol should be prepared by the team on the basis of this study. It should then be submitted for consideration and approval (with signature and stamp) to the most senior official in the sector.

Once the auditing protocol has been prepared, the length of time the audit will last, as well as the date and time of arrival of the team, should be planned in co-ordination with the management of the enterprise. Under no circumstances can the auditing be allowed to interfere with the normal functioning of the site to be inspected. Both the auditing protocol and the plan should be sent in advance to the management of the enterprise to be visited.

The presence of an environmental auditing team at a production enterprise should be regarded, in the first place, as a means of arousing the awareness of both the management and the workers in general, about the need to respect the legally established norms for environmentally sound development. The audit should be conducted in such a way that it is regarded as a form of help to the business community to improve the quality of the environment and the utilization of the natural resources under its influence, and consequently to derive more economic benefits and to create a positive image in relation to an increasingly environmentally conscious public and government.

If environmental auditing is viewed as a threat or hindrance or other sort of interference in the proceedings of the firm, then any chance of co-operation between the visiting team and the firm's management will be remote and the stated objectives will simply not be achieved. The following procedures should therefore be adopted for the conduct of environmental auditing.

i   Presentation of the auditing team
Immediately on arrival at the site to be inspected, the leader of the auditing team should introduce the members of the team, to the management of the firm. During the introduction, the team leader should highlight the following: that the audit is an environmental management tool and not a threat to the business community; the way the audit will be conducted; and who will receive the report containing the results of the audit. The team leader's description of the auditing process should include a rough estimate of how much time will be required to interview the relevant persons and to inspect the key sectors in the firm.

ii   Inspection of the firm
Before beginning the collection of detailed information, the visiting team should familiarize themselves with the key sectors and production processes or operations of the firm, particularly if it is their first visit to this location. They should therefore ask to be accompanied by a member of the management thoroughly versed in all aspects of the plant and buildings, as well as the production process and other functions, who can answer questions and clarify doubts that may arise during the inspection. Special attention needs to be paid to locations identified in the environmental impact study as being most at risk from the negative effects generated by the project. In some cases these locations will lie beyond the boundary of the enterprise.

iii   Data collection
Data collection is the core of the auditing process. It is the data which permit an evaluation of the degree of compliance with the recommendations of the environmental impact study, and of the effectiveness of measures intended to mitigate the ill effects identified. The data may be collected from the records kept by the firm for monitoring purposes, complemented by interviews with relevant persons in the firm. In some cases, tests will have to be made to check the accuracy of the data provided. The data collection should be carried out in accordance with the protocol, which has been given prior approval by the relevant senior official.

The inspector should always bear in mind the need to generate and maintain positive attitudes to the environment on the part of the business community. For example, the inspector should avoid the sort of questions likely to make the firm's management feel environmentally irresponsible.

It is vitally important to take notes on all the information provided, as well as of the names of the persons interviewed. The interviewees may be asked to sign a transcript at the end. Questions which may arise during the inspection include the following:

- Does the firm have the necessary materials and equipment to monitor the impact of the project?
- Does the firm employ staff trained to carry out environmental monitoring?
- How is environmental monitoring carried out in the firm?
- What results are obtained from the project's environmental monitoring programme?

These are just some of the questions that may be asked during an inspection in order to clear up any doubts that could arise with regard to the monitoring programme.

For an environmental audit of a factory or other industrial facility, the following additional documentation should be requested in advance: layout of the factory; diagram of the production process; raw materials flow chart; organizational diagram of the factory; list of dangerous substances used; list of waste (liquid, solid and gas) produced.

iv   Evaluation of the results of the audit
At the end of the inspection, the auditing team must select the information to be included in the environmental audit report, based on the protocol already approved.

v   Preparation of recommendations
The recommendations emerging from the audit must be practical and feasible. They should therefore be based on the human and material resources available at the site inspected. This does not, however, imply relaxing the established standards of environmental quality, but rather identifying short-term objectives which will ultimately achieve higher levels of environmental quality in the firm.

vi   Reporting the environmental audit
The report must include the name and location of the firm inspected, its activities and any other relevant details. This is primarily a technical report, with as little description as possible, but using graphs, tables, etc. where necessary. The main parts of the report are: a brief introduction; a short description of the location visited; a summary of the inspection process; the results of the inspection; recommendations and conclusions. The most important part of the report is the audit results. There should be no room for ambiguity. The results of the audit must not, under any circumstances, be confused with any opinion nor with the recommendations made. Should any differences emerge on matters of fact, the opinion of both the auditing team and the interviewee must be recorded.

The report should include an executive summary containing the most important results of the inspection, the recommendations and a description of the evolution of the environmental situation in the area of the project.

Complex projects may be sub-divided into different operational areas for inspection, as a matter of methodological convenience. For example, in a mining complex, the inspection may be divided between extractive and processing operations. Although these two operations may have different effects, the final report must not lose sight of the fact that the quality of the environment in the area of the project depends on a combination of both operations.

vii   Follow-up of an environmental audit

After receiving the final report of an environmental audit, the management of the facility inspected must prepare a programme of action, based on the report and especially its recommendations, aimed at correcting situations which failed to meet the minimum requirements for environmental quality. The programme should specify the objectives, the activities to be carried out and the timetable. This programme should be evaluated in the next audit.

17 Building Human Resource Capacity for Environmental Education

MÁRIO SOUTO

The promotion of sustainable development in any country is the responsibility of all individuals and groups in the different spheres of economic and social life. However, in recent decades the various inter-linkages that need to be made in guiding this process and its growing complexity have highlighted the importance of countries having specific mechanisms for promoting sustainable development. This is not a process which is likely to occur spontaneously nor can it arise from unilateral actions, however well conceived from the environmental point of view.

Following the first multi-party elections in Mozambique and the subsequent constitution of a new government, the Ministry for the Co-ordination of Environmental Action (MICOA) was established. This ministry evolved out of the government entity created in 1992 to co-ordinate environmental matters, the National Environment Commission (CNA).

An important CNA initiative in fulfilment of its mandate was the formulation of the National Environment Management Plan (NEMP), in collaboration with the World Bank, UNDP and various bilateral co-operation partners. The NEMP co-ordinates a series of sectoral plans aimed at helping to consolidate actions which will try to ensure the sustainable development of the country in the medium and long term.

For NEMP purposes the country has been sub-divided into three major zones: rural, coastal and urban. The NEMP describes the main problems and the specific interventions required in each zone in order to facilitate sustainable development. The on-going process of identifying problems and solutions and the subsequent implementation of the necessary environmental management measures adapted to each zone, will require the following: physical investments; legislation; monitoring and evaluation systems; human resource development; research and extension; and international co-operation.

This chapter presents a series of guidelines to help develop human resources for the promotion of sustainable development. The starting point is the need for a general framework of guidelines and actions for human resource development. This provides the basis for identifying, and later integrating, many of the current initiatives in this field, which at the moment tend to be dispersed and isolated.

The main premises

In parallel with consciously directed actions in other fields to promote sustainable development, it is essential that a relatively cohesive programme of human resource development should be prepared and implemented. Such a programme is further justified by the following:

(a) The absence of an 'environmental culture' in the country. Sustainable development is an integral part of a new paradigm, noticeably absent from the way of thinking and acting of both traditional Mozambican society and its current modern sector, which is still heavily dominated by a narrowly mechanistic view of development processes.

(b) Fragile human resources. Despite the enormous efforts made in the education field since independence with some degree of success, Mozambique's population still has high rates of illiteracy and low education indices. It was estimated in the late 1980s that about 70% of the population are illiterate, that 22% have less than 4 years of education, that 6% have 4 years (the current first level of primary education) and that only the remaining 2% have more than 4 years of formal education (Johnston et al., 1987:5). While recognizing that not everything related to proper environmental management has specific implications for academic qualifications, it is undeniable that under current circumstances some of the functions linked to the promotion and implementation of measures for sustainable development require people with more academic and technical-professional education. This often cannot be found, given the country's stock of human resources.

In order to improve this situation, using their own resources and in collaboration with other groups within the country and abroad, both the CNA and MICOA have been active in organizing a wide variety of education and training activities for many different groups. This has had a positive effect in helping to create the new 'environmental culture' that the country needs.

However, it is also evident that initiatives and actions have been somewhat dispersed and that this tends to provoke a lack of co-ordination and in some cases gaps appear which should not exist. In addition, there is a lack of continuity in education and training activities, and difficulties crop up in monitoring and following up people and projects. This is particularly serious in a context marked by an acute shortage of resources, as is the case in Mozambique.

In order to change this situation, a key dimension would be to move away from the excessive 'projectization' of activities, whereby successive projects are created in an attempt to achieve specific but partial objectives, to action based on a more cohesive programme in which the development objectives, the beneficiaries, the main activities, the organizational forms, implementation, resources, inter-linkages, monitoring and evaluation, are clear, comprehensive and harmonized.

Target groups and general development objectives

The promotion of sustainable development requires the following main categories of people:

(a) **People in command positions**. This category comprises those who make the policies and take the decisions on environmental issues in the country. In order to take the most appropriate decisions they need to have a reasonable amount of knowledge and understanding of the multiple questions involved in the sustainable management of resources. They must also be able to communicate with each other on these questions and with other categories of people. In general, this group includes: deputies to the Assembly of the Republic; members of the Council of Ministers, particularly those linked to sectors of particular relevance to environmental management; Provincial Governors; and other groups with general command and policy functions at different levels.

(b) **Technical and advisory people**. These comprise managers and technicians, usually of senior or middle rank, who study and evaluate development issues and measures, draw up guidelines and suggest alternative interventions in the various areas of economic and social life. This group includes national directors and heads of department in central government, the managers of large companies and technicians in charge of public and private activities in a wide variety of sectors, including NGOs.

(c) **Activists, extension and monitoring workers**. This group comprises those individuals and entities working with the various groups of agents who operate directly in the work process and in society at large, providing guidance and technical support and advice, and monitoring practices in order to encourage environmentally sound management. This category includes agricultural and other kinds of extensionists, health, education and information workers, community and social work agents, inspectors and others linked to technical assistance and the supervision and control of the everyday actions of various groups of producers and ordinary citizens.

(d) **Producers and communities**. These are people or groups working directly within the various fields of economic and social life. This category comprises producers in the primary sector (agriculture, fisheries and mineral extraction), and in industry and services, as well as the different units of human settlement throughout the country. In addition to being the largest group, they occupy a particularly prominent place in environmental conservation. The success or failure of the actions and measures taken to promote sustainable development is measured through their practices.

Actions to develop human resources

The promotion of the country's sustainable development presupposes that people in the above categories have the relevant knowledge, skills and attitudes to perform their functions in the environmental management field. Educational and training activities are needed which are appropriate to the specific characteristics of each group.

Types of education and training
(a) **Formal education**. Formal education is carried out in recognized institutions with clearly established hierarchical structures and relatively rigid forms of organization, conferring widely recognized levels of academic qualifications.

Of the categories outlined above, the technical and advisory people and the activist, extension and monitoring staff will tend to provide most candidates for this kind of education and training. These two categories of people need a solid and professional capacity to deal with environmental questions so that they can provide services of real value. It frequently falls to formal education to provide people with these skills.

In addition to training activities aimed at supplementing capacity in sustainable development subjects, through a 'licenciatura' (a five-year degree course), doctorate or other specialist courses for various kinds of professionals, work needs to be done to ensure that formal education in Mozambique increasingly incorporates environmental issues. On-going reform of the curriculum aimed at including some degree of environmental guidance in primary and secondary education must be progressively improved and extended to other levels and branches of education. This will make an important contribution to providing the country with citizens possessing a more solid awareness of conservation and environmental management.

(b)   **Non-formal education (training).** This covers all educational schemes organized in a more flexible manner with the aim of creating capacity to meet the needs
of more specific programmes and projects. Non-formal educational activities usually
take the form of seminars, workshops, lectures, and short- and medium-term
courses, dealing with specific problems directly related to people's lives and work.
Given its characteristics of flexibility and diversity, training of this kind may benefit
all the above categories in one way or another, but the first three groups in particular.

(c)   **Informal education (dissemination).** This is even more flexible than the
other forms, and occurs in a wide variety of places and situations. It usually encompasses instruction through daily inter-personal relations and can take the form of
practical internship, study visits, radio and TV programmes, books and magazines,
posters, pamphlets and other forms of social and inter-personal communication
which are not rigidly organized. In principle, all the above categories should benefit
from this kind of education, but especially producers and communities.

Institutional arrangements for training

Although the promotion of sustainable development is the responsibility of all seg-
ments of society, the biggest demands are made of the Ministry for the Co-ordination
of Environmental Action. This must be reflected in the quality of its staff, if it is to
fulfil the various components of its mandate successfully.

Given the specific situation of this ministry, in particular its relatively recent creation, its human resource development programme needs to be intrinsically linked to
other interventions in the human resource field. Interventions are required in the
following areas:

(a)   **Definition of staff complement and recruitment.** In parallel with the on-
going clarification of the Ministry's mandate and those of its individual operating
units (directorates, departments and sections at central, provincial and local level) in
the short and medium term, there is need for a more stable and precise definition of
which staff should work in the Ministry and how they should be recruited.

Efforts need to be made to define the precise attributes of each of MICOA's operational units and the posts to be created, in order to maximize operational performance. Recruitment for the various posts must ensure a close fit with these
definitions so as to ensure that the potential of those appointed matches the
Ministry's expectations of them.

(b)   **Internal training programme.** In 1996 MICOA had 87 officials paid directly
by the government (permanent line and contract staff), plus a few consultants, whose
numbers vary in accordance with the projects being implemented at any given time.
These figures refer only to the central level of operations.

The educational qualifications and general functions of the 87 officials are given in
Table 17.1. Most of these officials should receive careful guidance and on-going training so that, in partnership with staff in other sectors, they can perform the key functions for sustainable development promotion increasingly effectively. Capacity
building within MICOA needs to match the demands inherent in its mandate. It
needs to monitor closely the steps being taken to clarify this mandate and the subsequent recruitment of the necessary staff.

With the current staff complement, competent people will be required to carry out
MICOA's mandate in the following areas:

Table 17.1 *MICOA: Distribution of officials and technicians by levels of training and specialist area (1996)*

Educational Levels/ No. of officials and technicians	Higher				Middle	Basic	EP2	EP1
Speciality and functions	Doctorate	MA/MSc	Licenciatura (5 years)	BA/BSc (3 years)				
Administration					10	5		
Economics				1	2			
Documentation				1	4	1		
Computers					1			
Environment	1		1		4			
Physical Planning					6			
Sociology		1	1					
Biology			11	1				
Chemistry			3					
Agriculture and Forestry			2					
Geology			1					
Law			3					
International Relations			2					
General Support					2	5	17	1
Sub-total	1	1	24	3	29	11	17	1

Source: MICOA

A. Management of Natural Resources

- Natural resource management policies
- Environmental quality control, including environmental quality standards, global and integrated monitoring and evaluation programmes for air, water, and soil quality and for other environmental components; monitoring and evaluation of the environmental impact of development projects
- Evaluation of the environmental impact of socio-economic development
- Prevention and treatment of environmental accidents

B. Territorial planning, including rural settlements, urban development and coastal development

- National policies and strategies on territorial organization and use
- Establishment of norms and regulation of planning and territorial occupation at all levels
- Development of alternative territorial planning models

C. Environmental inspection

- Updating, systematization, and circulation of environmental legislation
- Control and inspection of the observance of environmental legislation

D. Environmental promotion and dissemination

- Co-ordination of large-scale environmental education and training techniques
- Participation in processes for the introduction of environmental education into formal education
- Environmental education and dissemination through the media

- Production and circulation of audio-visual materials for environmental education and dissemination
- Establishment and management of documentation centres, information and environmental extension

In addition to the initiatives taken by other government and non-governmental entities, public and private, national and foreign, it is expected that MICOA will play an important role in developing human capacity for promoting sustainable development in a series of organizations operating in Mozambique.

While adopting a mode of operation which does not hamper the initiatives and actions of others, MICOA must become, and be accepted as, the co-ordinator of this process, ensuring that the existing potential is used to the maximum and orienting it towards achieving objectives of national interest. Whilst promoting sustainable development should be the responsibility of all citizens and all have a real contribution to make, it is also a process which will be difficult to conduct without clear guidelines and effective multi-sectoral co-ordination. MICOA will collaborate with all its partners to identify and strengthen complementary aspects, overcome gaps and eliminate duplication of effort.

With regard to the management of natural resources and the environment, MICOA will have to work closely with the following ministries: Agriculture and Fisheries, Industry, Trade and Tourism, Mineral Resources and Energy, Public Works and Housing and Health. In order to implement a broader vision of the articulation between environmental management and socio-economic development, MICOA's privileged partners will be the Ministries of Planning and Finance, Public Administration and Education. MICOA will also establish direct forms of articulation with NGOs, particularly those with a relevant role in the management of natural resources. Activities resulting from these forms of co-operation must be translated into a solid partnership for the development of human resources, establishing various complementary types of competence.

Reference
Johnston, A., Kaluba, H., Karlsson, M. and Nystrom, K. (1987) *Education and Economic Crisis – The Cases of Mozambique and Zambia.* Swedish International Development Cooperation Agency, Educational Document No. 38, Stockholm.

18 Establishing Sustainability Criteria for Public Investment

ABÍLIO GUNE

The economic context

Although Mozambique is well endowed with a variety of natural resources, the gross national product (GNP) per capita is among the lowest in the world. The period from 1980 to 1985 was characterized by a fall in production, and a severe lack of import capacity, which lasted until 1986. The negative balance of payments, which was aggravated by the highly over-valued exchange rate, caused delays in servicing the external debt. Internally, the large fiscal deficit and the enormous subsidies to cover the operating deficits of state-owned enterprises resulted in an increase in the amount of money in circulation, despite the low production levels. Administrative measures rather than market mechanisms were used to control prices and allocate resources. Although their purpose was to promote social welfare, shortages of goods ensued, inflation rose and the parallel market for goods and foreign currency grew.

Structural problems in the economy have had a major impact on the agricultural sector. Many of these problems were the result of external factors, such as drought, floods, and the war, which came to an end in 1992, disrupting the rural economy and causing the majority of the population to abandon their land. Lack of qualified personnel and inadequate economic and social infrastructure made it difficult for the government to develop effective policies and plan activities. The poor performance of the agricultural sector is also explained by policies which fixed prices administratively and channelled public spending towards large-scale state farms which were capital-intensive at a time when capital was the factor of production in shortest supply. Scant attention was paid to the development of institutions and infrastructure to guarantee essential services for subsistence and commercial farmers. The adoption of a structural adjustment programme (PRE) in 1987 halted the economic decline. Basic marketing activities are still hampered, however, by the poor state of access roads, lack of transport, spares and fuel, and inadequate repair and maintenance services.

Economic development and sustainable development

One principal indicator of a country's level of development is its gross national product (GNP), which measures not only growth but also levels of consumption. According to this criterion, the higher the percentages of growth and consumption in a society, the greater is its development.

Sustainable development is a broader concept than the original concept of economic development, as measured by an increase in GNP, since it takes account of the future, not only in terms of forecasting growth and welfare, but also in terms of rationalizing the uses of renewable and non-renewable means and resources, which are critical factors in current economic growth patterns and in forecasting future trends. Sustainable development also takes account of the treatment or residual accumulation of waste from production or transformation processes and from consumption, relating it to the absorptive capacity of the ecosystems, with or without human interference. In practical terms, the concept of sustainable development encompasses two meanings: (i) the use of renewable resources, taking account of the balance between demand and the capacity for renewal of the natural stocks; and (ii) the use of non-renewable resources in a sensible way, applying enough of the outputs in research for alternatives and technologies to re-use and/or recycle them.

Economic development strategies should be compatible with present and future environmental objectives. The challenge is to find this equilibrium. There are no prescriptions or simple rules that automatically include environmental concerns in development processes. However, it is possible to design options and take certain decisions conducive to sustainable development; that is to say, they are environmentally balanced. On the one hand, it is necessary to identify the activities required to protect and conserve the environment, and on the other hand, purely economic national objectives should be linked to management of the environment.

It is frequently stated that correct environmental management is always economically sound. This means that each and every investment project that adopts environmental management principles conducive to sustainable development always guarantees a positive contribution to the national economy. However, clear guidelines should be proposed for investment so that it can be economically sustainable.

The characteristics of public investment in Mozambique

Progress has been made in investment programming and monitoring in line with the recommendations of the Economic and Social Recovery Programme (ESRP) of 1989. Since 1990, the basic policy instrument for programming investment has been the Triennial Public Investment Plan (TPIP). In reality, the TPIP is more a budget of projects than one of investment. It consists mainly of projects funded by donor aid, which includes significant sums for recurrent costs along with the investment. Currently the TPIP includes both sectoral and provincial investments. While there are difficulties in overseeing direct financing, this problem is tending to lessen because donors can enjoy exemption from customs duty on imports if their projects are registered in the TPIP.

The guiding principles for investment, according to the recommendations of the ESRP, are:

- the maintenance of macroeconomic balance by means of fiscal restraint exercised by imposing a limit on sectoral investment plans;
- giving priority to key sectors: agriculture, construction, transport and the social sectors (health, education and water supply);
- decentralization to the sectors of investment programming and project evaluation.

In practice expenditure on programming has exceeded the limit set, while that on execution has been lower than the programmed amount.

The sectoral trends for investment are determined partly by the preferences of the donors, who provide about 80% of the investment budget, while the remaining 20% state contribution is committed as the local counterpart in projects which are externally financed. Hence the sectoral allocation of investment does not simply depend upon the distribution of investment resources controlled centrally by the government, but also reflects each sector's potential for attracting donors.

Executing the investment budget presents real problems, given that budget resources are largely controlled by the funders, each with their own interests, practices and procedures. There is a considerable lack of transparency, since many donors provide little or no information on the execution of their projects. The problem is generally less prevalent with funds supplied as credit, since these are administered through the central bank, but is most apparent with grant-funded projects.

Sustainability criteria
Sustainable development is development which not only lasts but which has significant multiplier effects. The multiplier effects of each investment activity should be identified and many include guaranteeing the replacement of resources utilized. Sustainable development implies projects that try to minimize damage to the natural environment, since it is just about impossible to imagine a project that does not interfere in some way with the environment.

In order to establish sustainability criteria, those factors which make development unsustainable need to be analyzed. The criteria then identified need to be applicable both in the public and in the private spheres, even though the weight given to any one criterion may vary from case to case.

Economic criteria
In analyzing any investment, the economic criteria require an estimation of the probability that the investment will contribute significantly to the overall development of the economy and that the contribution will be significant enough to justify the consumption of the scarce resources involved. The economic criteria and the financial criteria, which will be discussed later, should be complementary, in that the financial criteria reflect the point of view of the individual participants, while the economic criteria adopt the point of view of society as a whole. However, the fact that discounted cash flow may be used as a measure in both methods of analysis, means that they are sometimes confused.

There are three main differences between the two methods, namely:

- In economic analysis, taxes and subsidies are regarded as transfer payments (to the government on behalf of society). They are therefore not costs. In financial analysis, taxes are regarded as costs and subsidies as revenue.
- The data used in economic analysis are obtained from the market prices used in financial analysis by calculating a shadow price which is an efficiency price reflecting social and economic values.
- In economic analysis interest on capital is not separated out and deducted from the gross return because it is part of the total return on the capital available to society as a whole, and it is that total return, including interest, that economic analysis attempts to estimate. In financial analysis, interest is deducted as a return to the owner of the capital.

If cost-benefit analysis is applied, the steps would be the same; only the definitions of what is a cost and what is a benefit are different.

Political decision-makers need to be concerned with how the investment of scarce capital resources meets national objectives, regardless of whether the capital comes directly from the government or from private sources. The objective is to identify the investments which can make a beneficial contribution to national income. In general, economic analysis makes it possible to remunerate labour and other inputs at market prices or at shadow prices, with the aim of approximating efficiency prices or the opportunity costs – the value we must give up if we transfer a certain resource from its current use to another purpose. The remainder is then compared with the capital required for the project. The projects which present the best return to capital, given the resources available, are chosen for implementation. The present study assumes that capital is the most important constraint on rapid economic growth. It is not implied, however, that capital alone can bring about economic growth. All the factors of production combined in a project contribute to the generation of new income.

Financial criteria

Financial effects usually receive the most attention. The financial implications of an investment include how it will impact on individual participants, public and private firms, institutions and even, in some cases, the national treasury, and conclusions must be drawn about the financial efficiency of the investment. The analysis and appraisal undertaken should provide answers to the following questions:

- What is the impact at household level, in particular for those on low incomes? Sustainability may be checked by analyzing the effects on income and expenditure, purchasing power and the capacity to repay loans.
- In a long-term investment, how can the undertaking be sustained until it produces its first outputs? What special alternatives can be created to guarantee sustainability in the initial phase?
- What incentives will be produced at the beneficiary level? This depends on the income they will receive as a result of the investment.
- In the financial administration of a project, in order to guarantee funding at the right time and in the right quantity, we need to establish what are the operating costs and how they will be met, and whether government policy will have to be changed to cover these costs.
- Is the investment fiscally sustainable as identified through the projected variation in the receipts from the investment, whether other resources besides the investment are needed to encourage participation by the beneficiaries and whether the administrative costs will continue to require resources from the state coffers? What is the effect on the treasury, besides the impact of operating and maintenance costs, for external investment in the form of loans or grants?

Social criteria

Analysts are becoming more and more concerned with examining the broader social implications of proposed investments. Among the aspects that may be included in these criteria in order to ensure sustainability are:

- taking account of the social patterns and practices of the target groups;
- weighting income distribution to ensure that the investment has greater impact in the form of benefits for low-income groups;
- ensuring the greatest possible awareness of the impact of the investment on defined national objectives, in particular, job creation, which is linked to income distribution, development of a specific region, and raising living standards through greater access to social goods and services;
- ensuring the compatibility of investment with maintenance of the environment, on which all possible effects must be analyzed (economic activities, health, conservation/preservation of the environment, etc);
- locating projects in places where the introduction of any technology does not cause problems that have to be corrected, which is always more expensive than preventing the problems in the first place.

Technical criteria
These focus mainly on the material inputs and the outputs of actual goods and services produced. It is important that the project framework be clearly defined in order to allow a thorough and precise technical analysis. These criteria guarantee sustainability, given that they ensure that the technical estimates and projections are related to existing conditions and that the facilities to be created by the investment will lead to the results foreseen.

Institutional, organizational and management criteria
All the preparations for an investment revolve around the institutional, organizational and management aspects of the projected undertaking, since they clearly have a significant effect on implementation. Thus, in order to ensure the sustainability of an investment, answers must be found for a number of institutional, organizational and management concerns, such as:

In the institutional sphere
- Have the customs and culture of the beneficiaries been taken into account in the design of the investment?
- Will implementation lead to the disruption of normal labour practices? If yes, what provisions are planned to help introduce the new patterns?
- What channels of communication exist for the transmission of new techniques?
- In view of the fact that adoption processes can be slow, is enough time being allowed for the beneficiaries to accept the new procedures or is the project plan over-optimistic with regard to average adoption rates?

In order for a project to progress, it should be properly linked to the institutional structure in the project area. It will therefore be necessary to deal with certain questions, such as the following:

- What is the situation regarding land tenure?
- What size of holding will be encouraged?
- Does the project involve local institutions in a complementary relationship?
- How will the administration of the project be organized in relation to other local agencies?
- If a separate authority will be required, how will it relate to the relevant line ministry?
- Will there be any reasons for competition or conflict between staff contracted for the project and staff in existing institutions?

In the organizational sphere
With regard to organization, all the institutions involved must have the opportunity to make comments on the proposed organization of the project. These comments must be taken into account when the final decision is made. Thus, the following aspects need to be considered:

- That the lines of authority are clearly defined within the organization.
- That authority is properly related to responsibility.
- Whether the organizational design permits delegation of power or requires that everything be submitted to the director.
- That up-to-date information on the progress of the project is available both to the project managers and to the supervisors in the central government authority.
- Is a special monitoring group necessary? Is one on training required? Is there

sufficient capacity to keep the project's financial affairs up-to-date, including timely disbursements?

In the management sphere
Management is crucial to project design and implementation. The capacity of the available staff must be analyzed in terms of skill in managing a large and complex public project. If this skill does not exist, it may be necessary to review the technical options in the project design, or the preference may be to contract expatriate staff. Even though expatriate staff may be well qualified, it may not be possible for them to pass on their experience to anyone during the implementation of the project, for whatever reason, and this could cause the project to collapse. In many cases, the best option has been to avoid the necessity of employing expatriate staff for management.

In considering the management and administrative aspects, the project design should be concerned not only with foreseeing possible problems that could occur, but mainly with a realistic evaluation of how they can be rapidly resolved. Delays in implementation are not compatible with the project's contribution to increased income.

Commercial criteria (market availability)
These criteria include the market for selling the product to be produced by the project and the market for inputs during the implementation phase, as well as during the operating phase. A level of demand at profitable prices must be guaranteed for the products produced by the project. Other aspects that need to be addressed are as follows:

- Where will the products be sold?
- The market must be large enough to absorb the production without affecting the price. If the price is affected, then by how much? Will the project continue to be sustainable at the new price?
- Do facilities exist to handle the new products?
- Is the product for domestic consumption or for export?
- Does the project guarantee production at the quality demanded by the market?
- What conditions are required to place the product on the market? Or what special measures must be taken during the implementation phase to ensure marketing?

With regard to inputs, concern should be directed towards the following questions:
- Do market channels for the inputs exist, and do they have enough capacity to meet the needs for new inputs on time?
- Should the project establish new channels or should special measures be taken within the project to encourage the establishment of new channels?
- One of the aspects of commercial criteria is the arrangements for procurement of equipment and materials. Is it possible to avoid delays in the procedures?
- Do procedures exist for competitive bidding to guarantee equitable prices?
- Who will have the responsibility for drafting the specifications for procurement?

Conclusions and recommendations

First of all, there must be consensus about the criteria to be observed in the public investment process among all the institutions involved, from the design of methodologies and proposals to appraisal and approval. The guidelines and methodologies for the preparation of the Public Investment Plan should include space to ensure compliance with the criteria to be established by consensus and approved by the competent authority. A strong position must be taken to avoid the authorization of projects that do not meet the requirements to guarantee sustainability. It is well known that the capacity of the personnel determine both the quality of the design and the character of the decisions made; training activities should therefore be carried out at all levels in each sector.

19 The Role of Environmental Impact Assessment in Development Projects

SARA TAIBO

The objective of this chapter is to describe and evaluate the efficiency of the process of Environmental Impact Assessment (EIA) for private investment in Mozambique. It relates the legal, institutional and political dimensions of the process to the technical and practical aspects. The chapter begins with the general definition of an EIA and the specific phases involved. It then considers the best way to carry out an EIA and this serves as a point of reference for the subsequent analysis of the situation in Mozambique. Some recommendations are then made for improving the EIA process to enable the country to progress towards a future of more sustainable development.

Environmental impact assessment

EIA definitions vary and are often based on different concepts. Some include socio-economic impacts and others are restricted to physical and ecological aspects. Some refer to decision-making and others are simply technical and predictive exercises. One definition of EIA which seems comprehensive may be summed up in the following three points. It is a procedure which encourages decision-makers to take account of the possible effects of particular investments on the quality of the environment and the productivity of natural resources. It is an instrument for collecting and combining data which the planners need to make projects environmentally sound and sustainable. It is used as a policy instrument to encourage the sustainable and rational utilization of resources.

The purpose of an EIA is to provide the decision-makers with information about the effects on the environment of proposed activities, before any decision is taken. This way the decision-makers can suggest not only modifications to any activities with a potential negative impact, but also the mechanisms required to minimize unavoidable negative impacts.

An EIA is a continuous process which should begin the moment the intention is formed to undertake a particular activity and end only when the activity is complete and its impact accounted for. The essential phases of the EIA process are:

i) screening;
ii) scoping;
ii) baseline studies and benchmark data;
iv) preparation and review of an Environmental Impact Study (EIS);
v) monitoring and post-evaluation.

Screening consists of the selection of the activities to be subject to an EIA. The type and nature of the project should be taken into account, as well as the sensitivity of the area. These considerations are important because of the limited financial and technical resources available. There are three methods for the selection of projects. The first is by means of a list indicating clearly what type of projects should be subject to an EIA. The second is to take a case-by-case approach to the decision to subject projects to an EIA. Finally, there can be some combination of the two approaches.

The scoping of an Environmental Impact Study (EIS) consists of trying to identify the environmental components about which there is public and technical concern and which should be covered by the EIS. The participation of the public is very important in this phase. An EIS should be restricted to important and significant questions, because of time and resource constraints. Baseline studies and benchmark data involve the collection of data on the parts of the environment which may be affected by a project (baseline study) and a future projection of the condition of the environment without the project (benchmark data). The preparation phase should demonstrate the necessity or not for the EIS, before any economic feasibility studies are conducted. In the preparation phase, various alternatives with regard to the project are considered and evaluated, notably location, design, size, construction technology, starting and finishing dates, as well as the non-implementation of the project altogether. Then the impact of each alternative under consideration is identified, forecast and assessed, thus allowing the EIS to pinpoint unavoidable effects and suggest measures to reduce their impact.

Given the degree of uncertainty surrounding whether the negative impact will occur or that the corrective measures will be effective, the EIS should contain provision for a periodic control or monitoring programme, once implementation of the project has begun.

The responsibility for the finalization of the EIS may rest with:

- the licensing authority;
- the proposer of the project or a consultant contracted for the purpose;
- the proposer (bearing the costs) in partnership with the licensing authority (establishing guidelines and carrying out the baseline and benchmark studies);
- an independent body, financed totally or partially by the state.

The review of the environmental impact study (EIS) may be carried out by an inter-departmental committee, by an independent committee of experts, by a committee composed of representatives from various bodies or even by a combination of all three, but there has to be public participation. The review consists of checking the quality of the EIS and, for the sake of efficiency, it should be delegated to an entity or person independent of the team, the project proposer or the competent authority. The review results will show whether project implementation can be given the go-ahead or if further studies are needed.

Monitoring and post-evaluation involve evaluation of both the accuracy of the forecast of effects and the effectiveness of the measures to reduce their impact and the efficiency of the environmental management and administrative procedures. This is of great importance to improving environmental impact assessment and environmental management. The post-implementation evaluation studies include a wide range of activities, such as environmental audits and the development of monitoring programmes.

The process of EIA in Mozambique

Foreign and domestic private investment in Mozambique is governed by law No. 3/93 and its regulations of 24 June 1993. This law is applicable to investments of an economic nature that wish to enjoy the guarantees and incentives it provides, as well as to investments in free industrial zones and special economic areas. A basic guiding principle in the current law is the requirement that investments must make a contribution to sustainable social and economic development in the country and must comply with the objectives of national economic policy and the legislation in force.

In relation to environmental management, the Investment Law states specifically in article 26 that investors are obliged to carry out an EIA during the design, implementation and operational phases of any projects. In addition, investors are obliged to take appropriate steps for the prevention of negative effects and the reduction of those that are unavoidable, and to ensure that their activities comply with the laws and regulations of the competent authorities. The Investment Law gives the Ministry of Planning and Finance the responsibility for the co-ordination of all investments. The Investment Promotion Centre (IPC) was set up as an advisory body to promote investment, analyze proposals and monitor and review investment projects.

According to the Investment Law regulations, the process of project evaluation begins with the delivery and registration at the Investment Promotion Centre of the investment proposal, which should be filled out on the special form and accompanied by the proper documentation in triplicate. After it has received and registered an investment proposal, the IPC, within a maximum period of seven days, should verify it at an internal level and in co-ordination with the appropriate authorities, such as the provincial government or the municipal council. This institutional co-ordination may include the Ministry for the Co-ordination of Environmental Action, depending on the nature, size and location of the project.

The IPC checks the following aspects of investment proposals:

a) their compliance with the provisions of the Investment Law and with the basic principles of national economic policy:
b) their technical, economic and financial viability;
c) their political, environmental or other implications; and
d) the provisions made or planned to guarantee that the required infrastructure, equipment and staff are available.

Organizations involved in the verification and the Ministry of Planning and Finance, through the customs and excise department, have to nominate their representatives who will inform the IPC about the position taken by their organization in relation to the proposal. The IPC conducts this process of consultation by calling a meeting to discuss the opinions and positions of the other sectors with regard to each proposal.

If the proposal is approved, the IPC prepares a proposal for authorization to be submitted for consideration and approval by the competent authority. This authority, in turn, must in principle give its opinion within three to ten days, depending upon its level of authority.

Once a decision has been made, the IPC is meant to notify the investor of the decision within two days. When a proposal is authorized, the investor must start implementation of the project within 120 days, unless another time period is specified or the authorization requires the presentation of other specific studies or additional documentation. The following phase is that of monitoring the projects, by both the appropriate sector authorities and the IPC, to check on compliance with the relevant legislation and regulations and the terms of the authorization.

Environmental impact assessment within projects

Environmental management in Mozambique, until the early 1980s, entailed little more than issuing and enforcing sectoral regulations that had practically no bearing on the conservation of natural resources, and the application of sporadic measures for the conservation of flora and fauna and the protection of the coast. Although efforts began in 1982 to create an institution which would integrate environmental principles into the development process of the country, ten years passed before the National Environment Commission (CNA) was set up. Two years later, in December 1994, the Ministry for the Co-ordination of Environmental Action (MICOA) was established.

The first attempt to create national legislation for environmental management was initiated by the CNA, with a draft Environmental Law. This had to be revised and adapted to meet the new challenges of sustainable development arising from the political and institutional changes introduced after the first democratic elections, which led to the creation of MICOA. The proposed legal framework for the environment establishes the basis for action by the government and citizens in the everyday use and management of natural resources. This specifically includes the process of EIA as an environmental management tool, which complements and co-ordinates the sectoral regulations. In this context, the provisions of the draft law include the requirement that all activities which may have a significant environmental impact, because of their location, nature or size, will be subject to an EIA and issued with an environmental licence, which must precede any other licence required by law in every case.

At present, the legal environmental framework is still awaiting discussion and approval by parliament. In the meantime, the EIA process introduced in 1994 is being implemented in a rather informal manner, since the technical, institutional and political structures are weak. Some sectoral legislation requires that an EIA be conducted for certain projects, and this is being carried out by the National Directorate for Natural Resources which is MICOA's department responsible for EIAs.

The EIA process started in 1994, after the peace agreement brought a rapid influx of investment projects into the country. This alerted the government to the need for economic development to be made compatible with environmental management in order to allow the country to progress towards sustainable development. In this context, and because the EIA regulations and the environmental legal framework are still awaiting approval, the EIA process is still not compulsory, even though the activities which must under certain circumstances be subject to EIA have been identified.

The EIA begins with the identification of the need to carry out an EIS for a proposed project. This identification can be done beforehand by the IPC or by the relevant government department, depending on the nature, size and location of the project, or subsequently by MICOA. Once the need to carry out an EIS has been identified, the project proposer is then notified by the IPC. It is the proposer's duty to conduct the EIS, using the terms of reference provided by MICOA. The EIS is then submitted to MICOA and a team is assembled, consisting of senior technicians from MICOA and the sectoral authorities, depending on the nature and location of the project. It is MICOA's responsibility to review the EIS and evaluate the results of the public consultation. MICOA's opinion will serve as the basis for issuing or denying a permit for the project.

The next phase in the EIA process is monitoring, which is the responsibility of the project implementers under the supervision of MICOA, to ensure that implementation follows the guidelines already set out in the EIS. The frequency and schedule of auditing are established according to the variables and the actual project to be inspected.

Despite the fact that EIA is fairly new to the country, it has already created environmental awareness among decision-makers, project promoters and the public in general, in the following ways. At the decision-making level, the tourism sector is regarded as being in the forefront in including an environmental component in the evaluation and authorization of development projects. This sector has played an important role in removing and relocating projects situated in the coastal zone which could have a negative impact on the environment. This was the case with tourism projects sited on dunes. At the level of project promoters, there has been the development, albeit gradual, of an environmental mentality and culture, which is mainly seen in the concern about whether their projects will have to be subject to EIA. The public has also become aware of the need to evaluate the advantages and disadvantages of specific activities within the environment in which these initiatives will take place. Moreover, the public has played an important role in informing MICOA of environmental pollution occurring from existing projects. This illustrates the importance of the role that EIAs can play in helping to achieve sustainable development.

An EIS covers specific aspects which are defined in the terms of reference and relate to compliance with the sectoral laws and regulations relevant to the particular type of project, such as protection of the country's natural, social and cultural heritage, soil conservation, pollution control, etc. In this way, the EIA reflects and integrates sectoral concerns in the management of natural resources. The role of the local authorities and non-governmental bodies is now being recognized. There is greater emphasis on the need for them to be trained and involved in environmental management.

The schedule of an EIA depends very much on the type of project and the implementation period of the EIS. The EIA schedule should be proposed by the project implementers in order to contribute to the efficiency of the process. Although the EIA process lacks legal force and currently enjoys very limited public participation, there has been considerable efficacy achieved with the EIAs conducted on the basis of pre-defined terms of reference. There have been very few cases of projects avoiding an EIA because the selection process has been made on a case-by-case basis. In addition, it has been found that in practice MICOA's opinion is binding.

The absence of an approved legal framework for the environment promotes the non-compulsory and informal character of EIAs in Mozambique. Some decision-makers take a negative attitude to EIA and regard it as an obstacle to development because it discourages investors, since it involves extra costs and may delay or hamper the process of authorizing projects. Because there is no clear and established definition of what activities should be subject to EIA, MICOA becomes involved in most cases only after the project proposal has been presented to the IPC. It has been found that the EIA is usually ineffective in cases where the project proposer has not contacted MICOA or has not observed the provisions in the terms of reference.

Although the phases of EIA that require public participation have been identified, the public has not participated actively in practice because the consultants regard EIA as simply a technical process of data collection and because there are no ready-made formats designed for public consultation. Moreover, it is argued that holding public meetings is time-consuming and complicated by communications difficulties. The only project that has involved active participation is MosaFlorestal, because of its nature and location and because it is large in relation to other projects (see Chapter 24).

Project review has only been started after the completion of the EIA. The review has been carried out by irregular teams formed haphazardly and composed solely of central government officials, most of whom are unclear about what is involved in the analysis of an EIA report. Thus there is a tendency to analyze the project rather than the EIA report. This, coupled with the lack of a data bank containing all the information required for environmental management, indicates the range of obstacles to an efficient system of EIA.

Control mechanisms have not yet been established, since the procedures for environmental inspection are still under preparation. For this reason and because of the ignorance of local authorities in relation to environmental management, many projects avoid EIA, particularly those which are not formally authorized or which receive permits from the local authority without the knowledge of the relevant line department.

Recommendations

Despite the great difficulties facing EIA in Mozambique, the potential conditions exist for it to become efficient, if certain steps are taken in both the short and the longer term. Greater emphasis should be placed on adapting the EIA process to local conditions, particularly to the specific circumstances of Mozambican decision-makers, so that EIA becomes an efficient aid to taking correct decisions. The following conditions must be met if this goal is to be achieved:

a)   There must be systematic technical training in environmental management topics for the officials involved in the process, as well as for consultants and the general public. This could result in the preparation of a technical manual for EIA.

b)   The institutional setting of EIA must be strengthened and its administration clarified. This would be done by formulating and publicizing rules for conducting EIA and by providing resources at all levels of involvement, including at the national level.

c)   A standard methodology needs to be established at national level for the selection, review and monitoring of projects liable for EIA. This could be achieved by designing standard forms and making them available to decision-making and co-ordinating bodies at central and local level.

d)   Supporting materials should be provided, particularly EIA guidelines which contain general terms of reference and terms of reference specific to differing types of projects.

e)   The role of the different parties at each stage of the process needs to be clarified, notably that of the licensing authority, the institution responsible for EIA and of civil society.

20 Managing Water Resources in the South

ISSUFO CHUTUMIA

Water resources in Mozambique: the current situation

Water is one of the most precious natural resources any country possesses. Managing those water resources wisely provides an essential challenge to sustainable development. We begin by looking at the existing water resources in Mozambique.

The rainfall distribution is variable both from north to south and from east to west. The annual average rainfall ranges between 800 mm and 1,400 mm in the coastal zones; between 1,000 mm and 2,000 mm in the mountainous interior in the centre and north of the country; and between 300 mm and 1,000 mm in the southern region. The potential evapotranspiration ranges from 700 mm to 1,600 mm in the north; from 1,200 mm to 1,400 mm in the Limpopo Valley; and from 100 mm to 1,200 mm to the south of the Incomati Valley.

There are three main types of vegetation: dense forest, permeable forest and savannah. The dense forest occurs mainly in small areas of the provinces in the centre and north of the country. The other two types of vegetation are found further south.

The mean annual volume of surface water potentially available in Mozambique is estimated to be about 217 billion (thousand million) cubic metres. Almost half (46%) of this volume results from rainfall inside the country and the remaining 54% comes in from international rivers that rise in neighbouring countries. The Zambezi River accounts for 75% of this water. The rainfall component occurs mainly in the river basins in the centre and north, while the main sources of water in the south are the international rivers.

There are three main aquifers occurring in the three principal geological formations: the Crystalline Complex (Palaeozoic and Pre-Cambrian); the Karoo; and the Post-Karoo sedimentary formations (Mesozoic, Tertiary and Quaternary). The spatial distribution of the two most important geological formations in the country may be shown as follows:

- The Crystalline Complex in the centre and north has average flows of from 1 to 2 cubic metres per hour. Exceptions may be found in faults, where flows can reach from 40 to 70 cubic metres per hour.
- The Post-Karoo covers almost all of the country south of the Save River and parts of the centre. Here the flows range from 4 to 5 cubic metres per hour in the deepest aquifers.

Mozambique in a regional context

Mozambique shares its main rivers with a number of upstream countries. These rivers are the Ruvuma, the Zambezi, the Pungwe, the Save, the Limpopo, the Incomati, the Umbeluzi and the Maputo. It is dependent, therefore, in terms of its water resources on its neighbours. Water is a driving force of development, hence it is important that development plans take into account water resource issues and relations of interdependence with the country's upstream neighbours. The national interests of Mozambique are unavoidably contingent on external factors.

These geopolitical realities have never been ignored, indeed they have been the subject of much political analysis. The southern African region has seen major social and political changes over the past 40 years. The liberation wars against Portuguese colonialism, the Zimbabwe and Namibian liberation wars and the struggle for majority rule in South Africa contributed to creating a climate of political uncertainty. This fostered the establishment of alliances between South Africa and Portugal, Rhodesia and Portugal and South Africa and Rhodesia. However, whatever alliances may have been established, they did not help the water sector, since generally no water-sharing agreements were reached.

Despite the universally accepted precepts on the need for 'integrated management of water resources' and 'regional sustainable development', the question of the equitable use of water by countries sharing rivers still poses a dilemma worldwide. Over 200 major rivers are shared by two or more countries. These river basins constitute about 60% of the total land area of all the continents put together. However, isolated planning by individual countries of the use of common water resources is the rule rather than the exception that it should be. There are over 300 treaties on water-sharing or on specific aspects of water-sharing, and reference is made to water in over 2,000 international treaties. Nevertheless, effective co-ordinated management of international rivers remains rare, resulting in economic costs, environmental degradation and international conflicts (World Bank, 1993).

Because of its geographical circumstances, Mozambique has been endeavouring for the past 30 years to make treaties with neighbouring countries on their common rivers. The priority has always been the rivers in the south that form the borders with South Africa and Swaziland. There are probably two basic reasons for this. Firstly, the region is semi-arid, with low rainfall and a very irregular water situation, alternating between long periods of drought and periodic floods. Secondly, there is the fact that South Africa is much more developed with a more intensive use of the common water resources. Mozambique also needs to secure the flow of the Umbeluzi River, which it shares with Swaziland, because this is the source of water for its capital, Maputo.

When Mozambique was still a Portuguese colony, bilateral and trilateral technical commissions were set up with South Africa and then Swaziland to discuss water-sharing in the Incomati and Umbeluzi basins. The first Mozambique-South Africa Commission was established in 1960 and Swaziland joined seven years later. Thus began a phase of regular consultation about the common rivers. In 1986, Mozambique joined the countries that share the Limpopo basin, namely South Africa, Botswana and Zimbabwe, to form the Limpopo Basin Permanent Technical Committee.

Despite the establishment of these technical committees, which meet twice a year, and all the efforts to establish water-sharing agreements, the first positive sign of action in this regard came in 1971, when the Massingir dam began to be built on the Elephants River. This was not so much a water-sharing agreement, as an indication of no objection by South Africa, since the dam when full would flood a part of the

Kruger National Park in South Africa. The first and only real water-sharing agreement was made in 1976 between Mozambique and Swaziland over the Umbeluzi River.

Agreements are usually founded on universally accepted principles. These principles are based above all on the equitable use of common resources, on the absence of limitations to development and on the minimization of loss in the preservation of the environment. Reaching agreement is not an end in itself, but a mechanism whereby the signatories establish rules to which they are committed. In fact, an agreement is only really valid if the parties comply with it.

The Umbeluzi Agreement uses the Helsinki Rules published by the Association of Human Rights in 1966 as its underlying principle. The agreement stipulates that Mozambique must receive at the border 40% of the annual flow of the Umbeluzi River and its tributary the White Umbeluzi.

Comparing the actual flow of 91 million cubic metres with the average annual flow of the Umbeluzi of 350 million cubic metres, based on 33 years of observations from 1951 to 1984, Mozambique in fact received 26% of the flow and not 40%. Moreover, the agreement does not establish the conditions under which this volume of water must be released. If a flood were to cause 100 million cubic metres at once to flow over the border, would Swaziland's obligations cease as of that moment? Another weakness of the agreement is that it contains no reference to the quality of the water.

An obvious question to ask is why did Mozambique sign this agreement? In the light of its history, of geopolitical confrontations with the white minority regimes, it would appear that there was a far stronger political rather than technical impetus behind the agreement. Portugal never agreed to the proposals made by Swaziland. The project to build the Pequenos Libombos dam was decided on unilaterally by Portugal. Mozambique became independent in 1975, and took a firm stance against apartheid in South Africa and the white minority regime in Rhodesia.

Because Swaziland is an African kingdom wedged between Mozambique and South Africa and Mozambique needed an ally, the agreement was signed. Geopolitical factors were the overriding consideration. What is required now is to consider whether it would be worthwhile reviewing the agreement in the light of the political transformations that have taken place in the region.

All that Mozambique claims with regard to the Incomati basin are guarantees of a minimum flow in the river from the border to the river mouth in order to preserve the ecology of the system. These claims have not yet been met. What has happened over the last 10 years is that the Incomati has turned into a river of sand. The reasons are mainly the drought that struck the region and the development and expansion of agriculture and industry in South Africa. Far from ensuring an equitable use of the basin, Mozambique has seen its part of the basin become a desert. What can be done? Mozambique needs to continue with the peaceful negotiation of its rights, while trying to persuade its neighbour of the need for integrated water resource management for regional sustainable development.

Protocol on water-sharing in the SADC region

One of the most important actions taken by the SADC countries is without doubt reaching agreement for a protocol to govern the use of water resources in common rivers in the region. The idea of the protocol arose when it was understood that joint planning for the Zambezi basin was needed, mainly aimed at environmental preservation. The United Nations Environment Programme (UNEP) was the force behind the Zambezi management project. UNEP first approached each of the countries that share the Zambezi basin in 1987 and came to the conclusion that the leadership of the process should lie with the SADC itself, more specifically SADC-ELMS (Environment and Land Management Sector).

It was agreed that the countries sharing the Zambezi basin should sign a protocol of understanding on the basin so that the project might go ahead. However, it was then decided to extend the protocol to cover all the shared river basins in the SADC region, since the countries sharing the Zambezi basin were a majority in the organization (South Africa was not then a member). This was a really ambitious decision, considering that a specific case, the Zambezi River, was turned into a more general and broad-based, but much more complex, arrangement. While the Zambezi has a plentiful flow and faces no great problems of water shortage, the other shared watercourses in the region have completely different characteristics.

The protocol is based on international rules and seeks to respect the national policies of each country and existing agreements, with the aim of bringing these into harmony with regional interests. The most telling proof of the difficulty in achieving this harmony is the fact that the protocol was only signed six years after the first draft was produced. Mozambique was one of the countries that had reservations when it signed. Some countries have still not signed. Mozambique is of the opinion that some basic definitions in the protocol ought to be revised, since they do not serve Mozambican interests, and to a certain extent run counter to them. The protocol was signed in 1995 and includes South Africa, by then a SADC member, among its signatories.

The implementation of the protocol by ELMS has aroused some controversy among the member countries, since ELMS is qualified to manage the environment rather than water, and seems to lack the necessary background for implementing its expanded mandate. In fact, the water sector professionals felt that a specialized co-ordinating unit for water should be set up, since water was being dealt with as a subsector of the environment and in a very fragmented way. In other words, water appeared as part of agriculture, of shipping, of fisheries, etc., but not as a thread linking all the different sectors, which is what is needed. It was ridiculous that water technicians attended meetings of the technical sub-committees to discuss and analyze joint water projects, but there were no water professionals at the decision-making levels: the technical committee and the committee of ministers of ELMS. Consequently, the ministers had to take decisions on matters for which they were not qualified. In the late 1990s a water sector was finally established within the SADC.

On 22 March 1998, World Water Day, a major international study of Water and Population Dynamics, undertaken by the International Union for the Conservation of Nature and the Population Reference Bureau examined the Zambezi basin specifically and recommended that 'a regional commission on water use, consisting of representatives of the concerned countries should be set up, based on the continuous evolution of the needs and of the available resources' (AIM, 26 March 1998).

National water policy

The National Water Policy of 1996 arose from a need to establish rules to co-ordinate the management of water resources at the national level. It was recognized that water is a vital resource that must be used in a rational and sustainable manner, with the aim of encouraging national development for the welfare of the people. Water supply in Mozambique is still far from meeting current needs. Despite the efforts made, the majority of the population do not have a safe water supply.

The National Water Policy recognizes that the top priority is the satisfaction of basic needs and the participation of beneficiaries in the management of water resources. Furthermore, it recognizes the economic and social value of water and the need to decentralize the operational management of water resources. It understands that government should not intervene directly to provide services, but should encourage and regulate service providers and foster the integrated management of water resources. The major innovations of the policy are undoubtedly the decentralization and the creation of opportunities for the private sector.

It is well known that water in all its forms in nature is a public good, owned by the state. On the basis of this principle, it was reasoned that the state should manage all water matters. Thus the state became a kind of super company, albeit one in deficit. On the one hand, it made large investments in the construction, operation and maintenance of water infrastructure and supply systems, and on the other hand, it demonstrated its inability to pursue its objectives since it was becoming increasingly decapitalized. It was unable even to maintain the existing facilities, far less to expand them.

This situation of stagnation had to be overcome. The strategy devised was that the state should regulate the sector and determine water charges as close as possible to the real value. Autonomous institutions, including the private sector, should implement the charges. These institutions must be self-sustaining.

Decentralization and the creation of RWA-South

As already mentioned, the decentralization of the water sector is part of a policy aimed at greater efficiency in the management of water resources. Law 16/91 of 3 August, the Water Law, establishes the resources that belong in the public domain, the principles of water management, the general conditions for the use of existing water resources and the general rights and duties of users, among other things. The principles of water management have therefore been established by law.

The Law provides for decentralization in Article 15. Article 17 establishes the National Water Council with the aim of sounding the opinion of other state bodies with interests in water management, a very important activity. The nature of the Council is consultative. It also acts as a facilitator in relation to domestic and foreign economic operators and to the Council of Ministers.

Article 18 created the Regional Water Authorities, the purpose being to satisfy the government's policy of decentralizing water management in Mozambique. Three interesting features may be noted in these Regional Water Authorities. The first is the boundaries of their jurisdiction. They are organized on the basis of water basin catchment areas and not the prevailing administrative divisions. This means in practice that a Regional Water Authority can cover more than one province and that one province can contain more than one Regional Authority.

The second feature is that, in terms of the law, the Regional Water Authorities are public institutions with a juridical personality and administrative, proprietorial and financial autonomy, under the umbrella of the Ministry of Construction and Water through the National Water Board. This feature is the key to achieving the self-sustainability of water management institutions.

The third feature relates to the organizational structure of the Authorities. Perhaps the most important division is the Board of Management, composed of representatives from the relevant ministries, namely Agriculture and Fisheries, Industry and Tourism and Mineral Resources and Energy, from local state bodies and from user groups. This shows that there is a genuine concern to make management participatory at the highest level of the Regional Water Authority.

The Regional Water Authorities planned are: RWA-North, RWA-Centre-North, RWA-Centre, RWA-Zambezi, and RWA-South. The first and only one to be established so far is the RWA-South.

The southern regional water authority (RWA-South)

The RWA-South is a statutory body established by Ministerial Decree No. 134/93 of 17 November (Statutes of RWA-South 1993), two years after the approval of the Water Law. The creation of RWA-South before the others was the natural outcome of a number of favourable factors, including the climate, the existence of water infrastructure established in the border areas and the availability of human and material resources to ensure the initial start of operations.

The boundaries of RWA-South's area of jurisdiction are the southern borders of the country and the Save River basin to the north. The three largest earth dams in Mozambique are located within this geographical area: the Massingir Dam on the Elephants River, the Corumana Dam on the Sabie River and the Pequenos Libombos Dam on the Umbeluzi River. There were three basic reasons for building these dams: to create water storage capacity and regulate the flow of the rivers; to create poles of development in agriculture; and to make Mozambique autonomous in relation to the neighbouring countries, especially during dry periods.

The RWA-South is divided into four management units in order to achieve greater efficiency. These units cover the Save, the Limpopo, the Incomati and the Umbeluzi Rivers. Each unit is in charge of water resource management in one or more river basins in its area of jurisdiction. In addition to the management units, the RWA-South has technical, administrative, legal and financial departments.

One of the factors favouring the establishment of the RWA-South was the availability of human and material resources. The human resources were technicians and workers formerly belonging to the Water Use Management Unit, set up specifically to monitor the Pequenos Libombos and Corumana Dams, and later asked to supervise monitoring the Massingir Dam, when technical problems were discovered there. This expansion of its responsibilities led to the creation of the Limpopo Basin Management Unit, and when the Water Management Unit was closed down its workforce and other resources were transferred to the RWA-South.

The main objectives of the RWA-South are the efficient management of water resources in its area of jurisdiction; the promotion of social welfare; and self-sustainability. In order to achieve these objectives, the strategy of the RWA-South is built around a policy of participatory management. This means that the parties directly involved, both managers and users, are represented within Basin Committees, which are consultative bodies. This allows permanent consultation and discussion among the various stakeholders, so that the efficiency of water management is increased, in particular because the users play an active part and begin to understand the true economic value of water. The management units are thus able to provide better services to users and raise the public credibility of the RWA-South and the government policy of decentralization.

Under this policy, users are encouraged to experience the problems faced by the organization managing water resources in order to understand them better. Users must therefore be involved from the start in water planning. The RWA-South believes that this is the only way to avoid major policy errors and to ensure that users will be in a position to accept decisions taken on the allocation of existing resources to meet demand. To achieve this objective, the management units will have to concentrate on raising public awareness among users. Users should be provided with timely information about the water available in any given season, they should be aware of the demand in that period and be informed of rainfall forecasts, etc.

Service delivery by the RWA-South involves costs for the operation and maintenance of dams and other equipment and infrastructure, which have to be borne by the beneficiaries. Hence, the management units should find appropriate mechanisms for improving service delivery, while the users for their part should collaborate in this improvement of services by meeting the costs.

Bulk water charges

Water has both economic and social values. The supply of water implies costs. How can these costs be prevented from falling heavily on the users? A simple answer would be to set a charge that satisfies demand at the real cost of meeting that demand. But establishing a fair price is not simple, as the opportunity cost of water needs to be taken into account. The cost of using water for the same purpose differs in times of scarcity from periods of abundance. The priority in water resource allocation depends on the purpose for which the water will be used and the social benefits derived from that use. Water should therefore be allocated, but to whom? Only to those who have money to pay or to the family sector, which would contribute towards social stability? Who should pay the bill? What price should be charged to some and what to others? These are some of the questions that need to be considered before setting user charges, in order to meet the interests of everyone in so far as this is possible.

A brief history of water charges

The history of water consumption in Mozambique shows that for a long time it was regarded simply as a gift from God. Piped water and standpipes in the rural areas have always been subsidized by the state. In the case of piped water, the consumer paid only a symbolic price or the water was free. The situation worsened over time in terms of financial sustainability, as inflation eroded even further the real value of the existing low water price.

The regulation of water by means of dams so that rivers can still have water in the dry periods was subsidized by the state. The state built the dams and covered their operation and maintenance costs without receiving any return on the capital invested. The first charge for regulated water was introduced only in 1987. The charge was 4 meticals per cubic metre, calculated on the average operation and maintenance costs of dams in the south. This charge, which was symbolic, had the virtue of giving consumers some awareness of the economic value of water. The situation changed from one in which neither the rich nor the poor paid, to one where both had to pay.

A study of charges was carried out in 1995 with the aim of bringing the charge in force up to date and establishing differential rates depending on the source of the water, the end-use and the quantities consumed. The possibility was left open of negotiation according to the ability of the consumer to pay.

The direct beneficiaries of water supply have shown some resistance to paying the fees demanded of them. This resistance is evident among both the family (subsistence) sector and the private (commercial) farmers. The industrial sector does not depart much from the rule. Paradoxically, it is the Maputo water provider, *Empresa Agua de Maputo*, that meets its obligations best, although its own difficulties in collecting fees are well-known. The Mozambican electricity company, for example, does not acknowledge that it should pay for water used in generating electricity, despite its own efficiency in collecting charges for its service provision.

At a meeting in 1995 with a large number of users and a mission from the World Bank, it was noted that the big companies took no account of the price of water in their cost structure, because the amount was insignificant in comparison with other costs. This meant that, despite the fact that the water charge was very low, it was not budgeted for. In the case of the large farmers, concern was directed towards the recruitment of labour and the purchase of fertilizers, pesticides and seeds, etc. but not towards irrigation. Why? Simply because the volumes of water required were already guaranteed.

Although Articles 42, 43 and 44 of the Water Law require consumers to pay user charges, this has been ignored. What then can be done? Is it enough to appeal to the conscience of the beneficiaries about the need to pay for water? Experience shows that this is not enough. It has often been the case that poor harvests are cited as the reason for non-payment, as though the water had not actually been used. What legal mechanisms exist to enforce the law?

Section 3 of the Water Law contains provision for the rights and duties of consumers. These rights and duties should be included in the regulations for licences and concessions, which specify the conditions demanded for a licence or a concession, as well as the penalties imposed for the failure of either party to meet such obligations.

The future of RWA-South: prospects and opportunities

The future of the RWA-South depends to a large extent on both internal and external factors. Looking first at the internal factors, the capacity of the institution must be strengthened in terms of material and human resources alike. The RWA-South currently has about 300 employees, of whom only 7 have higher education and 12 intermediate education. This number should be doubled, while at the same time the number of permanent employees whose qualifications are not suited to the purpose of the RWA-South should be reduced and these workers should be retrained. Training and upgrading courses need to be organized so that the technicians can have a broader view to help them move on from dam management to basin management.

To achieve its goals, the RWA-South needs adequate material resources and instruments for measurement in order to deliver better services to its clients. Currently the equipment and other resources needed for efficient water management are either obsolete or in some cases non-existent. These include: the hydrometrical network in the 25 river basins in the RWA-South area; the radio communications network; the fleet of boats and vehicles needed to cover an area of about 18,000 sq. km.; and computer equipment to establish and operate a data base for each of the basins (surface water and aquifers) and each of the dams. The great challenge now is to replace all these resources and to make new investments.

The fundamental external factor is the existence of water in the rivers. This is the purpose for which the RWA-South exists. The conditions of the rivers depend on favourable climatic conditions, both inside and outside the country. They also depend to a large extent on the amount of water released by the countries upstream.

The external constraints have more influence on the complexity of management than the internal factors. In terms of the volume of water crossing the borders, the situation is complicated. But it is even more so in terms of water quality. Since Mozambique is downstream, the country is vulnerable to upstream pollution, with little chance of correcting the situation. The joint commissions and constant discussion may eventually play an important role in this regard.

The RWA-South will grow to the extent that these internal and external problems are resolved or mitigated. The establishment of other regional water authorities depends to a certain extent on the experience gained by the RWA-South in this period. The mistakes can be avoided and the strategies improved and adapted to the specific conditions in each authority's region. There are indications that at least some of the problems will be resolved. Prospects appear to be good, but only time will tell.

Reference
World Bank (1993) *Water Resources Management: A World Bank Policy Paper*. Washington DC, September.

D CASE STUDIES

21 Participatory Development & Urban Management

MARIO DOS ANJOS ROSÁRIO

In 1920 it was estimated that the world's urban population represented some 20% of the total. This figure had risen to 40% by 1980 and is expected to reach 50% by 2000. This means that some 4.9 billion people could be living in urban areas by the turn of the millennium, a considerable increase in the urban population. About 70% of all city dwellers will by then be in underdeveloped countries, where rural economies are stagnating. This rapid urbanization is not being matched by a commensurate growth in the urban economies.

Whilst the urban population estimates given above are derived from United Nations statistics which are generally regarded as reliable and based on standard accepted indicators, differences in perception still occur. Hence what is considered to be 'urban' varies from country to country. Rapid urbanization, especially in the less developed countries, requires careful analysis, bearing in mind that the definitions of 'urban' and 'urbanization' are often inadequate to describe the generally spontaneous expansion of human settlements. The complex layers of urban economic existence need to be analyzed, as well as the difficulties people face in integrating into these economies.

The dominant trend in Mozambique is the 'ruralization' of cities and towns. Given this situation, and the predominance of children in the population structure, the health and education systems need to be adapted to take advantage of the economic, social and cultural wisdom of rural life and to develop its expertise to help people integrate into their new 'ruralized urban' surroundings. The systems currently prevailing cause people to feel uprooted; their working and social lives are based upon the *ad hoc* knowledge and the skills they have acquired for urban survival.

The political and socio-economic systems in place after independence induced in the population a state of lethargy and total dependence on paternal government structures. Private and individual creative initiative was so severely suppressed that citizens lost all sense of their rights, even the right of being able to make decisions about their own lives and the environment in which they lived. The process of rapid urbanization requires a redefinition of the functions of, and relationship between, the different sectors of the state, local administration and civil society, including private economic and social agents, non-governmental associations and grassroots community organizations, with the aim of reinforcing those resources and skills which exist in order to meet the challenges of environmental management and urban development.

The first section of this chapter examines new thinking on housing and urban management. The second section describes the urban situation in Mozambique, and the policies and strategies that have been applied. The third section tries to point to a new way forward in urban management and participatory development by presenting a case study of action research carried out in the peri-urban areas of Maputo by an independent indigenous NGO working with local communities, as a means of identifying strategies and methodologies to deal with serious urban problems in a sustainable manner. The involvement of the city dwellers themselves, making them jointly responsible for the management of the environment and development, within the limited resources available, made it possible to raise the issues of local community participation in the development process and of how best to utilize foreign aid. This involvement meant that people could share the responsibility for environmental management, the improvement of their living conditions and finding the best use for scarce resources.

New thinking on housing and urban management

The United Nations and other international agencies have recently promoted a global housing strategy based on the idea of helping governments to concentrate on the creation of mechanisms that make it easier to improve housing conditions by means of self-help construction and mutual aid. In other words, it increases access to locally managed basic resources. Factors that facilitate construction include: the simplification and modification of legislation on land tenure, access to credit, acceptable standards of construction and services, and incentives for private investment in such areas as land preparation, rental housing and the production of construction materials.

Strategies to safeguard human settlement must above all be rooted in a new division of responsibilities between the community and the authorities. The authorities should support programmes designed, organized and managed by the communities. This in turn assumes that new functions will be identified for central and local government, for the private sector and voluntary NGOs as well as for community organizations. These strategies are based essentially on the community, it being the principal stakeholder, which can count on support from both the government and the non-governmental sector and use the resources they provide. In terms of facilitation, the government should provide incentives for the private and community sectors and monitor their activities.

New thinking on the role of government includes decentralization of decision-making on the allocation of resources to the local authorities. Ideally this should involve local government at municipal and rural district level, as well as mechanisms for linking in to the community. Government at local level should have a counterpart in the community organizations.

Another function of local government should be to establish limited socio-economic monitoring on behalf of the community. This needs to be a technical service and not a supervisory function imposed from above. It is a technical service for the improvement of housing by means of a minimum quality control of product standards, together with technical assistance to improve production. The latter task could be carried out by private or non-government service providers.

NGOs are playing an increasingly important role in establishing links between community groups and the local government. They have a distinct advantage in being more flexible than government agencies, and they are able to start activities in new areas where government policy is not yet defined.

Governments should sub-contract the greatest possible number of services, creating economic incentives for small and medium-sized private businesses as well as for voluntary NGOs. In this way, the costs of services can be kept down by being provided by more efficient suppliers.

Often there are limited possibilities for spontaneous community organization, especially in less developed countries, because of their widespread levels of absolute poverty exacerbated by their history of social and cultural fragmentation, due in part to factors such as state repression or socio-economic disruption caused by migrant labour, but mainly to the fact that a large proportion of the population is totally absorbed in the daily battle for survival. This is why governments should promote extension activities through the creation or expansion of community development programmes and social welfare institutions, both governmental and non-governmental.

The function of central government in relation to human settlement is basically to:

- establish policy;
- draw up macroeconomic and regional plans;
- formulate and evaluate programmes;
- research and establish standards;
- create the legal and economic foundation for policies to succeed. This implies a very different role for the central government, which needs to relinquish control of resources and decentralize the decision-making process. This is not only the most efficient way of dealing with problems affecting the population, but it also strengthens community involvement in the political process.

The urban situation in Mozambique

The process of urbanization

The general population census in 1980 indicated that the urban population made up 10% of the total, although this only included the population of the 12 main urban areas. A territorial reorganization was carried out in 1986, when 23 cities and 68 towns were officially designated as urban centres (Decree-law 4/86 and Resolution 8/86, both of 25 June). The population of the urban areas has increased rapidly over the last three decades, because of the insecurity in the rural areas caused by war, with the rural economy practically destroyed. Around 2 million people were displaced inside the country, many of whom became squatters around the towns and cities.

In 1970 it was estimated that only about 9% of the population of Mozambique lived in urban areas. In 1990 the total population was estimated at 15.7 million, experiencing an annual growth rate of 2.7%. By 1992, it was estimated that an astonishing 50% of the population lived either in urban areas or in zones directly under the influence of urban areas.

Even now, with rural security restored, given the level of destruction of infrastructure and the loss of social and economic capital in many areas, a significant proportion of those who fled to the urban periphery are unlikely to return to the rural areas. Those who do return will have problems in resettling in the countryside. Combined with the natural population growth, this means that the urban population will increase rapidly and could reach about 9 or 10 million by early next century.

The General Peace Accord of October 1992 opened a new chapter in the history of population movements in the country. Previously the war had caused people to move to neighbouring countries and a great many remained displaced inside the country and far from their homes. A National Commission for Human Settlement was created towards the end of 1995 within the Ministry of Construction and Water, composed of officials and civil society representatives. The Commission sought to identify the general conditions in the urban centres, but there was little reliable information available. Around 10.3% of the total population lives in the three major cities, Maputo, Beira and Nampula, which are home to 67% of the urban population. The annual growth rate in Maputo was 4.3% compared with 6% for the urban areas as a whole in the period 1980–91. The rising birth rate in Maputo was 39.36 births per thousand, and the mortality rate 9.02 per thousand.

The degree of urbanization varies greatly from province to province, Zambezi and Nampula have very dense but less developed secondary urban areas, with longer periods of occupation. Maputo Province and the southern parts of Gaza and Inhambane are probably the most urbanized zones, reflecting the influence of South Africa. The levels of urbanization within provinces also differ from region to region, with secondary urban concentrations along the coast and the main roads and railways.

Characteristics of the urban population
A great part of the urban population lives on the verge of absolute poverty. In 1992, it was estimated that 35–45% of the urban population suffered severe poverty. The stagnant urban economy at that time and the existing infrastructure were not able to absorb the rapidly increasing numbers. Whilst growth has been recorded in the economy in general, job creation in the formal sector has been slow and the cost of living has soared. At the same time a process of local accumulation has taken place, based on an increase in the informal sector, mainly trade. Evidence of this can be seen in the rapid transformation of the built-up areas on the urban periphery, where cane or wood and zinc huts are being replaced by durable brick-built houses. For example, the average size of a Maputo household rose from 4.75 in 1980 to 6.7 in 1994. In Beira the increase was from 4.14 to 5.7 and in Nampula from 4.13 to 5.3 over the same period.

It is impossible to identify the *per capita* output of the urban population. It was estimated at US$5.8 in 1994, but this took no account of the informal activities in which a large proportion of the population is engaged.

The rate of illiteracy among those aged 15 years and over is high, for example 56% in Maputo and 90% in Nampula. Some 11% of Maputo children under the age of five suffer from malnutrition and the average life expectancy for both sexes is 58.6 years.

Some 73% of Maputo households have access to drinking water, but only 28% have a domestic connection. Of the remainder, 21% obtain water at public standpipes and others buy it privately from people who own wells. The situation is much more serious in Beira and Nampula. For example, less than 13% of Nampula households have a domestic piped water supply. The average price for 100 litres of water in the mid-1990s in the three cities was 30 US cents and in Maputo it was 50 cents. Roads in the cities are in an advanced state of disrepair, while they are practically non-existent in the periphery, and this hampers access by public transport. Sanitation, drainage and the collection and treatment of solid wastes are a problem in all of Mozambique's cities.

The situation with regard to health and education services is serious since these have not kept pace with the population growth rates. For example, there are 100 inhabitants for each hospital bed in Maputo, and 600 for each bed in the other two large cities. The under-five mortality rate is very high, 70 per thousand in Maputo, 110 per thousand in Beira and 86 per thousand in Nampula. Classrooms are overcrowded, averaging 45 to 55 pupils per class in primary and secondary schools in the three cities.

The state is the biggest landlord through the nationalization of buildings – a situation which will change with the sale of houses to tenants. In Maputo, house rent consumes 11.7% of household income. Most houses are located in the periphery and are of flimsy construction put up by the occupiers. However, the shortage of housing is very great and people's financial capacity to build houses is extremely small. The housing stock in the inner cities is plainly dilapidated because people have few resources to devote to maintenance.

The physical, social and economic situation of the urban system
The urban hierarchy in Mozambique shows a notable imbalance. Maputo is the largest urban centre, and the cosmopolitan capital. In 1992 its population was ten times larger than the population in the urban areas under its influence south of the Save river and more than three times greater than the population of Beira, the country's second city.

Most of the secondary urban centres are small to medium in size. Few have any influence outside their own immediate sub-region or local area. Provinces with inter-national transport corridors established before independence – the Nacala Corridor in the north, the Beira Corridor in the centre and the Maputo Corridor in the south of the country – have experienced the development of industrial and transport activ-ity, in particular close to the larger cities. But the majority of the secondary urban areas are built on commerce and agriculture. They are basically trading centres with some administrative functions.

Urban development is characterized by an increase in residential density in both the inner cities and the periphery, with the result that the basic service infrastructure is vastly overloaded. The unplanned growth of the peri-urban areas is complicated by the absence of land-use planning mechanisms and tools. Consequently, the majority of the urban population live in areas without access to social infrastructure and facil-ities and in precarious houses with no security of land tenure. In 1980, these areas represented approximately 60% of the total urban residential area and their popula-tion was 50% of the total urban population.

There are no plans to establish new urban centres, nor to extend services in the current areas so as to widen the urban perimeter. The majority of city dwellers today continue to have rural habits. Without jobs in the formal sector, they maintain a tra-ditional lifestyle and engage in all sorts of informal activity, avoiding all attempts at regulation. Hence the reality is the 'ruralization' of the urban environment.

Economic, social, physical, environmental and sanitation conditions in the urban areas have declined severely in the last 20 years. This situation could remain the same or even worsen for the following reasons:

- the absence of explicit policies on urban development;
- the lack of any policy to deal with areas of spontaneous occupation leading to an excessive increase in the density of built-up areas and the uncontrolled expansion of illegal or irregular occupation;
- the incapacity of the economic infrastructure to meet the demands of population growth;
- high levels of poverty and limited access to credit and income-generating oppor-tunities;
- deficient or non-existent physical infrastructure, social facilities and basic services;
- continued high levels of growth of the urban population and low levels of invest-ment in infrastructure and services, due largely to the illegal character of sponta-neous human settlements and the sporadic nature of public sector support.

As a result, there is a lack of criteria for urban planning and the spread of human set-tlements. No rules exist for urbanization and for arranging human settlements in a hierarchy. There is no clear idea of how to deal with areas of spontaneous occupation.

Insanitary conditions with a growing incidence of disease, rising crime rates, and declining possibilities to generate jobs and income undermine social stability. There are restrictions on house building or improvement, and on the improvement, recovery or expansion of basic urban infrastructure and services. Rapid physical and environmental degradation is occurring in the urban and peri-urban areas, caused by lack of maintenance and serious levels of erosion because of unregulated land occupation and destruction of the vegetation cover.

National policies
Aware of how this situation can affect social and economic development, the government has embarked on some programmes, projects and activities, with support from both domestic and foreign organizations, which should have an impact on the urban landscape in the future.

Until independence the role of the state was marginal and regulatory, limited to some indirect activities in basic urbanization and support for self-help construction. Various private, public and co-operative companies were involved in mobilizing savings for use in house building. After 1975, the Constitution vested the ownership of all land in the state. The nationalization of buildings by Decree-law 5/76 of 5 February 1976 gave the state the exclusive right to rent property. Rent subsidies were introduced to enable low-income families to occupy houses in the urban areas. Investment in house building rapidly declined thereafter, and all but disappeared.

Following the Third Frelimo Congress in 1977, the state's activities concentrated on a number of areas. Human settlements were reorganized in the rural areas to create 'communal villages', with the aim of reducing the imbalances in development between the rural and urban areas. Pilot areas in towns and cities were reorganized with local participation for the improvement of water, energy and drainage services and the promotion of informal production of building materials. In the housing sphere, there was direct intervention to provide housing for key projects and indirect intervention in the supply of social infrastructure and facilities and support for self-help house building and improvement, particularly in the rural areas.

A National Directorate of Housing was established. It carried out some pilot projects and focused its resources on physical planning, the provision of basic infrastructure and support for self-help construction. The first National Meeting of Cities and Communal Suburbs decided that the state should provide assistance to self-help house building through the Executive Councils created in 1978 to replace the municipal authorities.

A government plan for the 1980s drawn up in 1981 identified specific targets for the supply of housing: direct state intervention in new house building, with priority for agro-industrial and industrial projects in the urban centres; and indirect government assistance to self-help house building through the executive councils. In practice, state intervention was very limited because of the slow development of the executive councils in the cities and their restricted resources, dependent as they were on funding from the central government. The National Directorate of Housing concentrated on the training of technical staff to support them in the development of basic urbanization schemes in suburban and peri-urban areas.

From 1977 to 1982, the results of direct state action amounted to: the provision of 3,450 housing units; improvement in water supply and sanitation, particularly in the urban areas and communal villages; and subsidies estimated at 50% of the cost of the total amortization of the state housing stock. The only indirect action in the urban areas was a pilot project to reorganize the Maxaquene suburb in Maputo.

In 1983, decentralization of construction capacity and development of a housing policy with clear mechanisms to encourage self-help building projects were seen as the answer to problems in the control of planning and investment in house building. The National Directorate of Housing was transformed into the National Institute of

Physical Planning. The Ministry of Public Works became the Ministry of Construction and Water and drafted a national housing policy that reduced the state's involvement to a minimum. The responsibility for direct investment in housing was passed on to the executive councils, which still suffered from a total lack of capacity and resources and minimal awareness of financial support mechanisms. Efforts to take action were thereby weakened. In 1987, the government approved its Housing Promotion Programme and created a Housing Programmes Office (PROHABITA).

Since 1988, the World Bank has been financing the Urban Rehabilitation Project, which aims at restoring infrastructure in the cities of Maputo and Beira and creating jobs. The project includes the creation of financial mechanisms to allow people to become involved in low-cost self-help house building. It also involves the provision of basic infrastructure (access roads, water, sanitation and electricity) that will permit the rehabilitation of residential areas to minimum standards of habitability, the provision of local low-cost building materials, and research into and the transmission of alternative building techniques, by seconding technicians to strengthen the local bodies responsible for promoting house building.

A number of government policies are expected to have a significant impact on urban areas. The Economic and Social Recovery Programme and its monetary and fiscal policies are bringing about legal, institutional and financial reforms to promote private economic activities and redefine the relationship between the public and private sectors. The Urban Rehabilitation Project created a need to enhance the capacity of municipal councils and to institute mechanisms for cost recovery on investments. The national housing policy of December 1990 set out guidelines for the rationalization and privatization of the state housing stock and the creation of a property market, the promotion of social housing, the development of the building materials industry and the provision of institutional support and technical training.

The Local Government Reform Project provided for the establishment and autonomy of municipalities. This should create the conditions necessary for greater efficiency and effectiveness in local management so that it can foster development. A Social Housing Programme and the creation of a National Housing Development Fund will support self-help building projects by setting technical and financial standards. The National Environmental Management Programme contains specific activities for environmental protection, with provisions for building up local authority capacity to manage natural resources as well as for training, public awareness and the preparation of environmental profiles.

There are as yet no explicit policies on urban development, the distribution and grading of human settlements or urban planning, despite the many concerns about urban problems. But the serious situation in the urban centres demands integrated activities at various levels. The complexity of urban development and its multidisciplinary nature require a certain co-ordination among the different sectors and levels of government and between the government and civil society and economic agents. A national programme for urban development should be established to deal with this situation.

The only documents that could be regarded as forerunners to a policy on urban development are the conclusions and recommendations of the first National Conference on Urban Planning held in 1982, followed by various urban structure plans, the 'Methodology Manual for Implementation of Partial Plans' of 1986, and the Land Use Papers prepared by the Institute of Physical Planning as guidelines for urban planning and land use. These documents do not set out any policies, but they have influenced urban development by establishing provisional standards and models of development. However, despite all these efforts everything continues as before, because of the government's weak technical capacity, institutional debility and lack of resources, both at central and local level.

Management of the urban environment
According to the NEMP, the question of managing the urban environment in Mozambique's cities is particularly difficult because of the parallel existence of two socio-economic systems with sometimes contradictory needs and interests.

Every Mozambican urban centre has clearly differentiated zones. There is a formal modern zone where people of different classes and economic and cultural levels live, and where individual isolation is the dominant feature. And there is a suburban and peri-urban zone where settlement is spontaneous and anarchic. People arrive in search of security, work and other facilities, bringing rural habits with them while wanting an urban way of life, but still respecting tradition and maintaining a feeling of community. Life in parts of the peri-urban zone still has all the characteristics of a rural way of life. The traditional, informal, rural world meets the modern, formal urban world in all the zones in Mozambican urban centres.

The municipal councils that manage the urban environment have neither technical nor administrative skills of sufficient quality to deal with the major problems presented by an urban centre. In reality, the municipal councils are the government placed in the town or city. The city dweller has little opportunity to participate and take decisions to support and improve the urban environment.

The local administrations in the urban districts and wards have shown they are in control of their territory and know the people who live there. Each ward has its own internal dynamic with its own logic, created in the search for solutions to the problems of survival. Despite the present political complexity, the dynamizing groups and block chiefs still play an important role in the life of the cities.

Local elections, which are part of the process of decentralizing government, will give citizens the right to participate in the administration and management of the urban environment. Private economic interests and civil non-governmental associations can play an important role in mobilizing financial, human, technical and organizational resources to manage urban development, in conjunction with local institutions and grassroots associations. These associations, made up of residents in various communities, will be important in ensuring that measures to manage the urban environment are implemented. Co-ordination and dialogue among the different stakeholders are important factors for achieving success in urban environmental management.

The cities and urban centres are built on the economic base laid down during the colonial period. But the people who live in the towns and cities today come from a very different economic level, unsuited to the technology existing in the buildings and to the solution of problems related to basic services. People need to learn about sustainable development and to develop and internalize an appropriate culture. This implies reviewing the standards of reference in choosing which path to take, without, however, sliding backwards or stagnating. One way of solving certain social problems and at the same time reducing costs could be to opt for labour-intensive processes in urban management.

After independence, existing resources were meant to be directed towards integrated development in the rural agricultural sector, although this did not occur in practice. The present spatial redistribution of the population requires a national policy for urban and housing development, and resources should be devoted to achieving this aim. The result of the lack of investment in human settlement in the urban areas was the rapid and general decline of buildings and basic service infrastructure.

The chance for local governments to become autonomous is an important factor.

The process of decentralization can generate qualitative change and promote urban management and local technical skills as well as new investment. Local elections should strengthen the social and political base of the government and contribute towards the implementation of community initiatives.

The Pfuka Dzixile programme

Pfuka Dzixile is the name given to the programme of sustainable development by the women in the peri-urban wards of Maputo where it is now (1998) in its sixth year of implementation. They started to use this name to describe the movement it created and which has now spread to many wards. It expresses what each person and each community feels about working with the Mozambican Association for Urban Development (AMDU) to change their living conditions and restore the social fabric and its values. *Pfuka Dzixile* is a call to action, meaning 'Awake! Morning has broken'.

Pfuka Dzixile is a movement involving Maputo residents in the peri-urban wards, professionals, local government officials and the domestic and international donor community, in the search to improve the environmental conditions in which people live. It asks each participant for whatever contribution he/she can make to strengthening their ideas and convictions and achieving tangible results from their joint decisions and efforts.

Many people and organizations are participating in the programme. Residents in the suburban and peripheral wards of Maputo are involved, men, women and children, young and old people from all walks of life, skilled and semi-skilled workers. Women account for 50–65% of the participants. Various professionals from AMDU are participants, as well as university students and teachers who conduct research and hold classes and training sessions. Local firms contribute services and materials free of charge. The local administration at district, ward and block levels is active. The Maputo Municipal Council also participates.

Financial and material resources have been provided by: the central government; the World Food Programme and the Netherlands government; the Mozambican Association for Urban Development; various other donors; and finally members of the communities where the programme is being implemented.

Activities are taking place in eight peri-urban wards in Maputo:

1st action (1991–2) – Mavalane A and Hulene B wards;
2nd action (1993–4) – Mavalane B, Hulene A, FPLM and Malhazine wards;
3rd action (1994–6) – All the above plus Maxaquene and Xipamanine wards;
(1996) – New activities in Jorge Dimitrov, Ferroviario, Laulane, Munhuana and Mafalala wards.

The *Pfuka Dzixile* Programme is an integrated development programme based on local initiative and promoting the training and involvement of the beneficiaries. It is aimed at improving basic urban services and the sustainability of the activities undertaken. Education, training and production are emphasized by providing child care and giving skills training to women and young people. Support is given for income-generating activities as a way of financing educational activities and improving living conditions.

By 1996 the programme had carried out 49 different activities in six city wards, with a total of 235 blocks, each with 50 to 100 families. The total population of the six wards is 118,288 inhabitants. The communities involved in the programme belong to 50 blocks with 3,000 households totalling 15,000 members.

About 300 people are temporarily employed in the programme, but the number can rise as high as 700 at times of intense activity. A total of 4,100 people have passed through the programme, with a monthly turnover of about 20%. There are currently 350 women, 78 men and 2,500 pre-school children, 2,300 primary school children, 50 child care facilitators and 20 primary teachers involved in the programme's activities. In addition, 38 members of communities are serving on residents' development committees.

The AMDU volunteer technicians also benefit, since they gain rich social experience working with the communities and professional experience in planning, urban management and low-cost building in the self-help projects. Students and teachers of the Architecture Faculty of the Eduardo Mondlane University and of the psychology, pedagogy and adult education departments of the Pedagogical University also benefit from the programme as it has provided research opportunities in architecture, low-cost building, urban planning, urban economics, community, adult and pre-school education and field work with the communities.

Results of the programme
Direct results of the programme include the introduction of AMDU and the university professionals to new benchmarks and standards of reference for thinking about home-grown development. Community organization is strengthened to be able to undertake activities aimed at improving the state of the urban environment. People have gained experience in: self-help construction of social and community facilities; organizing a permanent system of refuse collection; rehabilitation and maintenance of roads; planting fruit trees and creating green spaces; organizing income-generating activities; and the discovery of potential resources and existing efforts to change and manage the urban environment. Local administrations have been strengthened by providing them with the skills to analyze and manage community problems.

Indirect results include the creation of a technical unit in the Municipal Council to deal with development in the peri-urban wards. There is increased awareness on the part of municipal directors and technicians of the new approach to the sustainable development of basic urban services. Low-cost appropriate technology that is durable and easily maintained has been introduced. Local people have been influenced by brightly painted schools in the construction and improvement of their own houses. New private sector production and service businesses have developed in the wards following the road rehabilitation. The electricity company has extended the public lighting system along the roads, and new routes have been added to the public transport services. A place has been set up for parents to leave their children when they go to work, and interest has been stimulated in their children's schools. New public services branch offices have been opened in the peri-urban wards. Progress has been made in the civic education of those involved in the programme, leading to the recovery of social values and professional ethics. Local civil associations have been formed and are now organizing an association of child care facilitators and women activists with the aim of ensuring that activities started by the programme continue, especially the nursery schools, the income generation and the training of women. In addition, there is an association of young people in the Ferroviario ward who want to improve conditions in their area which is not yet scheduled for inclusion in the programme, and a residents' and women activists' association has been set up in the FPLM ward with the aim of developing the nursery school further and working in production and the environment programme.

History and context
With *per capita* income estimated at around US$80, Mozambique is one of the poorest countries in the world. Two decades of war, and the shortcomings and errors of judgement of an inexperienced government led to the destruction of physical points

of reference and of the social and moral fabric, all of which must now be rebuilt. Some 6 million Mozambicans were forced to live as refugees in neighbouring countries or displaced within their own country. The end of the war produced a new group of people who need to be reintegrated – the demobilized soldiers.

People able to study or complete some form of training during the war had no chance to travel and get to know their own country, the rural areas, the localities and districts, the towns and villages. They were confined to the cities and to educational establishments, living a life of material shortages and of declining social and moral values. It is now essential to create opportunities for technicians trained at home and abroad to gain practical experience and local knowledge and to recover the professional standards that will enable the country to rebuild a framework of values to serve as a reference for the conduct of daily life.

The programme of action being implemented in the peri-urban wards of Maputo was designed in 1990/91, when the war had caused a mass exodus from the rural areas to the urban periphery, where people occupied land in a spontaneous and disorganized way, paying no attention to the minimum conditions necessary for human settlement. The solidarity of the peri-urban population is all embracing and offers a little more security, but the rising unemployment has brought with it an increase in theft and other crimes in the urban areas.

Children under school age or excluded from the state school system were a major concern for parents who had to go and farm their plots or seek other means of survival, leaving them all day in a strange place under the care of a local mother with no means to feed them.

The social facilities and services in Maputo were concentrated mainly in the built-up centre of the city, even though 75–80% of the population lived in the peripheral zones. The challenge was to extend the effective urban perimeter by expanding the area receiving basic urban and social services. It was also necessary to promote the improvement of the urban environment and to meet social needs with very limited human and financial resources.

The Municipal Council is now faced with a series of complex problems in that about 25–30% of Maputo's population consume all of the few existing resources. If the Council were to try to employ classical techniques of urban management for the whole of the immense peri-urban area, it would be unlikely to be able to meet the needs of the city's almost one and a half million inhabitants.

Against this background, a group of Maputo residents, mainly architects and physical planners, members of the Mozambican Association for Urban Development (AMDU), decided to start up an action research programme in search of creative ways of mobilizing local resources and skills and finding appropriate technological solutions. Their activities were based on interests identified by local social groups, which is an important pre-condition for sustainable development initiatives.

The first two years were taken up with research and identification of needs. At the request of communities in the Mavalane A ward, a project was begun using funds provided by the members of AMDU and resources from the communities themselves, such as materials, water and labour. According to the residents, no action had been taken to provide any assistance or improve conditions since independence. They had been subjected to numerous surveys on poverty and local conditions, but they never saw any returns from these.

The initial experience was not easy, but patience, persistence and the use of local knowledge, as well as flexibility in adapting the programme according to the local reactions, brought success, which had a strong impact on the residents of neighbouring wards. They quickly learned the methods of organization and asked ADMU to extend the programme to their wards.

The first 11-month module ran in 1993–4, covering communities organized in four wards, Mavalane A and B and Hulene A and B in urban district number 4 of Maputo city. Funds were channelled from the Italian embassy via MOLISV, an Italian NGO. The World Food Programme and the Netherlands government supplied food, hand tools and other equipment. CRIAA of France financed a similar module at the end of 1994 in the Malhazine ward of urban district number 5, and the consolidation of the residents' development committees. The Italian embassy furnished additional funds for training and other expenses.

The impact of the management and improvement of the urban environment, with the full involvement of the residents under the co-ordination of AMDU, sparked the interest of the Municipal Council and the central government. In January 1994, the Municipal Council set up a technical co-ordination unit for the programme of basic urban services. The central government provided a budget for joint activities with AMDU. In 1995 the roads and refuse collection components of the programme were extended to urban district number 3.

AMDU received new funding for 1994/5 under a contract signed with the National Planning Commission. These funds covered the second module over a period of 30 months, which continued work in the wards already included and extended it to the FPLM ward. Extension to the Xipamanine, Mafalala and Munhuana wards was then prepared for 1996, in collaboration with the Municipal Council and the World Food Programme. The establishment in 1996 of resource centres related to different aspects of development in the various wards could provide support to local initiatives for sustainable development.

The programme began during a study of the peri-urban zones of Maputo in 1991. AMDU members made contact with households in these areas, particularly in Mavalane A, an area which was spontaneously settled in the 1960s. A series of activities that the community wanted to undertake to improve the care of pre-school children was identified, as well as a list of priority actions proposed by the community.

Mavalane A ward was chosen because the settlement was about 30 years old and had never had any assistance from the local or central government. There was also a group of young, unemployed and retired people who had taken the initiative to become involved in managing the ward and implementing small programmes that were within their capacities. A more detailed study was then carried out with the local administration, the so-called dynamizing group.

AMDU gradually got to know the local leaders and prominent persons in the area, the child-care specialists and the literacy teachers. Over a period of six months, AMDU members visited the homes of some of the block chiefs. A block comprises between 50 and 80 houses. AMDU sought to build up mutual trust with as large a number as possible of residents in the ward, by visiting them and showing interest in their concerns. When AMDU had reached some preliminary conclusions and drafted its ideas, a public meeting was organized with the residents in order to receive more contributions.

At the same time, AMDU was asked by residents in Hulene B for help in building a nursery school in block 30. Hulene, established more recently and assisted by the social welfare department of the city, was home to many war-displaced people.

These first two programmes were a test of the voluntary participation of local communities in a time of war. The impact was great and it mobilized neighbouring wards. People in contact with the areas that had already benefited understood the methods of organization and asked AMDU if they could join the movement. The situation was then evaluated by means of contacts with the administration of urban district number 4, which includes many very different wards, some very old, others more recently established with a large proportion of war-displaced people, some again with some urban facilities, and yet others with plainly rural characteristics. At the same time, contacts were made with the Maputo Municipal Council and each of its directors managing the various urban functions in order to obtain a full understanding of existing urban policies and to explain AMDU's ideas about jointly promoting improvements to the urban environment, contributing to civic education and strengthening local institutional capacity.

The programme is now running in eight wards of the city: Mavalane A and B, Hulene A and B, FPLM, Malhazine, Maxaquene and Xipamanine. Preparations are under way to extend it to Jorge Dimitrov, Ferroviario, Laulane, Munhuana and Mafalala.

Principles and objectives
The central government is in the process of decentralizing functions, responsibilities and resources to local organs of government. This will enable ordinary citizens to become involved in public affairs and environmental management. AMDU has proposed to the Ministry of State Administration that it carry out a bottom-up exercise in order to develop a sense of citizenship and awareness of civic rights and duties among the population of the city and its surroundings. This would help restore social values by building relationships based on mutual tolerance and respect and through teamwork with the peri-urban and rural communities.

The general principles of the programme seek to: strengthen local community skills in identifying, designing and implementing rehabilitation and development projects to improve living conditions and manage the environment; promote grassroots social organization in order to participate in local administration; improve basic urban services by using labour-intensive methods combined with resources provided by different institutions.

Practical experience has enabled AMDU to redefine the following concepts. 'Community' is the social setting where a series of ideas, attributes, habits, beliefs and rites, meanings, symbols, values, aesthetic images, social organization and customs, which make up the environment, are superimposed on all the cultural acquisitions and inputs. It implies an organized way of living that seeks to preserve cultural traditions as the heritage passed on by individuals and by society. The individual is the basic building block of the community and of the social movement as a whole. Working with the community means working with individuals in the search for solutions to common problems in the daily struggle for survival. It complements the work of the government and tries to make the best use of the few resources available.

'Participation' is the process whereby people influence decisions that affect them and through which they become engaged in their own development. Participation is not simply involvement in the implementation of ideas or in the benefits from development activities. The key to participation is the individual. The tool of participation is organization. The motive for participation is interest and benefit (moral or material, individual or collective). Levels of participation include exchange of information, consultation, decision-making, and initiative in action or execution.

'Development' is the biggest challenge facing the human race. It is a constant process in which different interests, both individual and community, come together to clash or to converge. It is a process of building and managing the environment in which people live, consuming and renewing resources. It is a process in time and space, during which some cultural values and features may lose their validity while other new features gain strength. The secret of development does not lie in eliminating conflict, but rather in knowing how to manage it so as to utilize its energy for the common good. Development should be viewed in all its dimensions: cultural, economic and technological, social and environmental. To develop is to transform the world, not deform it.

'Sustainability' is the capacity to keep activities that meet basic needs functioning. Three main obstacles to sustainability exist: the lack of moral commitment; the unequal distribution of power; and the separation of environmental management from economic development.

'Sustainable development' is the process which aims at securing adequate levels of consumption of the basic necessities and of the income to obtain them, for ourselves and for future generations. It is a process that ensures the continuity of life in the long term.

The general objectives of the programme are: first, to mobilize Mozambique's technical capacity in order to deal with local problems creatively, competently and ethically. Secondly, it is to train Mozambican technicians in the management of development processes for urban infrastructure, who could also serve as facilitators in development activities with more distant rural communities. Thirdly, it is to develop a new type of relationship, based on mutual respect and co-operation, among civil organizations in the South and between them and similar organizations in the North. Finally, it involves strengthening local institutional capacity.

The specific objectives of the programme are to rehabilitate and build social and community infrastructure and promote basic urban services with the participation of the beneficiaries, to promote food security by means of job and other opportunities, to promote better care for pre-school and school-age children and help train and organize women to undertake sustainable activities, and to promote better living standards by means of care and education in health, nutrition and the environment.

The programme of action

A number of activities were planned and then adapted specifically for each module.

Construction and rehabilitation of social and community infrastructure involved nursery and primary schools, health centres, culture and recreation centres, resource centres and markets. Organization of basic urban services addressed the rehabilitation of access roads, water points, drainage ditches and alternative sources of energy. Environmental health and management involved the collection and treatment of refuse and other solid waste, public and household latrines, cemeteries and funeral services, tree-planting and the creation of green space, and environmental education.

Training and employment for the active population entailed the establishment of resource centres for training in production techniques, assistance for self-employment, temporary employment as a means of training and the adoption of programmes and technologies that use labour-intensive methods. Training for women included home economics, literacy training and schooling as a means of access to information and knowledge about women's rights and vocational training for income generation. Education of children covered the organization of care for pre-school children, leisure activities, and increased access to schooling for all children.

Finally, social and civic education for participation in municipal life covered cultural traditions and urban life, the establishment of centres for information and social communication, community radio, training residents for development and support for the local administration offices.

In order to implement development activities in the peri-urban areas of Maputo and strengthen local capacity, a methodology was designed that would allow all activities to be monitored so as to be able to make an investment without having to start from scratch every time. There were three main points to the methodology: promoting complementarity among the various activities carried out in each ward by different agencies and institutions; developing the social and community infrastructure required, using appropriate technology, with the aim of durability, use of local labour, operation by the beneficiaries and sustainability; and promoting the training and employment of young people and demobilized soldiers and contributing to household income through temporary jobs.

The local administration sought to invite various organizations working in the city's wards to periodic meetings to discuss progress and avoid duplication of effort so as to achieve better results. Every attempt to bring all the agencies in the field together in a meeting met with failure, however.

With regard to the technical choices, it was shown to be possible to build solid and durable buildings at low cost. They were spatially of good quality, functional and formal, demonstrating the poor judgement of international organizations making investments on a similar scale but using flimsy materials such as cane and poles, which can be destroyed by termites in less than two years. Even treating the wood is no solution, since the treatment is expensive and a poor deterrent to the insects. The design of the buildings took into consideration the training and employment of local labour, thus building techniques were simplified. The choice of finishing materials took account of the running and maintenance costs that the communities would have to bear in future.

All the activities in the programme began with working sessions for organization and to train the residents who volunteered. Thus 30 to 45 days were spent in each community in organizing and training both unskilled and skilled workers recruited locally.

Men and women of all ages and social classes participate in the programmes. Among the participants are various professionals and technicians, including architects, physical planners, engineers, teachers, psychologists, lawyers, sociologists, nurses and other health workers, cartographers, designers, skilled and semi-skilled local workers, such as tinsmiths, carpenters, glaziers and electricians, as well as teachers and students from the universities, who carry out research and hold classes and workshops.

Everyone collaborates in and develops different pieces of applied research. In this way they gain a new perspective on the problems of rebuilding the social fabric, on actual living conditions, on managing the environment, and on the problems of rapid urbanization and the relationship between the city and the countryside. An important lesson in creating new working relations was learned by all the people involved. These relations are based on interdependence and balanced demands. Everyone learned how to control human and material resources and to find sustainable solutions within the reach of each individual and his/her community as a whole.

Women of all ages are the driving force behind all the activities. They are joined by young unemployed people, older retired people, demobilized soldiers and other unemployed persons, all of whom contribute their ideas and dreams, along with their labour, experience, practical knowledge and organizational skills. Together they design the programmes of action for local development, and together they put these plans into operation.

The local administrations and residents formed various working groups and committees to co-ordinate the activities in each block of the wards. Residents' development committees were set up at urban district and ward level. It is these committees that assess the needs, collect proposals for projects and monitor their implementation and operation. The Maputo Municipal Council and the central government provide the legal and institutional framework required for contact with the international donor community. They help with human and financial resources and provide the criteria for implementing projects within existing policies and plans. AMDU co-ordinates the programme technically and collaborates with the Municipal Council and the district administrations to extend the good practice established to other areas.

AMDU is a national civil association set up by a group of Mozambican professionals from various disciplines, each with their own ideas and creativity, initiative and training. With years of experience working in public institutions, they know the country well and are aware of the shortages and lack of resources, but, above all, they are keen to take part in national reconstruction and development, in restoring the fabric of society and rebuilding infrastructure destroyed by years of war and neglect. For several years now, AMDU members have been working with people in the rural areas in times of flood, and with urban communities in developing building techniques for schools.

AMDU's current programme has been running for five years, with a continuous discussion of ideas. Faced with the realities of Mozambique, the realization has dawned that each individual has the right to his/her own ideas, to be different from others, to think differently from the received wisdom, to experiment and gain new experience and to struggle for social mores and professional ethics. The members of AMDU accept their duty as citizens of their country in an active and critical way, while also being constructive and participative.

The local people let it be known that their main concern was about the pre-school-age children whom parents have tended to leave behind when they go to work in the fields, offices or factories. At the same time, the worsening war situation and the lack of jobs had caused children's nutritional status to decline, since many households did not make even one meal, but survived for days on bread and tea, when that at least was available. The education of pre-school-age children, and the family's interest in it, was not regarded as very important. More emphasis was placed on primary schooling. The construction of a nursery school was taken as the core of the programme. It also functioned as a civic centre where all the community involvement developed and all the projects were prepared.

The programme was broken up into increasingly bigger implementation modules as community interest in it grew. The initial stage, in which the residents assessed the community's needs and ranked the solutions in order of priority, was accompanied by a small intervention on the ground, funded by AMDU, to help learn how the local administration functions and discover the social dynamics of the community, as well as the existing skills and talents.

The outputs expected and in part achieved from these interventions have been various. In terms of training, about 150 volunteers from the communities were trained, particularly women, young people and retired people. They attended courses in the following skills: project planning and management; community facilitation; supply and control of stocks; human resource management and labour control; self-help building (masons, painters, carpenters, management of materials, labour, etc); dressmaking and needlework; and organizational principles. A team of 200 was trained for road rehabilitation. Fifteen child-care facilitators were trained in nutrition and health education. Women involved in the programme received literacy training and environmental education. Those managing the nursery schools were organized and trained to manage budgets and handle pedagogical and administrative matters. A nutrition programme was organized in the nursery schools and food was distributed to everyone working in the programme. A resource centre was set up to provide pedagogical and organizational support to the nursery and community schools by producing teaching materials from local resources, holding seminars for facilitators and teachers and setting up a library (Mavalane A). Another resource centre was built and organized for cultural and artistic development and the organization of local craftsmen and theatre and dance and song groups (Hulene B, block 53). Training for and organization of economic activities was conducted as follows: construction and organization of a training and production resource centre for metalwork, carpentry and building (Hulene B, block 20); a dress-making and needlework training and production centre (Mavalane A); the *Papo Seco* Bakery (Mavalane B); and organization of groups to collect and recycle refuse as a source of income.

The building of infrastructure was an important output of the programme and included:

- 12 pre-school nurseries managed by the community in 6 wards;
- 2 official primary schools rehabilitated (Mavalane A);
- 3 workshops for income-generating activities built;
- a health centre rehabilitated and extended (Hulene A);
- ward administration offices built or rehabilitated (Mavalane A and B and FPLM);
- a recreation centre for the ward rehabilitated (Mavalane A).

A third aspect was the organization of basic urban services, which included the construction of 100 improved dry latrines, organization of a refuse collection and recycling system with community involvement, rehabilitation of 10 kilometres of tarred road, rehabilitation of 3 water points and pumps, and finding solutions to problems of rainwater drainage at critical points.

A summary of the achievements gained through the programme runs as follows:

i)   an increase in awareness of the municipality and support for the local administration;
ii) facilitation among local communities to increase awareness of their civic rights and duties;
iii) the promotion of dialogue and co-operation among civil society, local administrations and the central government;
iv) skills training for unemployed women and young people;
v)   the promotion of self-employment through training in production processes;
vi) the local involvement of retired old people in activities useful to the community;
vii) the introduction of appropriate sustainable technologies in building infrastructure;
viii) better care for pre-school and school-age children;
ix) professional training for AMDU volunteers and others to work in programmes of sustainable development.

Conclusions and recommendations
In the course of the seven years of the programme's existence, a number of difficulties have emerged, which AMDU and the local communities studied in order to put forward solutions to the local and municipal authorities. The following are the principal issues:

i)   Participatory development has rather slow rates of implementation, since the programme must respect the pace of community life. It has been possible to encourage the donors to accept this.
ii) The ownership of the infrastructure built remains an open question, since the community, in legal terms, is an imprecise concept. A possible solution could be the formation of local associations.
iii) The correct use of the resources created and their further development in the future require regular monitoring by AMDU and the local administration to ensure that the social and community facilities do not become privatized.
iv) The management and maintenance of the facilities can be ensured by the

establishment of a technical assistance unit composed of residents trained during the programme.

v)   The role of the local administration needs to be discussed in seminars to be held. It will also be necessary to ensure the continued participation of ward residents in all the processes of local administration.

The impact of the programme has gradually built up in the peri-urban areas. Communities seek out AMDU to be allowed to join the *Pjuka Dzixile* movement. At the same time, AMDU is of the opinion that the government and other public institutions are prepared to adopt the principles, strategy and methodology of the programme because of the results it has achieved, despite some initial scepticism and doubt.

It is already possible to evaluate some of the programme's impact, which includes:

i)   improvement of the quality of the peri-urban environment;
ii)   positive effects in the local economy and the delivery of services;
iii) the creation of conditions for mobilizing potential existing resources;
iv)   the development of services that can generate revenue for the municipality;
v)   the recognition and integration of local vital forces and skills;
vi)   giving due worth and respect to each person's culture, and achieving a spirit of tolerance;
vii) the possibility of replicating the programme in other wards and other cities;
vii) the development of models and criteria for evaluating participatory programmes.

AMDU's experience in working with communities in peri-urban areas has demonstrated that potential skills and knowledge exist among the city dwellers to resolve the basic and serious problems affecting Maputo. There are people in the city who are extremely keen to take an active part in national life, at their own level, and who have great capacity to mobilize and organize. Others have a type of knowledge that would be useful if properly integrated and directed.

The methodology and strategy used in Maputo were adapted for use in the rural areas of four districts in Inhambane Province in the *Tsima Ga Ku Aka* Programme. This programme likewise had a significant impact on restoring settlements and on the reconciliation process to strengthen peace.

Recommendations
i)   The first recommendation is that the methodology and implementation strategy of the *Pfuka Dzixile* Programme should be studied together with the municipal and central government authorities and the urban district administrators of Maputo and of other cities. Field visits to talk to local participants could be useful for checking and practical work. Questioning the practices developed would be a way of improving what could be adopted as a policy for sustainable development.
ii)   Urban planning and basic urbanization cannot wait until the conclusion of the master plans foreseen in the local government reform programme. These will take at least five years to prepare and then more time to be reviewed and approved. The Municipal Council should muster the available technical skills to draw up partial plans to reorganize the peri-urban zones where reorganization is still possible. Basic urbanization, namely, the supply of access roads, water, sanitation and energy, is a task the state should shoulder, as it is likely to generate further development, since people, however few the resources they have, are ready to invest their efforts in the creation of housing and services.
iii) The state should encourage research into appropriate technology and review

building designs and standards in order to match these to the general economic level of the population. This process should include the promotion of:

(a) the production of building materials and other building components;
(b   local production and access to credit;
(c) marketing of building materials and other building components;
(d) technical assistance and quality control services for self-help building projects, perhaps through the creation of an extension service.

iv) The mass media should be encouraged to promote civic and environmental education. The creation of community radio and ward information centres could serve as important channels for publicizing new technologies, educating the public and developing a culture of sustainable development.

v)   The state could facilitate indirect mechanisms to regulate the functioning of informal markets. Informal activities are a means of survival for the poorer sections of the population, and as such they are absolutely essential to deal with unemployment, crime and delinquency. The creation of space for informal markets, with basic water and sanitation services, could introduce some discipline and contribute to urban development.

vi) The law which is applied to international donors should be revised so as to encourage firms and services to contribute to participatory community development.

22 Rapid Appraisal as a Tool of Sustainable Development in Bagamoyo Suburb, Maputo

LORNA GUJRAL

After 16 years of civil war, Mozambique is currently undergoing a process of socio-political, economic and institutional change. This process offers an opportunity for reorienting the country's approaches to the management of its natural resources and for building the human resource capacity to promote sustainable development.

The World Commission on Environment and Development report, *Our Common Future* (1987) provides some guidelines for the orientation of this new approach, which are outlined by Barry Munslow in Chapter 2 of this book. Success in the implementation of these guidelines will only be achieved if there is participation by the state, the private sector, NGOs and the wider civil society. To be effective, such participation will require co-ordination which will not only identify the basic priorities as perceived by the population, but will also ensure that these are made known to the managers and policy-makers so that they can be taken into consideration when formulating new policies.

Rapid appraisal methods are an important tool in the context of this new vision. These methods comprise a group of techniques and approaches which not only provide rapid and precise information needed to ensure development in a decentralized context, but also empower the local population to share, strengthen and analyze their knowledge in order to plan and take action to improve things (see Chapter 12 by Ong and Munslow; Chambers, 1992; Ong, 1996).

Rapid appraisal methods

Rapid Rural Appraisal (RRA) and Participatory Rapid Rural Appraisal (PRRA) offer a group of techniques aimed at collecting information which can be used throughout a project cycle, to discover the main characteristics of the problems facing the population, the people's own priorities of their needs, and possible solutions to be found within the community. For instance, these can include:

i)   Exploring an area to understand the problems people face and the key opportunities, with a view to helping in planning research or in project development.
ii) Researching a topic, question or specific problem.
iii) Monitoring or evaluating research or the development of an activity.
iv) Finding solutions to conflicts between different social groups.
v)   Applying the techniques in the daily work of scientific workers, field researchers, extension workers, etc. (IIED, 1991).

Although both methods require the participation of local communities, there are some authors who prefer the RRA method, as it covers most areas of application adequately, whilst reserving the PRRA method for cases when the participation needs to be done at a deeper level to ensure community participation in the planning process, interviews and analysis of the results obtained (Whiteside, 1994).

These methods are sustained by five basic principles:

i)   *in the community* – community involvement, increased participation, capacity for acting locally and producing the greater part of the results in its own area;
ii) *interactive* – combined participation of all the group members and subjects to make communication easier;
iii) *innovative* – no standard model, an easy research methodology looking at each subject from different points of view;
iv) *informal* – adoption of a less formal focus;
v)   *iterative* – the possibility of changing the process and objectives and the newly generated information allows for an understanding of what is or is not relevant (Chambers, 1992).

Opportunities and constraints in using RRA and PRRA methods

The use of these methods offers considerable advantages, namely: (i) it avoids problems deriving from formal, long-term and expensive research, for instance, excess data collection, collection of non-relevant data, the production of late and inadequate results; (ii) it avoids the risks of hasty and structureless research, such as obtaining a rapid impression of the area or topic, excessive confidence in previous research, work undertaken without a clear framework to collect and analyze information; (iii) it overcomes distortions inherent in conventional methods, namely, looking only for apparent and quantitative data, missing the more qualitative information, counting only on those who are most accessible or in a superior social position as groups or individuals, looking only for the average and normal and missing the extremes which provide the limits and the exceptions; and (iv) it promotes collaboration between researchers and the community in collecting, analyzing and presenting information, deciding on priorities and developing a mutual learning experience (IIED, 1992; Whiteside, 1994).

Nevertheless, there are also some limitations to the effective use of these methods. For instance: (i) they are complementary to other research methodologies, such as statistical research and long-range anthropological studies; (ii) although they produce rapid and low-cost information, the development process itself is slow; (iii) sensible or complex matters can be missed or misunderstood, as, for instance, with social conflicts; (iv) they can generate heightened local expectations and the information obtained can be distorted, giving advantages to a special social group; (v) they elaborate only questions or hypotheses for future development, rather than presenting answers; (vi) their effective use demands a significant period of preparation and training for the orientation of personnel and participants; and (vii) they cannot be easily moved from one culture to another and need to be adapted to local conditions (IIED, 1992; Whiteside, 1994).

The focus proposed by the RRA/PRRA allows a choice to be made from a rich variety of techniques and the particular combination will depend on the existing resources and on the results expected. Table 22.1 presents a brief description of these techniques.

Use of RRA and PRRA methods in Mozambique

In Mozambique these methods have been used mainly in the rural zones, usually in areas such as agriculture, forestry and natural resources, to identify problems as they

Table 22.1 *Description of RRA and PRRA techniques*

Technique	Description
Secondary data revision	Learning from official records, census reports, documents, maps, photographs, etc.
Direct observation	Direct contact with local living conditions (people, problems, agrarian practices, existing relations, etc)
Semi-structured interviews	Individual or group informal discussions, based on a flexible list of topics, whose interviewees can be common residents or key informants
Group discussions	Discussions conducted through target groups or focus groups (to know the interest groups or the attitudes of experts) or through open discussions (for general discussions)
Participatory diagrams, mapping and modelling	Local production of diagrams on the ground to improve communication and learning and clarification of information provided by the interviews
	It can include participatory mapping of the surroundings or community models; transversal walks; seasonal time-tables and daily routines; diagrams of flows and schemes (story profiles, tendencies and scenarios)
Prioritizing	Research on the preferences and reasons which determine a certain choice, through the comparison of items
Local quantification	Comparison of simple classes, consideration of criteria or evaluation of proportions, using local material
Games and representations	Adjustment of traditional table games as learning instruments (populations and/or teams) aiming to increase communication and learning and encourage discussion
Stories, pictures and sayings	Record of the stories told during the interviews, description of pictures of the houses and inclusion of exemplifying sayings (secret practices, beliefs)
Seminars (workshops)	Open discussions (brain-storming), analysis and presentations in the area
Feedback reports to the community	Presentation of the findings to the local population to be discussed and reviewed

Source IIED 1991

are perceived by the population, their own prioritization and possibilities for poverty alleviation.

In the field of health, these methodologies are little used as yet in Mozambique, though, internationally, Bie Nio Ong (1996) and others are pioneering work on rapid appraisal and health policy. However, there are a number of qualitative studies available which focus on understanding existing traditional beliefs about diarrhoea, sexually transmitted diseases (STD) and mental health, and aim to draw comparisons with modern medicine.

This situation is now changing. On the one hand, there is an increasing interest in community perceptions of their diseases and health problems; on the other hand, there is growing recognition that the knowledge of the population about their own local conditions is often greater than was previously assumed. Health System Research (ISS) is a research tool that makes possible an improvement in the community health situation. The ISS is oriented towards priority problems in community health and is directed towards action and finding solutions. It aims to provide the relevant and necessary information for decision-making by policy-makers, managers at different levels, and planning personnel, as well as community leaders. It is important to emphasize that one of the characteristics of this kind of research is its participatory approach involving community intervention (Varkevisser *et al*, 1993).

What follows are the early results of an on-going study being implemented by the Health System Research Unit (UISS) of the National Health Institute (INS). This study began in the Bagamoyo Health Area, in Maputo city, in 1996. It is expected that the results of this research will contribute to a deeper knowledge of this Health Area and of the perceived health problems which are considered to be a priority in the local community. This will facilitate (i) the availability of information to the Bagamoyo Health Centre to improve the level of health care given to this community; (ii) the availability of information to the Maputo City Health Directorate so that the next educational campaigns can be oriented towards priorities identified by the population; (iii) support for the community in understanding and analyzing its own problems; and (iv) guidance for the community in searching for local solutions, and offering the opportunity to participate in the implementation process.

Health problems perceived by the community in the Bagamoyo health area

The objectives of this initiative were to:

- Identify the health problems as perceived by the population in the Bagamoyo Health Area.
- Identify the evaluation criteria and priorities for these problems.
- Identify the population's concepts about the diseases, symptoms or indications that can induce a diagnosis.
- Discover the population's perceptions of individuals most vulnerable to diseases.
- Discover the population's perceptions about the seasonality of the diseases, symptoms or indications that can induce a diagnosis.
- Identify the opportunities perceived by the community that could reduce the sanitation problems existing in the suburbs.

The Bagamoyo Health Area is located in the suburban zone of Maputo city and has a population of some 86,300 inhabitants, distributed between the suburbs 25 de Junho 'A' (17,747 inhabitants) and 'B' (8,726 inhabitants), Bagamoyo (20,765 inhabitants), Jorge Dimitrov (30,137 inhabitants) and Malhazine (8,934 inhabitants). It is surrounded by Magoanine to the north, Nsalene to the south, Hulene to the east and Nhavel to the west.

The average family unit comprises 8 persons and the main activity of the majority of the population is agriculture. Most houses are made of brick and mortar (cement houses), covered with corrugated iron, and are fenced with spiny plants. There are also houses made of caniço (reeds) and some other dwellings.

Piped water is supplied only in the mornings, which obliges the residents to transport and store the water, often in inappropriate containers susceptible to contamination. There are a number of wells and some bore holes.

Although refuse collection undertaken by the Municipal Council is inadequate, except in the areas of high population density, there is no rubbish piled up or scattered on the streets, as the local residents collect and bury it. The houses are clean, and in general do not have glass windows and curtains. Firewood and charcoal are generally used for cooking in the yards and verandas, and oil lamps are the main source of light.

This area has 3 markets, the main one being the Mercado 25 de Junho; 7 primary schools and 1 secondary school; 1 paper factory; 1 judicial court; 4 bakeries; 1 police station; 1 administrative office (station); 13 commercial properties (8 shops and 5 bars) and the Regional Sanitary Development Centre (CRDS) (Oluemena *et al*, 1995). There are 10 churches, mostly Protestant, ('Anglicana', 'Exercito de Salvação', 'Bom Pastor', '12 Apostolos', 'Assembleia de Deus' and 'Zione' churches) in Bagamoyo, and in 25 de Junho 'A' a Catholic church and in Jorge Dimitrov Catholic and 'Universal do Reino de Deus' churches.

The Bagamoyo Health Centre is the only primary-level health care unit in this Health Area. It faces many different problems, namely, lack of food for the patients, lack of hygienic and cleaning materials, of water and energy, and of vehicles to transport the patients, and a lack of manual workers (Director of the Bagamoyo Health Centre, personal communication, 1996). The main diseases diagnosed in children are malaria, malnutrition and intestinal parasites (Oluemena *et al, 1995*). In adults infectionary parasite diseases such as malaria, sexually transmitted diseases (STD), tuberculosis, respiratory diseases and skin itching are prevalent (Director of the Bagamoyo Health Centre, 1996). There are also some cases of hypertension and a small number of mental health cases (Oluemena *et al*, 1995).

For this study health problems are defined as a group of diseases and symptoms or indicators that can induce a probable diagnosis, problems of the Health Centre, and environmental sanitation problems which inhibit the physical, mental and social well-being of people in the Health Area.

Methodology

A non-intrusive exploratory and qualitative study was implemented using RRA and RPPA techniques. These included discussion techniques of focus groups, matrixes in pairs and option criteria and season timetables as well as informal interviews (Groverman, 1992).

Informal interviews with the patients and workers at the Health Centre enabled an understanding to be gained of existing approaches and ideas about health problems as defined above and a better understanding of the points of view and terminology used by the community. By means of a convenience sampling 5 workers and 10 patients were interviewed about: (i) the main diseases in the Health Area; (ii) their description; (iii) who was most affected; (iv) in what season of the year; (v) the main problems of the Health Centre; and (vi) the main problems of community sanitation.

With the support of the administrative structures of the Health Area, the leaders of all the religious institutions and the traditional healers were invited to separate meetings for the purpose of explaining the objectives and the work methodology and asking for volunteers (a minimum of 6 and a maximum of 12) to form two focus groups (DGE), one of religious leaders and the other of traditional healers. For each focus group, two sessions were carried out, the first on the topic 'diseases and symptoms or indicators that can induce a possible diagnosis' and its description, and the second covering the other two topics. After the first DGE session, the religious leaders were asked to present a list of 60 women, aged 18 or over, together with a completed identification form for each, 40 of whom were selected to form four DGEs. The selection was done in such a way as to include different ages and those with and without children and holding different religious beliefs, which made it possible to gather information from the Health Area as a whole. The invitation to the participants was given by the various religious leaders, 72 hours in advance, to ensure the attendance of all the women.

For each of the four groups, two sessions were held. At the beginning of each session, the objectives and the work methodology were explained to all the informants. The first session discussed the first topic, and the second was devoted to the other two topics. The DGE involved a facilitator (researcher), two reporters and one interpreter and took place in the 'Grupo Dinamizador' headquarters of Bagamoyo suburb.

Preliminary results

Only part of the DGE's findings with the religious leaders, the traditional healers and the first group of women will be presented here. The study had not yet concluded at the time of writing.

The key issue was the identification, description, seasonality and individual susceptibility of the most frequent diseases. The first diseases to be identified in any of the groups were malaria and diarrhoea with a show of blood; the latter is also called dysentery. Rheumatism, also called feet disease, was also identified by the three groups.

Malaria
The bites of insects not visible to the naked eye, of mosquitoes, of tsetse fly (less frequently), well water and food covered with mosquitoes' eggs, the lack of vaccines and the lack of spraying were identified by the religious leaders and traditional healers as causes of this disease. The women showed an ignorance of the cause, but admitted the possibility of it being an infectious disease, hence it was possible to become infected from sick persons, for instance, people living in the same house.

In general, the groups described the disease as follows: a feeling of cold and bites similar to injections, when one is exposed to the sun and the body feels tired; vomiting, fever, itching and lack of appetite; bitter saliva (spittle) in the mouth and the feet are heavy. Sometimes the brain does not work properly with headaches and talking nonsense, and the vision can also be affected. The traditional healers added that the malaria can also cause headaches, weakness and sometimes diarrhoea. The women emphasized that, besides headaches (mainly in the forehead and sides of the head) one feels burning (in the back and middle) and a lack of energy (blood).

With the exception of the women's group, our informants said that malaria is a disease that occurs throughout the year; according to the women, it occurs only during the change from the hot to the cold season. Concerning susceptibility to the disease, children and adults are affected equally.

'Paludismo'
It is considered that malaria is a main root cause of this disease, along with the swallowing of food not properly washed, such as flour, bread or sugar on which mosquitoes and flies have landed. 'Paludismo' occurs throughout the year and affects both children and adults in the same way.

Diarrhoea
The traditional healers' group demonstrated ignorance of the causes of this disease.

The religious leaders indicated the swallowing of food which was not properly digested and breast-feeding with breast milk in a poor condition as the main causes.

The characterization, seasonality and susceptibility of individuals to this disease varied with the informant group. For the religious leaders' group, this disease affects adults and children in the same way and occurs throughout the year. The patient feels stomach cramps, the stomach becomes warm and there can develop an urge to go to the toilet up to 10 times a day. According to the traditional healers, it affects only adults and appears during the cold season. The patient feels the worms moving in the morning, vomits, becomes weak and has no appetite.

Diarrhoea with a show of blood or dysentery

According to our informants, all individuals may be affected by diarrhoea with a show of blood, irrespective of age. The traditional healers specified that children under five or six do not suffer from this disease. With the exception of the women's group, we were informed that this disease occurs in the early period of mango development, that is, in October and November.

The descriptions given by the groups were not identical. For the religious leaders' group, diarrhoea with blood or dysentery is similar to normal diarrhoea but, when going to the toilet, blood is expelled. For the traditional healers' group, the patient feels bites between the stomach and the bladder, blood comes out of the mouth and, generally, there is no fever. The description given by the women's group was similar to that of the religious leaders; according to them the patient feels bites in the navel (umbilicus) and is constantly going to the toilet where blood is expelled.

Cholera

Food not properly washed and salads, rubbish and lack of defences (vaccines), were the causes highlighted by the religious leaders and traditional healers, respectively. The description given by the two groups was different. For the religious leaders' group, the patient experiences a bitterness in the mouth as if he/she had eaten hot chili, and vomits a 'bitter water'; he/she loses strength and can even die. The traditional healers' group pointed out that the patient has a cough, his/her eyes become red, and he/she experiences fever and lack of appetite. According to the religious leaders, this disease occurs only during the cold season and affects all individuals irrespective of age, while for the traditional healers' group it occurs in the cold season and affects only children from 4 to 12 years old.

Paralysis or Thrombosis

The religious leaders' group ignored the causes of this disease which occurs throughout the year, potentially affecting all individuals irrespective of age, while the traditional healers indicated personal problems as the cause of the disease. According to their perception, it can occur throughout the year and only affects adults.

According to the traditional healers, the disease comes on suddenly, the victim starts to lose the power of speech and parts of the body become paralyzed. The religious leaders' group mentioned that the patient feels tired and starts having difficulties in moving about, then loses strength and feels hot and cold at the same time. He/she starts to slobber and suddenly cannot stand up, because of the pain and the feeling of heaviness.

Intestinal Parasites or Worms

The groups showed an ignorance of the cause of this disease, which only affects children and can occur throughout the year. According to the traditional healers, the disease is dangerous, as the patient can even die; he/she starts to feel worms moving in the stomach, vomits and the worms come out of the mouth and nose. The patient becomes weak and is unable to breathe properly. The description given by the women's group was different; according to them, the patient lacks appetite, has a lack of blood and the stomach swells.

Foot disease or Rheumatism
Various potential causes are put forward for foot disease or rheumatism, namely: working in swampy zones with salty water or with chemical products, standing up for long periods, lack of movement in normally fit persons, inadequate diet and lack of prophylaxis. For the women's group, the cause of the disease is unknown.

The descriptions offered by the traditional leaders and the women's groups were similar. To them, this disease is very dangerous; the bones hurt (intense pain in the feet, arms, veins, ankles and spinal column) followed by headaches, a burning head and weakness. The women added that one feels dizzy and it is best to keep the legs covered, to allay the pain. According to the religious leaders' group, one feels pain in the veins, the feet swell and consequently the person cannot walk. According to our informants, this disease may currently affect any individual though previously it affected only the old and occurred throughout the year. The women's group said that the rheumatism appeared only in the cold season.

Coughing
Smoke, working with paints/inks and lead and unloading 'brume' and charcoal were the causes given for the appearance of this disease, which affects only men and occurs in the cold season. Coughing begins with the appearance of a discomfort in the throat, caused by something that a person has eaten. Later, the coughing starts in earnest, the chest hurts, headaches set in, and the nostrils become blocked up. Later, after some time, blood can also appear in the phlegm.

Pain in the chest (lungs)
This is a disease of unknown cause, characterized by the appearance of a pain that starts when one is eating; before the end of a meal the lungs hurt and the person feels like going to the toilet, but there is no evacuation. When the patient walks he/she feels very tired. It is a disease that can affect all individuals irrespective of age and can occur at any time during the year.

Pain in the kidneys
Heavy work, lack of nutrition, poor living conditions and the carrying of heavy loads for long distances, were reasons put forward for the appearance of this disease, which occurs at any time during the year and affects all individuals irrespective of age. Pain in the kidneys consists of feelings of tiredness when carrying heavy loads for long distances, pain in the spinal column and lack of strength in the elbows.

High blood pressure
The existence of many socio-economic problems, divorce, inadequate rest for adults and the transmission of the parents' blood to the children, were the causes identified for this disease, which may occur throughout the year and mainly affects women. Tiredness, the impression of having walked long distances, an increase in the heart rate, loss of strength and fainting were symptoms used to describe this disease. Hot chili, salt, sugar and oil were identified as foods that may worsen the disease.

Skin itching ('sarns')
We were informed that the causes of this infectious disease were not well known;

deficient nutrition or the dust in the suburbs were identified as possible causes. The disease affects children at the beginning of the hot and the cold seasons. It is described as the on-set of itching that causes pimples and, later on, fever. These pimples are different from 'hot season pimples', where one only feels itching; the pimples appear and then after a couple of hours disappear.

Lack of vitamins
Inadequate nutrition and the lack of fruit in the diet were the aspects identified as being responsible for this disease. Lack of vitamins is characterized by weakness, headaches and loss of appetite and may occur throughout the year, affecting all individuals irrespective of age.

Lack of blood
Poor nutrition was identified as the cause for this disease, described as weakness and tiredness. It can occur throughout the year and may affect individuals of any age.

Headaches
Long periods of exposure to the sun and taking meals at irregular intervals were identified as causes of this disease, which is characterized by pain in the sides, the forehead and the middle of the head, and by fever. The headaches may occur at any time during the year and affect individuals of all ages.

Fever
Poor nutrition and bad housing conditions, mosquito bites and constant physical effort were identified as the causes for this disease, which is characterized by headaches and cold shivers. Fever is a disease that may occur throughout the year and affects individuals of all ages.

Bronchitis
This is a disease of unknown cause that occurs in the hot season, and affects only children. The patient has a fever and, later on, sores appear on the tongue and mouth.

Asthma
The causes of asthma in adults were unknown but in the view of our informants pregnant mothers can pass it on to their children. We were informed that this disease mainly affects children and occurs when there are changes of temperature. Two 'types' of asthma were identified: in the first, the patient experiences a lack of air and a cough and, in the second, the patient suffers only from a lack of air.

Conjunctivitis
This is a disease of unknown cause, in which the patient suffers pain in the eyes and has the feeling of having sand inside the eyes. The eye becomes yellow and after a time a white 'thing' appears between the cornea and the retina. This is very painful and may require surgical intervention. It is a disease that mainly affects children and occurs during the hot season.

Stomach pains
This is a disease of unknown cause which, according to our informants, can be caused by the fact that food does not settle well in the stomach. The pain is described as bites and stomach burn, with diarrhoea. It is a disease that may occur all the year round and affects children.

Tooth ache
This is a disease of unknown cause that mainly affects adults and occurs during the cold season. It is described as the appearance of a hole in the tooth which becomes very painful when 'something' gets into it.

Heart pains
The cause of the disease is related to particular problems which cause the patient to be worried. An individual affected by this disease has a high heart rate, is listless and becomes easily irritated. It is a disease that may occur all the year round and only affects adults.

Selection criteria and prioritization of diseases

The groups expressed difficulty in quantifying the diseases according to the criteria mentioned by them. However, when filling in the pairs matrix, the criteria were discussed and analyzed as a whole in the prioritization of the diseases. The most important criterion for all the groups was that 'it is a killer disease'. What followed in the view of the religious leaders was: the difficulty of treatment, prevention, prolonged treatment and the period needed to restore the patient's health. For the traditional healers it was: difficulty of treatment, vaccinations, frequent occurrence and many people becoming ill. For the women's group it was: having to go to hospital to be treated, the period needed to restore one's health, the fact that the disease affects most children, the intensity of the pain and finally seeing blood and being frightened.

The prioritization of the diseases is presented in Table 22.2.

Table 22.2 *Group prioritization of diseases*

	Religious leaders	Traditional healers	Women
Diarrhoea with blood or dysentery	14	4	8
Malaria	12	5	4
Cholera	15	6	–
Diarrhoea	13	2	–
Paralysis or thrombosis	9	1	–
Foot disease or rheumatism	4	0	1
Intestinal parasites or worms	–	3	2
'Paludismo'	11	–	–
Pain in the kidneys	9	–	–
Pain in the lungs	8	–	–
Asthma	–	–	8
Heart Pain	–	–	8
High blood pressure	7	–	–
Stomach pain	–	–	6
Cough	6	–	–
Lack of blood	6	–	–
Bronchitis	–	–	5
Headaches	3	–	–
Fevers	2	–	–
Conjunctivitis	–	–	2
Skin itching	1	–	–
Tooth pain	–	–	1
Lack of vitamins	0	–	–

Source Health Systems Research Unit 1996

Sanitation problems perceived by the community

The sanitation problems identified by the community were as follows:

Pulverization or lack of assistance The non-existence of pulverization in the suburbs was identified as the main factor responsible for the proliferation of mosquitoes and cockroaches.

Lack of inspection ('fiscalizaçao') The lack of inspection in the markets by the Municipal Council was identified in some cases, namely, the sale of contaminated products in the market, the unregulated sale of medicines, the selling of out-of-date medicines and of medicines for abortions, without any clear instruction as to how to use them and their possible side-effects.

Existence of rubbish in the suburbs The existence of large piles of rubbish in the suburbs, sometimes referred to as 'poor functioning of the Municipality', was considered an important cause of disease, because, according to our informants, 'the people clean their houses, put the rubbish/dirt outside the house but the Municipal Council does not collect it'.

Existence of rubbish in the markets Although this is related to the lack of inspection and inadequate conservation of food in the markets and 'dumba-nengues' (informal markets), our informants were of the opinion that this aspect should be dealt with separately because, although inspection has an important role to play, the sellers also had to take some responsibility. According to our informants, 'the sellers sweep only in the places where they sell and put the rubbish anywhere, instead of burying it'.

Negligence by neighbours This situation was explained by two examples: 'there are neighbours who keep pigs in the yard but don't bother to clean the yard properly', and 'we clean our houses but our neighbours do not clean their houses and the toilet. When we try to talk to them about it they get angry.'

Inadequate conservation of food in the 'dumba-nengues' According to our informants, all the food in the 'dumba-nengue' is exposed to flies and dust. This problem is worst for food that is not washed before use, for instance flour, sugar and bread. Nevertheless, although people recognize that these products are better conserved in the shops they still prefer the 'dumba-nengues', because 'the food is sold in cups, and is thus more affordable, while in the shops the food is sold by the kilogram and is more expensive'.

Need to license market traders This concern was explained by an example: 'a person with tuberculosis can sell in the markets and "dumba-nengues". Meanwhile he/she coughs over the food. A person who is not sick buys this food and can be infected.'

Rain water Rain water is a problem because, according to our informants, it washes the rubbish from the piles in the suburbs and spreads it into the yards and sometimes inside the houses.

Removal of corpses from public places This situation was explained as 'a lack of respect on the part of the authorities concerned', because, after reporting the incident to the authorities, 'the body can remain for 24 hours in a public place before its removal'.

Personal hygiene Our informants exemplified this situation by the attitude of some people who 'do not have a bath, do not wash their clothes or their baby's nappies', because of the lack of water in the suburbs.

Selection criteria and prioritization of sanitation problems

The selection criteria for the sanitation problems existing in the suburbs were identified by the different groups as follows:

Religious leaders

Socio-economic problems such as unemployment and the low minimum wage; large numbers of flies; non-existence of vaccines to prevent diseases; rubbish dispersed by rain water; inadequate rubbish collection; sale of medicines in unsuitable places; selling meat in the markets (pork and goat meat) without refrigeration

Traditional healers

Lack of rubbish collection; large numbers of mosquitoes; animal breeding in inappropriate places; contamination of products in the markets; sick market sellers who continue working

Women

Economic problems; rules of hygiene not complied with.

Some criteria presented were related to the diseases identified previously, namely:

i)   the existence of piles of rubbish close to houses and of swarms of flies was related to malaria, 'as the flies land in the food (sugar, flour and bread) which is then eaten without being washed', and to skin-itching, 'the children play in the midst of the rubbish and then eat without washing their hands'.
ii) lack of pulverization and immunization (vaccines) was referred to as 'aggravating the existence of mosquitoes which cause malaria'.

Our informants emphasized that social and economic problems were the cause of many of the constraints existing in the suburbs: 'most people are unemployed. To cook a meal for a family of 8 or 9 persons costs 10,000,00 mts just for firewood. Then they have to buy the curry. How can an unemployed person or someone on a minimum wage eat for a whole month?' In this context, unemployment and the minimum wage were associated with the lack of vitamins and lack of blood because, according to our informants, 'the lack of blood is dependent on the diet, while vitamins are found in fruit'.

Proposals by the groups to minimize the problems identified
Proposals put forward by the groups relate only to the government's role. The religious leaders and the traditional healers said that they did not know what to do. According to them: 'the government has to increase inspection in the markets and the suburbs; immunize people before they become infected and not wait for them almost to die before starting to give vaccines; carry out regular pulverization in the suburbs, and also regular collection of rubbish'.

The women were of the same opinion. 'The Government knows the solution to the problems in the suburbs. So, it should issue directions to get something done about them.'

Preliminary discussion of the results

Diseases identified
During the focus groups, the perception of informants about the diseases identified was sometimes vague, confused or even incorrect. Headaches, pain in the kidneys and

pain in the lungs are examples of diseases about which the descriptions given were vague and confused and the informants showed some difficulty in describing. Sometimes a prejudice was noticed, as for instance, in relation to bronchitis and cholera. This extended to some of the denominations used by the participants; some of the diseases had 'synonymous denominations'. Examples of this situation were: diarrhoea with a show of blood and dysentery; paralysis and thrombosis; foot disease and rheumatism; intestinal parasites and worms.

The descriptions of diseases such as cholera, diarrhoea and diarrhoea with blood or dysentery given by the religious leaders and the traditional healers do not conform. The existence of 'traditional' prejudice about these diseases could be the reason for this. However, it was not possible to confirm this, as the lack of knowledge alleged by the women and the traditional healers about the causes of the diseases, and the vague and sometimes confused descriptions given, gave the impression that information was being withheld. This could be caused by two factors. On the one hand, by the format of the integrated discussions, since all the participants knew each other, and this may have inhibited some individuals from displaying their knowledge rather than agreeing with the majority. On the other hand, the fact that the diseases mentioned (with the exception of malaria) were only treated by the Health Centre led us to think that there were other diseases identified by the population, whose diagnosis and medication were not the responsibility of the Health Centre, that is, of so-called modern medicine. In the case of malaria, the traditional healers' group referred to the fact that they used to supplement the treatment given by the hospital with traditional medicines (roots), and the person could be cured in two or three days.

The opposite situation also occurred. There were cases of different diseases being described in a very similar way, as with high blood pressure and heart pain, malaria and 'paludismo' and stomach pain and diarrhoea. High blood pressure and heart pain were identified similarly by different groups. Their origin and seasonality as identified by the groups were similar, although the perceptions of the groups about the individuals most affected were different. In the view of the religious leaders' group, high blood pressure mainly affects women, while for the women's group, all adults are affected by this disease.

With regard to malaria and 'paludismo', the two diseases were separately identified by the same group of informants, and although the origin, characteristics, seasonality and susceptibility of individuals to the diseases given by the religious leaders' group were identical, in their perception it was not a matter of different names being given to the same disease but rather of different diseases existing, with malaria being a more recent and dangerous disease than 'paludismo'. Major campaigns in the colonial period against 'paludismo', which simply means malaria in Portuguese, associated with a lack of knowledge amongst the population, could be the key factor responsible for this wrong perception.

When identifying the seasonality of the diseases, the informants demonstrated some difficulty in specifying the months corresponding to some of the expressions they used, for instance 'cold season', 'hot season' and the 'change from cold to hot weather'.

According to our informants' perception, the diseases given priority occur throughout the year, affect individuals irrespective of age and can kill the affected individuals or cause immobility. Asthma, although it was identified only by the women's group, was considered important as it attacks all children, including the new-born.

Sanitation problems identified by informants
These included lack of pulverization or of assistance, lack of inspection in the suburbs (of houses and markets), piles of rubbish in the suburbs, and the rainfall in Maputo.

However, the perceptions of the problems differed according to the group of informants. For instance, in the view of the traditional healers, the existence of rubbish in the suburbs and in the markets are two different issues. The lack of rubbish collection by the Municipal Council and the contamination of products sold in the markets are considered to be the cause of the problems, the seriousness of which varies. This perception can be related to their subjective identification of the causes of diseases as illustrated previously.

Concerning the sanitation problems existing in the suburbs, the failure to identify solutions involving the participation of the population may be due to a lack of knowledge of potential opportunities or to a certain degree of passivity on the part of the population who prefer to leave the solution of existing problems to the government.

Finally, it seemed important to us to work together with the population in such a way as to involve them in the search for opportunities to overcome the constraints they identified. This process will not only strengthen the community, but will also make it more responsible, and in the process make development more sustainable.

Preliminary conclusions

- The diseases considered most important by the groups were malaria, diarrhoea and paralysis or thrombosis.
- There is insufficient knowledge about the causes of the diseases.
- The sanitation problems considered most important by the groups were a lack of inspection, lack of pulverization, the rainfall and the existence of piles of rubbish in the suburbs.
- There is an awareness of the importance of hygiene in the community.
- It is important to involve the local community in the process of discovering solutions to their problems and in their effective implementation.

Preliminary recommendations

As only a part of the results of the research have been analyzed, it is premature to propose definitive recommendations. Nevertheless, we would like to highlight certain aspects, namely:

- Practical and multi-disciplinary surveys, specifically oriented towards the diseases considered most important by the community, should be carried out, mobilizing human and material resources from the different community sectors, such as Health, Social Affairs, Environment and Education, and aimed at finding opportunities for solving the problems that can be implemented by the community itself in a sustainable way, such as a small industry initiative to separate and treat the rubbish.
- Sanitary education campaigns should be undertaken. The Health Centre should co-ordinate this activity, involving the religious institutions and leaders, in such a way that the activity should be on-going, directed to the majority of the people and meeting the community's real needs.
- There should be collaboration with the practitioners of so-called 'alternative medicine', with a view to learning their real perceptions about diseases and mobilizing them to participate in the sanitary education process.

References

Chambers, R. (1992) *Rural Appraisal: Rapid, Relaxed and Participatory*, Discussion Paper No. 311, Institute of Development Studies, University of Sussex, Brighton.

Groverman, V. (1992) *Rapid Rural Appraisal (Participatory Rural Appraisal). A Tool for Gender Impact Study – A Choice of Methods.* Amersfoort.

International Institute for Environment and Development (and Cabo Verde bilateral cooperation) (1991) *Relatório dum seminário em Diagnóstico Rural (Rapido Participativo)*, The Netherlands.

Oluemena, C., Walle, C., Mascarenhas, C., Somá, D., Hibraímo, E., Andrade, E., Maia, E., Adamo, F., Cuambe, F., Pinto, G., Mússa, H., Chavale, H., Boize L., Sitoe, S., Muchanga, S. (1995) *Reconhecimento da Area do Centro de Saúde de Bagamoyo. Relatório.* Universidade Eduardo Mondlane, Maputo.

Ong, B.N. (1996) *Rapid Appraisal and Health Policy.* Chapman and Hall, London.

Varkevisser, C.M., Pathmanthan, I. and Brownlee, B. (1993) 'Designing and Conducting Health Systems Research Projects', *Health Systems Research Training Series*, Vol 2. International Development Research Centre.

Whiteside, M. (1994) *Manual de tecnicas de Diagnóstico Rural (Rapido) Participativo.* National Environmental Commission, Maputo.

World Commission on Environment and Development (1987) *Our Common Future.* Oxford University Press, Oxford.

23 Community Participation in Wildlife Management

AFONSO MADOPE

This chapter presents a preliminary appraisal of a project for community participation in wildlife management in Tete Province. The province of Tete is located in the north-west of Mozambique and comprises a total area of 100,274 sq. km. Lying mainly in the Zambezi basin, Tete shares 1,514 km of international border with Zambia, Zimbabwe and Malawi. The mean population density of the province is 12.4 inhabitants per sq. km. This average masks variations between and within districts, which are determined by the complex of factors affecting population distribution. These include climate, water and the access to means of livelihood, for example arable land and other natural resources, as well as such things as security, in the context of the recently ended war and the currently unknown location of landmines.

Because of an abundance of water, more than 80% of the land is covered with a variety of natural vegetation. Mopane forest covers about two-thirds of the land, mainly in the south, while the vegetation in the north is miombo (*Brachystegia* sp). This rich and diversified vegetation has produced a distinct socio-ecological system characterized by a diversification of habitats and rich ecosystems.

The devastation caused by the prolonged period of war in the country was reflected in the paralysis of activities in the forestry and wildlife sector, since control and supervision systems were no longer feasible. Once the armed conflict ended, the need to restore the activities of the sector took on considerable urgency. At the same time, current government policy gives priority to more traditional productive activities, such as livestock and agriculture to alleviate the poverty and malnutrition of the population.

Organizational structure

The National Directorate for Forestry and Wildlife (NDFW) is the government body in charge of implementing policy on forestry and wildlife resources for the Ministry of Agriculture and Fisheries. Its mandate includes the protection, development and promotion of the sustainable use of resources, as well as the design, co-ordination and monitoring of research and similar programmes (Ministerial Diploma No. 41/87 of 25 March, published in B R 12, series I of 25 March 1987).

This mandate is generally in line with the policy of development in the country. It reflects an organizational structure originally set up for a centrally planned economy with centralized control of forestry and wildlife management. However, the Municipalities Law confers significant responsibility for conservation and resource management on local authorities.

The 1996–2001 five-year programme of the NDFW declares its immediate objective as being 'an increase in participation by the rural population and communities as stakeholders in and beneficiaries of the integrated management, use and conservation of forest and wildlife resources' (DNFFB, 1995). This is intended to ensure inclusion of the human factor by increased community involvement in the management of these resources. Two outputs are expected from this process, which should have a significant impact in both the medium and the long term on the principles of community participation. These are the implementation and expansion of a network of pilot projects with community participation, and an improvement in the technical capacity of the NDFW to give assistance to community-managed projects, by means of a special structure to be set up under the NDFW.

The land policy that has been approved (MAP, 1996) reinforces the importance of decentralization by recognizing the part played by local authorities, traditional and otherwise, in managing the land issue. The policy achieves this by the importance it gives to customary rights and which is embodied in the fundamental principles. The land policy, via the land law, is the main vehicle for the recognition of customary land rights, as well as of the role of local leaders in the prevention and resolution of conflicts and the legitimization and legalization of the occupation of any given area.

Modern natural resource conservation in Mozambique has its origins in Decree 40.040 of 20 January 1955. The merit of this decree is that it sets out the general concepts to be observed with regard to the protection of the land and the flora and fauna, and stipulates that the regulations necessary to implement its provisions should be established in legislation. Its main defect lies in its failure to recognize the important role of communities in the management and protection of their natural resources.

Regional experience

Since the 1970s, there has been a growing awareness of the importance of involving local people in wildlife management. Southern Africa is in the forefront of the movement for community participation, as seen in the case of *Campfire* in Zimbabwe, *Live* in Namibia and *Admade* in Zambia. The experience of these three countries plus Botswana has shown that rural communities can use wildlife as a complement to mainly subsistence agriculture and can contribute to rural development. This has been significant in semi-arid areas or marginal land where community-based management of resources has the potential of becoming a source of income for the rural people.

A prime example of this is the Communal Area Management Programme for Indigenous Resource Exploitation (Campfire) in Zimbabwe. This innovative programme is based on the ability of rural communities to own, manage and benefit from their natural resources. The Campfire programme is currently being implemented in at least 15 rural districts where it generates an annual income of about $1 million, the major part of which is paid directly to the rural communities that are in charge of wildlife management. The decision to adopt this form of land use is taken by local community institutions, basically for economic reasons. Campfire offers opportunities for improving living standards, especially for people living in marginal areas which are less suitable for agriculture and livestock. Another important benefit is that it contributes to the development of local community institutions and strengthens mechanisms for local decision-making.

According to Tello (1984)

It is neither possible nor practical in Mozambique to apply protectionist principles, because of the level of socio-economic development, except in selected areas, such as the protection of certain species on the way to extinction or some habitats or biomes extremely sensitive to human interference that have shown a sharp decline. Wildlife has not been and is still not a public good. For this to happen and for wildlife to have a future in Mozambique, its multiple and varied uses must be democratised in ecologically correct ways. About 80% of Mozambique's population is rural. Half of this population lives in areas with natural conditions unsuitable for profitable or at least economically significant agriculture or livestock production because of the ecology. It would seem therefore that correct and varied use of wildlife is the answer to rural development in a large part of the country.

The above quotation provides a starting point to discover a viable alternative that would make rural communities responsible for the control and management of natural resources. The different approaches in the region were explored, including the ideas of Tello presented above. Ways had to be found to recognize and restore the important role played by rural communities in managing wildlife and thus reduce the costs borne by the state in supervision. According to Cumming (1991), the state would otherwise need to spend about US$200,000 a year on the maintenance of each square kilometre of conservation area.

Objectives

A more proactive role for rural communities is now being incorporated into the new concepts and approaches to the conservation of natural resources. Communities must be involved in a genuine way in conservation activities so that the management and use of resources result in real benefits for rural people. This is the lesson gained from practical experience in many southern African countries.

Thus, the main objectives of the preliminary appraisal of the first project for community participation in wildlife management in Mozambique are to:

i) Evaluate the local community's acceptance of the idea that it should be responsible for the management of the natural resources existing in its region.
ii) Approach the government authorities at various levels in order to raise their awareness of the importance of natural resources and the need for their rational management with the active involvement of the local community.
iii) Identify certain problems arising from the co-existence of rural people and wildlife.
iv) Identify the existing villages and define an area in which to begin the programme according to various criteria, namely:
    (a) the population density in the various villages;
    (b) pre-evaluation of the existing natural resources;
    (c) accessibility, especially by road;
    (d) the scale of the human-wildlife conflict.
v) Evaluate the socio-economic impact of programme implementation and isolate the factors which indicate the value of expanding this approach.

Methodology

A hypothesis was developed based on the following four premises:

i) Mozambique was once considered to be a unique wildlife paradise because of the number and variety of its game.
ii) About two-thirds of the country is infested by tse tse fly which hampers livestock production.
iii) The long period of war has contributed significantly to reducing the national herds of free-range livestock and wildlife.

iv) Mozambique is underdeveloped and consequently suffers from shortages of: financial resources to meet its numerous needs; skilled human resources to meet the projected needs of production and development; material resources to satisfy current levels of demand; and technical resources to cover the whole country.

The following hypothesis was derived from the above premises. Programmes for the management and sustainable use of forest and wildlife resources, utilizing community participation and thereby enabling the community to derive direct and indirect benefits, offer one possible solution to problems of rural development.

The community participation approach is an essentially sociological procedure that rests on various assumptions:

- ample availability of natural resources in the project area;
- knowledge and esteem of natural resources on the part of the local community;
- a level of socio-economic development that can be improved by benefits derived from the use of natural resources;
- a settled population;
- areas unsuited to agriculture and livestock;
- legal provision for the recognition of areas of community management of natural resources;
- legal mechanisms to secure the return of benefits without prejudice to government fiscal policy.

The principal features of the methodology will be:

i) various appraisals by means of questionnaire surveys and rapid participatory methods to evaluate the socio-economic conditions of the population, before and during the first year of the project, and two years after the project start-up;
ii) making an inventory of resources by (a) a questionnaire survey, (b) absolute and relative aerial surveys, (c) a ground survey by observation;
iii) data analysis in tabular form.

Project appraisal

The Chintopo administrative post in Magoe District was proposed as the site for a pilot programme for natural resource management involving rural communities. Magoe was formerly a municipality or sub-division of a district, created by Decree No. 3196 of 10 November 1937. It became a district under the combined effect of Decree No. 6/75 of 18 January and Resolution No. 6/87 of 18 April. Magoe District covers an area of 8,792 sq. km., with an estimated population of 30,000. The district, which is divided administratively into Mpende, Mukumbura and Chintopo posts, lies at the western side of Tete Province, south of the Zambezi River. To the north are the districts of Zumbo and Maravia, to the east the district of Cahora Bassa, to the south the Republic of Zimbabwe and to the west the Republic of Zambia. The co-ordinates are as follows: latitude: 15° 48' 30" South; longitude: 30° 34' 40" East.

The Chintopo post covers an area of 2,932 sq km, composed of the localities of Chintopo and Mussenguezi. It is located at the extreme west of the district, with the following co-ordinates: latitude: 15° 22" South, longitude: 30° 34' 40" East. The limits of Chintopo are as follows:

i) from the confluence of the Aruangua and Zambezi rivers, the line follows the middle of the Zambezi River and the Cahora Bassa lake, eastwards to the Mukumbura bay;
ii) following the course of the Mukumbura River upstream to the point where it crosses the Zimbabwean border; and

iii) following the Zimbabwe border to the west and north to the confluence of the Aruangua and Zambezi rivers.

Chintopo is characterized by a predominance of mopane forest, some stretches of mixed riverine forest and a large flood plain. In terms of water resources, it is crossed by many rivers and streams that empty into the Zambezi River. The main rivers are the Mussengueze, Hangua and Mpanhane, the last two of which flow together at the seat of the administrative post to form the Mpanhane river.

There are some 8,086 inhabitants, of whom 741 are returnees, according to June 1994 records (Madope, 1994). Three ethnic groups are culturally dominant: the Chicunda, the Chitwe and the Shona. The people live in abject poverty, largely because of the recently ended war, low levels of farm output for geographical and climatic reasons, frequent loss of agricultural produce destroyed by animals and the lack of farming tools and improved techniques.

With regard to natural resources, the area is rich in bird life and mammals, especially baboons, elephants, kudu and small antelope. There is a large indigenous forest, rich water resources and abundant fish in the Zambezi and its tributaries. Access by dirt road is only possible in the dry season, since the roads become impassable during the rains because the various streams are full. The World Council of Churches currently has a project under way to distribute beans, oil, sugar and soap in a food-for-work scheme in which the local people are re-opening the dirt roads.

Chintopo was selected for the following reasons:

i) The area is characterized by poor soils and low annual rainfall (200 to 400 mm), making agriculture impractical.

ii) The high density of tse tse fly infestation makes cattle farming impractical.

iii) The abundance of wildlife creates severe conflict between humans and animals.

iv) The inhabitants are heavily dependent on natural resources.

v) The proximity of the area to Masoka in Zimbabwe, and the use of the same language, Shona, facilitates contact among the rural population, which helps to ensure the transmission of knowledge and experience from the programme.

Following this line of thought, the first field visit was made from 27 June to 5 August 1994. After a short meeting with the provincial authorities, the team travelled to the district, where meetings were held with the district authorities. After briefing the Chief of Chintopo Administrative Post on the reasons for the visit, a meeting was held on 1 July 1994 with the secretaries of the villages. One outcome of this meeting was a schedule of meetings at the following villages: Chitete, Champonhongo, Chintopo, Bawa and Nhantgendge. The other villages in the district were not included because of difficulties of access.

After meetings with the residents of the villages mentioned, a meeting was held with the traditional authorities, the local headmen, and finally with the Chief of Chintopo Administrative Post, José Chikolo.

A Ministerial Diploma from the Ministries of Agriculture and Fisheries, Planning and Finance and Justice established the framework for project implementation. The revenue deriving from the use of wildlife is to be divided into three parts: one for the state treasury according to normal procedures; one for the district administration; and one to be deposited for the activities of the population in the Chintopo administrative post.

There is potential for conflict in the Chintopo locality which may be characterized as follows:

• It is common practice to use the low-lying land along the banks of the Zambezi River for subsistence agriculture because of the natural poverty of the surrounding land and the low rainfall. This situation implies a scarcity of land for farming, so that the valley bottoms are overcrowded. Conflict exists over space.

- The Zambezi River is permanent and has many seasonal tributaries. Thus it is the main, and in some cases the only, source of water in the dry season. Conflict may arise over water.
- Viewing, photographic and hunting safaris were authorized, by way of an exception, in 1989, to a firm which banned subsistence hunting by the local population. Conflict may exist over the use of game.
- The area is well-known for the passage of large herds of wild animals, especially in the dry season, to water at the Zambezi. The migration of herds of wild animals can mean conflict among species for water.

The resolution of these conflicts will have to be found by changing the approach to procedures and by encouraging and ensuring community participation in the management and use of existing natural resources. Moreover, finding a resolution depends on the diversification of sources of income or the alleviation of problems of survival in the region, such as to guarantee direct benefits from tangible activities and indirect benefits from other activities which are reflected in better living standards for the people.

The potential benefits to be derived from the use of wildlife, as regards this case in particular, should not allow other sources of income to be ignored, such as fisheries, petty trading with Zimbabwe, goat breeding, although on a small scale, wage labour and any other means of subsistence.

In November 1994, facilitators were sent in to explain the project and to help set up wildlife committees. Under the scheme, communities will have to guard against poachers. Plans were made to set up electric fences to guard against crop destruction. Committees were set up in the twelve villages. Their role is to control the facilitator and oversee the Zimbabwean safari company. Under this scheme the communities will be rewarded not with cash but in other material benefits.

References

Comissão de terras, MAP (1995) 'Anteprojecto da Lei de Terras, versão preliminar'. Government of Mozambique, Maputo.

Cumming, D. (1991) 'Developments in Game Ranching and Wildlife Utilisation in East and Southern Africa' (mimeo).

DNFFB (1995) 'Programa Quinquenal de Direcção Nacional de Florestas e Fauna Bravia: 1996–2001', Ministry of Agriculture, Maputo.

Madope, A. (1994) 'Maneio de Recursos com Participacão Comunitaria em Mocambique' unpublished paper.

Tello, J.L. (1984) 'Consideração sobre a situacao actual de fauna bravia em Mocambique e suas perspectivas futuras' (mimeo).

24 An Analysis of Eucaliptization

ATANÁSIO TIVANE

Origins of the MosaFlorestal project

The MosaFlorestal project was first mooted in 1987, in the context of the political and military situation existing at that time. South African support for Renamo was continuing and the war was creating untold suffering. The military situation was particularly difficult, but the Mozambican government hoped that by initiating this project it could help create a more favourable political and economic situation in the future. Hence the top policy strategists determined the parameters within which this, along with other projects at that time, emerged. Essentially it was hoped that by granting some economic concessions to South Africa this would help discourage South African destabilization of Mozambique.

In 1987, the government invited the South African company SAPPI Forests (PTY) Ltd to enter a joint venture with the state-owned enterprises SOCIMO and SOCHIEF to create a eucalyptus plantation, the MosaFlorestal Project. The detailed political-military background to these events is as secret today as it was then. The process of approval of the project remains obscure. The voices raised more recently against the project went unheeded then, because they were muffled. It is to be hoped that the secret version will soon be published because yesterday's secrecy may create a vulnerability to corruption.

The project was to be located in the south of Mozambique, in Maputo Province, in Matutuine District. The boundaries were the Maputo River to the west, the Indian Ocean coast to the east, the Maputo Elephant Reserve to the north and the South African border to the south. Together with other proposed enterprises, it was intended to serve as a buffer or shield for Maputo city against any Renamo military incursion from across the South African border. In quantitative terms, the project represented an area of 150,000 hectares, of which an economic feasibility study carried out by a planning consultant identified 32,400 ha. as suitable for afforestation.

The big mistake made at the outset was wrongly locating the project in technical and scientific terms. These aspects should have been considered from the start, but they were ignored because a number of relevant state institutions were not consulted. The limited number of institutions that were consulted were sympathetic to the political and military objectives of the promoters of the project.

Another serious mistake was the failure to draw up a land-use plan for the project area. MosaFlorestal has never presented a land-use plan, even after public criticism of the project was voiced. This is why its application for a land concession remained for so long in a drawer at DINAGECA (the National Directorate for Geography and

Maps), the government department responsible for issuing such concessions. It is difficult to criticize the project in detail at its application level because of the lack of a land-use plan or a forestry project document, both of which would be essential for carrying out an environmental impact study.

From the beginning, MosaFlorestal was given *carte blanche* by the strategists of the day because, according to reliable but confidential sources, they were aware of the risks and therefore listened to no-one. Commitments were made, and the authorities have remained reluctant to relinquish the project, which was only finally overturned by the government in December 1996. The original site has now been designated for ecotourism use, but an alternative timber plantation site was offered, further north.

The environmental impact statement

In 1993, the voices raised against the MosaFlorestal project began to be heard in public. Changes taking place in the country, with the move towards democratization, meant that attention was finally being paid to criticisms of the project. The National Environment Commission then took charge of this opposition and demanded an environmental impact study. The project's proponents and the Commission drew up the terms of reference and the project proponents contracted the Institute for Natural Resources of Natal, which specializes in environmental impact studies.

An EIS is intended to have the following objectives:

i) To ensure that environmental questions are taken into consideration throughout the drafting process, thus facilitating integrated environmental management. This includes the timely identification of the main environmental concerns, with the aim of informing the planning and decision-making processes.

ii) To collect relevant data on the environment so as to enable an evaluation and continuous monitoring.

iii) To prepare a draft of the EIS for comment by all the interested parties and stakeholders prior to the finalization process and before the ultimate decision is taken by the authorities.

The environmental impact study was to be carried out by a multi-disciplinary team comprising qualified professionals in the following fields: environmental impact assessment; earth sciences; agronomy; forest management; ecology; wildlife management; hydrology; economics and rural sociology. It was also recommended that the team should include local professionals with knowledge and experience of the project area. Essential points from the terms of reference included: that respect should be ensured for the legislation in force and current directives on environmental conservation; and that the EIS should be monitored by the National Environment Commission (now MICOA) and the NDFW.

The environmental impact study should have considered the possible alternatives to using the land for afforestation, with due regard to the size and location of the plantation areas, the tree species and the agricultural techniques to be employed. It should also have considered the project activities and their impact in the various phases of implementation – infrastructure construction, planting, management and cutting in the areas of afforestation – as well as the relevant activities and their impact in the recuperation phase.

The study should have included the following tasks and activities:

i) a description of the project and its activities;

ii) a definition of the project's area of influence;

iii) baseline data for the project's area of influence;

iv) analysis of the environmental impact of the project;
v) proposed mitigating measures;
vi) programme of supervision and monitoring of impacts;
vii) prognosis of environmental quality in the project's area of influence; and
viii) a non-technical summary.

In general terms, the EIS did not meet these expectations. A great deal of information was missing because there was no land-use plan nor a development plan for MosaFlorestal itself.

By superimposing the maps of vegetation, human settlement and areas of silviculture it became apparent that areas of peasant agriculture and of pasture would disappear. The EIS did not deal with the resettlement of this population numbering some 8,000 people. Before the war, there were over 20,000 people in this area. The population is returning at a steady rate; people are resuming their pre-war activities and new opportunities are being created.

The project would only employ a total of 1,250 workers. In 50 years' time, the possible duration of the project, the population could total 70,000, but where would the remaining people find employment? The project lacked adequate vision.

Beyond missing essential data, the EIS was criticized on professional grounds, namely, the team's denial of the incontestable visible evidence that the area has a high level of animal and plant diversity, and the lack of a land-use plan indicating where settlements, grazing and arable production would occur, and of a plan for the afforestation project itself. The report is full of gaps. Analyzing the report with regard to its compliance with the terms of reference, it is possible to classify the total of 43 questions studied and discussed according to the following criteria:

Good   means that the study was detailed and conclusive with regard to a particular reference point.

Fair   indicates that overall the study was conclusive, although some aspects could have been more detailed.

Poor   indicates that, although the topic was presented, the discussion was superficial and the study was inconclusive.

Not done indicates that although the topic was part of the terms of reference, it was not dealt with or discussed.

The final classification was as follows

- 7 classified as *good*   (16.3%)
- 7 classified as *fair*   (16.3%)
- 19 classified as *poor*   (47.2%)
- 10 not discussed   (23.2%)

A main conclusion drawn from this study is that most of the terms of reference were not complied with or the compliance was unsatisfactory.

It was not possible to justify the MosaFlorestal project on the basis of the existing report, mainly because the EIS was incomplete. The description of the plantation project, as well as the analysis of the possible impact during implementation and operation, remained very weak. Many of the proposed effects needed to be investigated by means of forestry and management studies. The EIS made no reference to the Save River forest gallery. In 1964, it was proposed that this forest gallery become a forest reserve. It is regarded as one of the most interesting and important communities south of the Save River. Since it is within the project area, the possible impact on this gallery should have been studied in more detail. Extracts from a letter to President Chissano from Professor van Wyk of the University of Pretoria Botany

Department illustrate the importance of the area for its rich biodiversity (see Appendix).

The hydrological model used in the EIS assumes that under plantation conditions the water table is not replenished. The big question is whether or not eucalyptus uses the water table through capillary attraction. This possibility is noted in many studies on eucalyptus and should have been examined in more detail. Another major failing in the model is that it does not deal with the water balance on a regional scale. Given that the aquifers in the region are highly permeable, any local change has regional effects. This aspect of the EIS suggests that a different model should have been used that allowed regional simulation of subterranean flows and better modelling of the existing ecosystems. There is a lack of knowledge on the quantities of surface and ground water.

Basically no discussion took place about the quality of the surface or ground water. One extremely important aspect is the movement of saline fronts. Many of the lakes in the region have slightly salty water. This saltiness could be the result of saline intrusion. Given the importance of this issue and possible impact on the ecosystems of the region, the balance of salts and the movement of saline fronts in the rivers and ground waters should have been analyzed in much more detail.

The proposed centre for rural development arises from the recognized need to stop the foreseeable adverse effects of integrating the population into a monetary economy, while the resources for survival are reduced because the land is being occupied and placed under intensive use. Thus, a centre for rural development should be conceived of as a system of support for farming, including cattle and community life as a whole. The creation of a centre is therefore a necessary part of the strategy to achieve the project's objectives. Because of its nature and importance, this centre deserves special consideration and a specialized study. The EIS also omits any consideration of how the initiative would be integrated into existing national plans.

Conclusion

The MosaFlorestal project was intended to be beneficial for the country in physical, environmental, economic, social and political terms. It was in fact very badly located because the political and military criteria were the predominant considerations at the expense of the physical, social and environmental concerns. The reasons for this have been explained. In December 1996, the government decided to cancel the former political concession granted by the previous Council of Ministers, and to give MosaFlorestal the chance to select another site for development. The original site chosen was to be dedicated to ecotourism and cattle production, since the physical and natural characteristics and even the infrastructure make this the most appropriate land use.

Future development undertakings should not be based on political considerations alone, but should encompass economic and all other relevant considerations so that serious clashes can be avoided between the technicians and the politicians. The mechanisms established by the government for the approval of projects should be followed. This procedure should be carried out within government institutions, and horizontal and vertical co-ordination needs to be ensured to avoid undue delays and inconvenience to the project proponents.

Appendix

EXTRACTS FROM A LETTER TO PRESIDENT CHISSANO,
dated 12 October 1995
COMMERCIAL AFFORESTATION IN SOUTHERN MOZAMBIQUE

The signing of the International Convention on the Conservation of Biological Diversity in Rio de Janeiro, June 1992, has focused renewed attention on the rapid global loss and degradation of natural ecosystems. During the 1980s a major international collaborating project was initiated by the IUCN (The World Conservation Union) and WWF (World Wide Fund for Nature) to identify the world's main Centres of Plant Diversity (CPD). The principal aim of the CPD project was to identify areas of prime botanical importance, with the hope that these will receive adequate levels of resources to ensure their conservation. These are the areas around the world that, if conserved, would safeguard the greatest number of plant species.

In 1994 the CPD project culminated in the publication of a volume listing 82 botanical sites of global conservation significance in Africa. Only one major site, the Maputaland Centre, falls in Mozambique. In fact, the core area of this Centre lies in southern Mozambique, between the KwaZulu-Natal border and Maputo. Prior to this publication, the uniqueness of the Maputaland Centre as a region of exceptional plant and animal endemism (species and communities occurring in this region and nowhere else in the world), has largely escaped the notice of biologists. Recognition and demarcation of the Maputaland Centre are largely based on my own research and that of my students.

1. From a plant diversity point of view, the Maputaland Centre is the most remarkable area in Mozambique. It is the only major site in Mozambique recognised by the CPD project as being of global significance (a minor site is located on the border with Tanzania). Moreover, the region is an outstanding centre of animal diversity, with many forms of mammals, reptiles, birds, fresh water fish and other animal groups endemic or near-endemic to the region. Many parts of the Centre still abound in wildlife. People living in the region have accumulated extensive indigenous knowledge on the local plants and animals and have lived in harmony with this environment for probably hundreds of years.

2. The coastal grasslands of the Maputaland Centre and in particular those of southern Mozambique, are unique. They are a natural feature of the region and are certainly not the result of recent human disturbance. These tropical grasslands have a structure and species composition which are unmatched by other grasslands in southern Africa, or anywhere else in the world.

3. The Maputaland Centre is most probably Mozambique's principal natural asset. Proposals to link the Tembe Elephant Reserve in northern KwaZulu-Natal and the Maputo Elephant Reserve in southern Mozambique could result in a major tourist attraction comparable with some of the great game reserves of East Africa. The extensive grasslands in such a reserve would enable tourists to view elephant and other game in large numbers in the open. Existing so-called big-five nature reserves in southern Africa are predominatly located in areas of dense bush, making gameviewing difficult.

4. Commercial afforestation of natural grassland with exotic trees is the most extensive, environmentally destructive activity in southern Africa today. In South Africa alone, it destroys about 200 square kilometers of natural grassland every year. The associated impacts on water run-off, as well as animals and plants, are devastating. For example, over the last few years many streams and rivers that

flow east through the Transvaal lowveld and into Mozambique have showed progressive reductions in flow, particularly during the dry-season when water is needed most. Despite persistent denials by the forestry industry, it is a fact that large-scale, irresponsible afforestation in the catchments of these rivers is contributing significantly to these reductions.

5.   Massive commercial afforestation in the core area of the Maputaland Centre would be a destructive activity of international concern. The grasslands are partly a response to the very shallow water table in the region. In addition to the destruction of grassland and associated habitats, afforestation is expected to have serious long-term effects on the hydrology of the region, thus destroying a significant part of one of the most remarkable natural ecosystems in the world, and a Mozambican natural resource asset of national and global importance.

Prof. A.E. VAN WYK
Department of Botany
University of Pretoria
PRETORIA
0002 SOUTH AFRICA

25 Gold Mining in Manica District

ISIDRO RAFAEL VICTOR MANUEL

This chapter has a number of objectives. First, it will identify the main environmental problems related to large-scale and traditional artisanal gold mining exploration in Manica District. Secondly, it will propose measures to prevent, reduce or eliminate these problems. Finally, it will identify opportunities for sustaining the livelihoods of the traditional mine workers, who on the whole are peasant farmers, by enabling them to increase their off-farm income from mining.

Geographical characteristics

Manica District is located in the west of Manica Province between parallels 19° 20' and 19° 09' latitude South and 32° 41' and 33° 17' longitude East. The district is bordered on the west by the Republic of Zimbabwe, on the east by Gondola District, to the north by Barue District through the Pungue River and to the south by Sussendenga District whose border is marked by the Revue and Zonue rivers. The district covers an area of 4,396 sq km (Manuel and Muacanhia, 1995).

Close to the Zimbabwean border is a mountainous area, ranging in altitude from 800 m to 2,000 m. The interior forms a plateau. The Revue river-basin covers an area of 8,350 sq km and has an extension of 243 km. Part of it is located in Manica District and comprises the Revue River, the main river, and its tributaries: the Mussambe, Ndirire, Chua, Mazi, Inhamazonga, Chimezi, Messica and Ndopodzi on the left bank and the Nhamatsambe, Nhahombue, Mechinza, Zambuzi, Munene and Zonue on the right bank (*ibid.*).

The climate is moderately tropical and varies with the altitude. The temperatures vary between 7° and 23°C. The Manica region has two seasons: a cold dry season from April to October and a hot wet season from November to March. The mean annual rainfall is 1,000 mm in the low land and 2,000 mm in the high altitude areas, such as Penhalonga and Moriangane Mountains.

The population of Manica District is estimated at about 185,000. Whilst Mozambique has an average population density of about 22.3 per sq km (SARDC, IUCN & SADC, 1994), the density of Manica District is higher at 42.1 per sq km (Manuel and Muacanhia, 1995). Within the Revue basin in Manica District, the people live in very well defined areas with good access and communications.

The geology of the district makes up part of the 'Cratao do Zimbabwe', a stable nucleus of antiquity. The Greenstone Belt of Manica is a 'green' belt with an extent of 35 km and an extension of 15 km, characterized by having the shape of a 'synclinorium', a general east-west direction and a stratum inclination of 50–85° south or north. In the Manica Greenstone Belt rocky sequences of 'ultramaficas', 'maficas', 'metasedimentares' and alluvials can be found (Manuel, 1992). The soils of the Manica district are closely related to these geological characteristics and are mainly sandy, sandy-clay, clay (reddish-brown) and alluvial soils.

The most important mining activity in Manica District involves: gold, bauxite (aluminium oxide ore at Alumen and Marondo mine), copper ores (Mundonguara mine) and mineral water (Vumba mountain water).

Characteristics of large-scale and artisanal gold mining exploration

Gold has been extracted from the alluvial deposits and gold filaments for many centuries. Archaeological and historical data prove conclusively that gold had already been exploited by the states of Zimbabwe (1250–1450 AD) and of Muenemotapa (1325–1600 AD). After the discovery of gold in Witwatersrand, South Africa, in 1888, many Europeans moved to Manica looking for gold. This is how the gold fever in Manica began, known by the name of 'Macequece' at that time. As a result, there were 23 gold mining companies operating in Manica by 1900 and 140 requests for mining exploration. From 1900 to 1949, 9,530 kg of gold were extracted, 60% of which was derived from alluvial deposits. Production declined drastically between 1949 and 1975. Nevertheless, after independence, gold production did continue (Manuel and Muacanhia, 1995).

The company 'Aluvioes de Manica' (ALMA) founded in 1987 as a joint venture between the British company LONRHO and the Mozambican government is dedicated to gold mining research and prospecting in the alluvial deposits. It has subcontracted the South African company BENICON to carry out the research and exploration of alluvial gold. The concessions for survey and exploration by ALMA, in the Revue Basin, cover vast areas, which include agricultural areas with alluvial soils and permanent water supply courses. This is the only company dedicated to gold extraction activities in Manica. Nevertheless, other companies are currently concerned with research and prospecting for gold, with the aim of undertaking actual mining in the future if it is deemed economically viable.

In Manica District the main zones for gold digging are: (i) MuKudo – close to the Revue river-head; (ii) Marondo – close to the Chua river-head; (iii) Chihururu – in Chua; (iv) Nhahombwe – IFLOMA sawmill, Penhalonga; (v) Ndirire – down to the Revue river, after the IFLOMA sawmill; (vi) Nhamachato – one of the Ndirire suburbs; (vii) Chua – 'Pothole' mine where there is an immobilized drag; (viii) Andrade – in the Andrade region, on the Revue's left bank; (ix) Revue II – in the region between Manica city and the Mavonde bridge over the Revue; (x) Chimese – on the Chimese River; (xi) Musa – in the Musa River; (xii) Nhamacuarara – the Nhamacuarara mine; (xiii) Mimosa – in the Mimosa zone.

Both before and after independence, artisanal mining exploration was forbidden. Gold-digging only began to be tolerated from 1990, when the ALMA company started alluvial gold exploration in the Revue basin. Between 1992 and 1995, artisanal exploration activity became much more intensive, which was not unconnected to the fact that during this period the Manica region was badly affected by drought.

An analysis of data collected through a major survey, in which more than 250 gold-diggers and 300 peasants were interviewed, allows the following conclusions to be drawn:

- Gold-digging is currently a survival activity for most of the diggers who have inadequate sources of income.

- The majority of the gold-diggers are peasants.
- The population actually prefers agricultural activity to gold-digging. Agriculture is the main source of income and the basis for food security in the district.
- Gold-diggers do not have sufficient knowledge of basic or more advanced geological mining techniques, nor are they aware of the safety measures required.
- Gold-digging is seasonal work for some people, whilst for others it is a full-time activity. Where it is a full-time activity, the diggers contract seasonal labour to work on their own farm plots.
- Gold-digging is a more profitable activity than agriculture. The returns are used in many different ways. Only a few diggers put the money gained to productive use, however.
- Usually the tools used in artisanal gold exploration are hoes, picks, levels (hand-spikes), spades, basins, wheelbarrows, waterpumps, cords and bags.
- Production levels are very inconsistent, which makes gold-digging a high risk activity.
- The gold extracted from the Revue valley alluvial deposits and mine-dumps is in practice not submitted to amalgamation because of its size and pureness.
- Gold-digging is not adequately controlled by the state. Hence it is normal to find hundreds of gold-diggers working in very small areas (for example, 1,000 diggers in Andrade work in an area of only a quarter of a hectare), thus causing great pressure on people and the environment and the destruction of the gold deposits. In gold-diggers' camps, work and living conditions are very precarious.
- Gold-digging is done by men, women, children and old people. Most of the diggers are Mozambicans coming from different parts of the country, but there are also foreigners coming from other African countries. Many live a nomadic existence.
- Gold-diggers' ages vary from 6 to 75 years. Diggers under 14 years of age, certain women and the oldest men (e.g. 70 years old) are often involved in activities that require less effort. They collect the gold from the surface of the less consolidated mine-dumps and in the alluvial deposits on the riverside. Strong men and women in general work in places that require more physical exertion, such as in wells, trenches and semi-galleries.
- Individuals originating from many different professions work in gold-digging. Whilst a majority are peasants, others include secondary and primary school teachers, accountants, mechanics, cooks, students of all levels, miners, bricklayers, carpenters, and basic and medium-level technicians in agriculture and health. Some of the miners are demobilized soldiers from the government army and Renamo.
- Living together with the gold-digging communities are informal traders (bakers, grocers and vegetable vendors). Prostitution and excessive consumption of alcohol are very common.

Environmental impact of the mining

Mining exploration often generates alterations to the earth's surface. The dimension of these alterations depends on the type of geological formation or structure, on the exploration technology and mining processing used, and the type of waste produced and its storage (Hollaway and Associates, 1992; SARDC, IUCN and SADC, 1994). Alterations have occurred to the natural topography following the gold mining exploration in Manica as a result of mine-dumps, trenches and wells, siltings and deviation of the river beds.

The mine-dumps are superficial deposits of wastes, disintegrated from the rocky mass by mechanical and/or chemical means (Manuel, 1992). They are largely confined to the Revue River and the Chua and Zambuzi tributaries. According to the age of formation, the mine-dumps can be classified as:

(a) Dumps formed between 1912 and 1949, most of which resulted from dragging.
(b) Dumps formed since 1992. These resulted from gold mining by the ALMA company and companies that it sub-contracted.

In the oldest mine-dumps, the material was often separated according to granulometry.

According to their height, the mine-dumps can be classified as: (a) high dumps between 10 and 35 m but in a small area; and (b) dumps with a height of less than 5 m but covering the largest areas.

According to the material consolidation of the dumps there are: (a) dumps with non-consolidated material, and (b) dumps with consolidated material.

The physical environmental impact of the mine dumps in Manica District is decidedly negative. They reduce the arable land area available. This is particularly significant as they occur in rich agricultural land where the population can produce all the year round. They profoundly alter the landscape and the natural beauty of the Revue valley and its tributaries. The material in the dumps can cause serious silting. The mining dump zones are extremely vulnerable, as they are exposed to constant physical alterations caused by gold-diggers looking for high concentrations of residual gold.

In the mining zone of Manica District there are two types of wells and trenches: research wells and trenches and exploration wells and trenches. The physical impact of wells, trenches and galleries in the district has had certain negative environmental effects. Wells, trenches and galleries sometimes collapse into the Revue, Chua and Zambuzi rivers, causing river bed enlargements with all of the attendant effects that an altered flow has upon the multiple uses of the river resource to ensure that livelihoods are sustained. Abandoned wells, trenches and galleries are also a serious danger to animals and people. As a result of over-ambitious exploration, the random development of wells, trenches and galleries destroys the gold deposits. The beauty of the landscape is altered and safety is sacrificed. Abandoned wells and trenches with stagnant water are also sources of disease, namely: bilharzia, filariziosis and malaria.

The silting is the accumulation of waste (blocks, pebbles, sands, clay and organic matter) in the zones of a weak unevenness of the river bed. The physical and environmental impact of the silting is revealed by the accumulation of high quantities of clay which reduces the depth of the Revue river bed and its tributaries in the less steep zones and in the Chicamba reservoir. High quantities of clay can also bury organisms of small dimensions in the river beds and in the Chicamba reservoir.

Gold processing, both large-scale and at artisanal level, can cause the suspension of high quantities of clay material in the water, making it brown or reddish-brown. The mud along the river is visible from the Penhalonga sawmill up to the Chicamba reservoir. The extent of the muddy water depends on the intensity of activity of the mining company. Some tributaries of the Revue river still have clean water, given the absence of any mining activity in the river beds or their proximities, as is the case in the Inhamazonga and Chimezi rivers.

The muddy water created by the mining in the Revue river-basin has a negative effect on the life of the people of Manica District. Specifically, the impact of the mining is revealed in the following ways. The mud created influences the deposit of clay materials, reducing the depth of the rivers and of the Chicamba reservoir. The increased mud in the river seriously affects the quality of life of the population as the water quality is no longer suitable for household consumption (for drinking, cooking, washing, bathing and for the use of cattle). The aquatic fauna and flora are seriously affected because they are buried by the mining waste and the plants are no longer capable of photosynthesis. The accumulation in excess, of the conglomerated clay particles, can cause the obstruction of irrigation channels. Given its conglomeration capacity, clay can be a vector of harmful substances, namely fertilizers and nutrients, eutrophication, pesticides and heavy metals, and poisonous organisms.

The opening of wells in the riverbanks and holes in the villages can increase the cost of living of the local population. The fish catch has fallen dramatically in recent years in the Chicamba Dam. The 'Tilapia' (*oreochromis mossambicus* and *tilapia rendalli*), big mouth 'perca' (*micropterus salmoides*) and the red eye 'labeo' (*labea cylindricus*), the cat fish (*clarias gariepinus*) and other species such as *Barbus spp.* are declining in numbers in the Revue river.

Socio-economic and cultural impact

Agriculture is the main economic activity in Manica District. Yet the arable area in the district is restricted as a result of the orography (marginal soils) and concessions given by the government both to mining companies (e.g. ALMA/BENICON) and for commercial forestry (e.g. IFLOMA E.E.). For the peasants, land forms the basis of their subsistence. With the gold exploration in the Revue basin and the consequent destruction of some of their arable land, some peasants are deprived of their main source of wealth in the form of their 'machambas' (farms) and fruit trees, and with it the hope of being able to produce continuously for their subsistence and for the market. The tradition of the land remaining for the use of their children as they had received it from their ancestors is being undermined. This implies a profound change in traditional social, economic and cultural relations within the local communities in Manica District. These effects of mining activities have similarly been noted in the wider SADC region (MacDonald and Sithole, 1992).

Gold exploration in Manica District does not benefit the peasants; on the contrary it constrains them financially. They lose their farm land, much of which contains fruit trees or small plantations, all without receiving adequate compensation. The limited benefits that they do receive do not allow them to initiate new activities to sustain their livelihoods. The wage work available through the mining exploration companies is limited and the majority of workers are recruited from outside the district. The change from an agrarian to a monetary economy had already tended to undermine the stability of the population and social cohesion in the mining zones. Following the gold exploration, the ALMA/BENICON companies rehabilitated no more than a nominal 200 ha of land in the Revue valley and its tributaries. The extensive area affected was transformed into marginal land no longer appropriate for agriculture.

The availability of water in Manica District for animal and human consumption, for irrigation, for household activities such as washing clothes as well as for energy production (e.g. Chicamba Hydroelectric-SHER) and to facilitate industrial activities (e.g. the shoe factory, the wine and mining industries) is limited. The main contributing factors to the water scarcity are: prolonged droughts; mining exploration; irrigation; erosion; and silting.

Besides ALMA/BENICON, there are three other mining companies in Manica carrying out primary and alluvial gold research and prospecting. Relations between the mining companies appear friendly once the licensing documents are legalized by the Ministry of Mineral Resources and Energy. Amongst the gold-diggers, relations are also good in spite of the occurrence of regular conflicts over the possession of certain portions of land where a high concentration of gold is supposed to exist.

The institution that provides the mining titles in Mozambique is the Ministry of Mineral Resources and Energy through the National Directorate of Mining. These include: research and prospecting licences; mining concessions; operating licences; and mining certificates. The Mining Certificate is the title of certification required by the gold-diggers, while the others pertain to the small and large-scale companies. Mining Law 2/86 of 16 April, prevents the commercialization of mineral resources which do not result from a mining title.

In reality the majority of gold-diggers in Manica do not have any mining certificates. Thus they cannot legally sell the gold, and indeed are subject to the prospect of their gold production being confiscated and having to pay fines in addition. The best way for the gold-diggers to sell their gold is through intermediaries, who are open every day to buy the gold produced. The buying price offered is relatively low, but is higher than the price paid by ALMA. Later, the intermediaries sell the gold inside or outside the country at very high prices, thus becoming the main beneficiaries of the artisanal gold extraction.

The local, district and provincial governments are unanimous in saying that they should be consulted about large-scale gold exploration in Manica and that the population of the district should benefit directly from the gold exploration. But there is an excessive centralization by national government and a lack of governmental and intersectoral co-ordination in the decision-making process.

Recommendations

Poverty and environmental degradation are interlinked in a vicious circle in which the population do not have the means necessary to take care of the environment. Degraded ecosystems produce fewer renewable resources to provide food, firewood, charcoal and building materials. Populations who live in these ecosystems are vulnerable because the environment cannot produce enough for their subsistence (Archer *et al*, 1987; SARDC, IUCN and SADC, 1994).

Human and natural resources are the foundation for socio-economic and cultural development in any country. Sustainable economic development depends on the relationships established between human and natural resources. Measures can be taken to establish greater harmony between the two in relation to agriculture, forests, wildlife, cattle and mineral resources in Manica District. In view of the complexity of the environmental impact of the gold exploration and the need for environmental conservation, the following recommendations are made:

i)   Deeper knowledge is needed of the current problems related to the natural and human resource situation in Manica District.

ii) The active participation of civil society is required by means of tripartite negotiations involving the local population, the government and mining companies.

iii In Manica the mining companies should:
- Initiate mining exploration in the case of its proving to be a profitable activity which brings benefits for the country.
- Build reservoirs for purification of the water used in the gold exploration before it is returned to the river.
- Rehabilitate the degraded land in the old mine zones.

iv) Respect for the contractual and legal principles of both mining companies and the state should involve:
- Real indemnification or compensation to the legal occupants of land for the damage caused to crops, goods and infrastructures or as a result of the resettlement of the mining area occupants.
- Soils recovery and rehabilitation in view of the sequence of the existing strata in the initial profile.

- Payment of taxation.
- Control and inspection of the mining exploration.

v) There should be promotion of artisanal gold mining activity. Nowadays, to turn gold-digging into a sustainable, productive and safe activity the following initiatives are necessary:

- Identification of the geologically gold-rich zones that can be used by the gold-diggers.
- Granting of mining certificates for gold exploration to gold-diggers' groups, families or individuals, taking into consideration the quantity and quality of the gold deposits, and the availability of water resources and arable soils and vegetation.
  The gold-diggers to be licensed should meet the following requirements: have experience; be of a suitable age; and have a certain degree of physical fitness.
- Organization and professional training of the gold-diggers in management, geological mining and mining safety techniques are required.
- Gold-digger training should be carried out by the various institutions existing in Mozambique such as the Geology Department of the Eduardo Mondlane University, the Mining Promoting Fund, specialized NGOs, the Small-Scale Mine Workers Association.
- Financing is required with low interest and taxation.
- Continuous technical support is required, e.g. in management and mining techniques, and economic feasibility and rational water use studies.
- Conversion of the gold and/or money deriving from the gold sales into capital is needed.
- Gold sales facilities should be initiated at fixed and competitive prices in order to reduce the cut of the intermediaries.

By carrying out the above initiatives, gold-digging can become a safe, profitable, regulated and sustainable activity. The sustainability will imply harmonization between agrarian activities and the gold-digging as well as the possibility of more integrated development.

vi) There should be rational utilization of the available water by the different sectors (mining companies, gold-diggers, agriculture, forestry, population, etc.).

vii) Assistance should be given to population groups in the mining areas.

viii) Sectoral harmony should be instituted in the land-use tenure system via the definition and demarcation of the protection, agricultural and forestry and mining exploration zones.

ix) Adequate complementarity it should be instituted between formal and customary law.

x) Adequate and complementary land and mining laws should be ensured.

xi) There should be integrated development of Manica District, ensuring intersectoral co-operation for sustainable development.

xii) Monitoring should be established of the environmental impact in the district.

xiii) Good co-ordination should be established between government institutions at different levels, and between the government and the private sector as well as the government and civil society.

Implementation mechanisms

Sustainable development is an attempt to combine the development process with environmental conservation. In order to develop mining activity in Manica, without jeopardizing other areas of development as well as the environment, the following mechanisms are recommended:

i) The catch phrase to be applied should be: 'If the people concerned understand their problems, then they will be able to find the solutions'.
ii) Identifying those stakeholders who are really concerned in the issues.
iii) Setting up workshops or seminars involving the Governor and representatives of Agriculture, Planning and Finance, Housing and Mineral Resources, central government, provincial government, district and local government, representatives of mining companies, peasants and fishermen from the Chicamba reservoir dam. The seminars would facilitate the discussion of the gold-diggers' and miners' problems as well as the gold exploration problems in Manica.
iv) Visiting the gold-digging areas, informally winning the gold-diggers' confidence and discussing the existing problems with them. Involving them in the reassessment of problems in order to define a consensual plan of action.
v) Persuading the gold diggers to organize themselves the better to achieve the objectives of the action plan, using the abilities and capacities of the group members.
vi) Supporting the gold-diggers already organized with practical courses in management, administration and geological mining techniques and introducing concepts of natural resources protection and basic concepts on Land and Mining law.
vii) Assisting the organized gold-diggers in obtaining their own mining certificates.
viii) Establishing through the banks and government organizations mechanisms for purchasing gold at real commercial prices, thus reducing the role of the intermediaries, and ensuring greater security for the gold as it will be kept in the banks' coffers.

References
Archer, A.A. Lüttig, G.W. and Snezhko, I.L. (1987) *Man's Dependence on the Earth*, UNESCO, Paris.
Hollaway, J. and Associates (1992) 'Environmental Effects of Mining in the SADC Region. Emissions to air, effluents to water and their standards'. A presentation to the SADC Mining Sector Mining and Environment workshop, Lusaka, 1–3 December.
MacDonald, M. and Sithole, B. (1992) 'Discussion paper on the social and cultural disruption associated with mining activities in SADC'. A presentation to the SADC Mining Sector Mining and Environment Workshop, Lusaka, 1–3 December.
Manuel, I.R.V. and Muacanhia, T. (1995) *Impact Ambiental da Exploração do Ouro no Districto de Manica* Minstério para a Coordenacao Ambiental, Maputo.
Manuel, I.R.V. (1992) 'Geologie, Petrographie, Geochemie und Lagerstätten des Manica Greenstone-Bel, Mosambik', Doctoral Thesis, Aachen Technical University, Germany.
SARDC, IUCN and SADC (1994) *The State of the Environment in Southern Africa*, SARDC, IUCN and SADC, Harare.

Index